Building Basic Therapeutic Skills

Building Basic Therapeutic Skills

A Practical Guide for Current Mental Health Practice

Jeanne Albronda Heaton

Jossey-Bass Publishers • San Francisco

Substantial discounts on bulk quantities of Jossey-Bass books are available to
corporations, professional associations, and other organizations. For details
and discount information, contact the special sales department at Jossey-Bass Inc.,
Publishers (415) 433–1740; Fax (800) 605–2665.

For sales outside the United States, please contact your local Simon & Schuster
International Office.

www.josseybass.com

Manufactured in the United States of America on Lyons Falls Turin Book.
This paper is acid-free and 100 percent totally chlorine-free.

Library of Congress Cataloging-in-Publication Data

Heaton, Jeanne Albronda, date.
    Building basic therapeutic skills : a practical guide for current
mental health practice / Jeanne Albronda Heaton. — 1st ed.
        p.   cm.
    Includes index.
    ISBN 0–7879–3984–6 (cloth : alk. paper)
    1. Psychotherapy. 2. Psychotherapy—Case studies. I. Title.
    RC480.5.H3475 1998
    616.89'14—dc21   97–45300

FIRST EDITION
HB Printing   10 9 8 7 6 5 4 3 2 1

Contents

Because they taught with love and wisdom—
My parents, Mildred and Henry Albronda
And our friends, Edward and Claire Liska

Preface

I wrote this book to answer a fundamental question: How can I do what's required and still maintain a good therapeutic relationship with my client(s)? As students of helping relationships, we share a common interest in making our work compassionate, efficient, and effective. This book has been designed to provide assistance to students, supervisors, and educators in doing therapeutic work in a therapeutic manner.

Very often we flounder with how to implement the tasks of therapy while striving to maintain an effective and compassionate alliance; this book describes how to accomplish that goal. There are lots of down-to-earth suggestions for what to do, what to say, and how to manage the common demands of current mental health practice. These suggestions are not meant to be applied in a dogmatic fashion. Quite the contrary—it's my intention that the ideas presented here be used as a starting point for discussion about even better ways of providing services to people in trouble. As such, this book would be useful as a text for introductory courses for mental health professionals in therapeutic practice, prepracticum, or practicum. In addition, this book is useful for case managers, social workers, peer counselors, and allied health professionals who work with mental health problems and issues.

Acknowledgments

First and foremost, I'd like to express appreciation to my clients. Without question, they are my best teachers. You know who you are, but you may not know what you've taught me. It's been my privilege to learn about you, from you, and with you—and I'm grateful.

Then I want to acknowledge my supervisors, who are now my friends and colleagues—especially Jim Gleason, John Garske, and

Bill Osher. Their early confidence in me mattered much more than they know.

My students and my supervisees continue to provide a very special spark. They certainly keep me humble, as they teach me more than they learn. I especially would like to acknowledge Nona Wilson, who was my student, then my supervisee, and then my coauthor. But all that pales next to the deep and abiding friendship we've crafted. Thank you, Nona.

I also want to acknowledge my colleagues, who added insight and criticized when necessary, and who make getting up and going to work gratifying. But especially, I want to express gratitude to Fred Weiner. He took on this particular project with enthusiasm, support, and a willingness to patiently read and make critical comments on every page. His help and friendship made the unmanageable seem possible, and I'm very appreciative.

There is no way to express the depth of my gratitude to my family and my friends who patiently put up with my obsessions while maintaining the support that sustains me—especially my husband, David Heaton.

Finally, I'd like to thank my editor, Alan Rinzler, whom I respect more than he knows and who once again had the courage to stick with me as well as the wisdom and insight to help and encourage me when I needed it most.

Athens, Ohio   JEANNE ALBRONDA HEATON
February 1998

Building Basic Therapeutic Skills

Introduction

It's a privilege to be allowed access to the most intimate thoughts and secrets of others, but with that privilege comes substantial responsibility. Fulfilling that commitment to our clients requires respect, common sense, compassion, and most important, basic therapeutic skills.

Those skills are evident when a therapist tries to help

A twenty-six-year-old woman as she explains how, as a child, she hid in the closet with her doll when her mother was drunk, again

A young man when he agonizes over his decision that it is now time to tell his fundamentalist mother he is gay

A mother who wonders why she keeps shoplifting

A seventy-year-old man who cries over a letter from a friend he hasn't seen in forty-five years

Each therapeutic contact provides unique opportunities to ameliorate suffering and cultivate change—that is, of course, if therapists can find a way to create the conditions that will allow those who seek their services to reveal personal difficulties, experience painful emotions, and take the risks necessary to solve their problems.[1] Meeting that challenge is what this book is about.

Fortunately for all of us trying to learn this profession, there is ample evidence that therapy can be effective. Most clients who participate in psychotherapy claim substantial and lasting benefit.[2] It doesn't seem to matter whether the helper is a counselor, psychologist, social worker, or psychiatrist. When the helper is

1

skillful, therapy not only alleviates symptoms and speeds up natural healing but also provides coping strategies for handling future
problems.[3]

Traditionally, most therapists have relied on theory to provide
the direction necessary to develop basic skills. A strict theoretical
orientation supplied the practitioner with explanations for the
development of symptoms, guidelines for therapeutic intervention,
and methods for evaluating the results. In addition, a theoretical
framework enhanced the therapist's confidence by furnishing a professional identity.[4] Therapists identified themselves with labels such
as "I am . . . a behaviorist, a psychoanalyst, a Rogerian," and so on.

What is intriguing about this tradition is that there are so many
processes, techniques, and interventions—all labeled *psychotherapy*
or *counseling*, each different, and most claiming superiority. But
after decades of debate over which "talking cure" is preeminent,
researchers have drawn some compelling conclusions about different therapies and how they work that question this traditional
reliance on theoretical orientation:

1. Different therapies accomplish comparable therapeutic benefits.[5] (We should keep in mind, however, that the therapies covered in psychological research are by and large mainstream—
   dynamic, cognitive, behavioral, family systems, or combinations
   of those modes—not past-life regression therapy or primal
   scream.)
2. In "real life" most therapists do not follow just one theory or
   use one method. Eclectic therapists draw on about four different approaches, which most often include combinations of psychodynamic, cognitive-behavioral, humanistic, and systems
   techniques.[6]
3. There are common factors—variables that cut across theories
   and techniques—that consistently account for positive therapeutic results. We know that skilled therapists must be able to
   establish rapport, instill hope, provide explanations of problems, and facilitate opportunities to learn different ways of
   thinking, feeling, and behaving.[7]
4. There are factors, not covered in research, that also may
   account for change. These include the "charisma" of the therapist, the "mystique" of the setting, the "magic" mix of the odd

teachable moment—in other words, those occurrences not covered in theory or technique that seem to foster insight and positive change.

5. Unfortunately, there remains the dreadful possibility that harm can be done. Whether because of a therapist who ineptly applies treatment or a therapist who is poorly adjusted, lacking in empathy, unethical, or overly controlling, some clients are damaged.[8]

These results make clear that in addition to theory, therapists must focus on the acquisition of basic therapeutic skills. But that isn't all. Therapists must also learn how to integrate those basic skills with the demands of current clinical practice. And those demands have changed dramatically.

The public perception and practice of psychotherapy has shifted for therapists and their patients. The focus is no longer exclusively on in-patient treatment for the seriously disturbed nor on long-term analysis for the affluent elite. Therapy has become democratized: it's something everyone can undertake if they're having a problem; it's not shameful or (as) stigmatized; it's usually brief and focused on problem solving. It's something people do now, almost like going to the dentist.

Furthermore, this democratization makes it essential that therapists are able to respond to a multicultural society. Given that a majority of mental health professionals are non-Hispanic whites, it is imperative that all therapists are prepared to expand their understanding to include diverse cultures.[9] Therapists must be not only sensitive to cultural differences but also able to delineate between cultural influences and individual psychopathology and make modifications in treatment approaches (if necessary).[10]

Another important aspect of this global context is that more than 50 percent of all behavioral health care is now managed by third-party payers, and that figure changes daily; by the time this book comes out, it may be closer to 70 percent. Without health insurance, most people can't afford mental health services. And although mental health clinics are supposed to take up the slack, there are strict limitations on the amount of available care.

Consequently, accountability and cost effectiveness are now key elements in the way therapy functions as a profession. Insurance corporations, managed care companies, health maintenance organizations, and government agencies all demand broad-based coverage at the lowest cost. There is tremendous pressure for efficient and effective therapy that has a specific treatment plan with measurable goals and outcomes.

All these issues raise the question, "What do we need in order to work in this environment?" What we need to know is how core therapeutic skills can be merged with the needs of consumers and the demands of behavioral health care systems. It is imperative that basic skills include an integration of art and science. The art comes from experimentation and intuition, the science from practice and research. Training provides the synthesis.

That training must be inspired by theory, guided by research, tempered by common sense, and practical enough to withstand the turmoil of real therapeutic practice. This book is designed to be a practical synthesis of the crucial aspects all therapists must consider as we strive to

- Become effective observers
- Establish rapport
- Manage an initial interview
- Communicate essential information
- Create meaningful therapeutic contracts
- Manage awkward moments
- Balance personal responses with professional obligations
- Communicate effectively with supervisors

Learning these core skills leaves a lot of space for interpretation. The acquisition of these skills can take a lifetime and still leave plenty of room for improvement. This book provides a place to start.

Notes
1.   Strupp, H. H. (1986). Psychotherapy: Research, practice, and public policy (how to avoid dead ends. *American Psychologist, 41,* 120–130.
2.   Seligman, M. E. (1995). The effectiveness of psychotherapy: The Consumer Reports study. *American Psychologist, 50,* 965–974.

3. Lambert, M. J., & Bergin, A. E. (1994). The effectiveness of psychotherapy. In A. E. Bergin & S. L. Garfield (Eds.), *Handbook of psychotherapy and behavior change* (4th ed., pp. 143–190). New York: Wiley.

4. Garske, J. P., & Lynn, S. J. Toward a general scheme for psychotherapy: Effectiveness, common factors and integration. In S. J. Lynn & J. P. Garske (Eds.), *Contemporary psychotherapies: Models and methods* (pp. 497–516). Columbus, OH: Charles E. Merrill.

5. Luborsky, L., Singer, B., & Luborsky, L. (1975). Comparative studies of psychotherapies: "Is it true that everybody has won and all must have prizes?" *Archives of General Psychiatry, 32,* 995–1008; Smith, M. L., & Glass, G. V. (1977). Meta-analysis of psychotherapy outcome studies. *American Psychologist, 32,* 752–760. Stiles, W. B., Shapiro, D., & Elliot, R. (1986). Are all psychotherapies equivalent? *American Psychologist, 41,* 165–180.

6. See note 3, pp. 143–144.

7. See note 3, p. 181.

8. See note 3, pp. 176–180.

9. Vargas, L. A., & Willis, D. J. (1994). New directions in the treatment of ethnic minority children and adolescents. *Journal of Clinical Child Psychology, 23,* 2–4.

10. Rogler, L. H., Malgady, R. G., Costantino, G., & Blumenthal, R. (1987). What do culturally sensitive mental health services mean? The case of Hispanics. *American Psychologist, 42,* 565–570.

Chapter One

Developing
Observational Skill

From the first therapeutic contact to the last, there is one over-riding skill that provides the foundation for how you will implement all other competencies. That skill is observation. Observation allows you to collect the information you need to understand your clients, their problems, and the means to move toward solutions.

Right from the start you'll make observations that will provide information to help you understand what's going on during therapy: Is this client scared, this one drunk, or that one taking too many risks? Furthermore, your initial observations will give you the material you need to build rapport and create workable therapeutic contracts. It's your observations that provide the data needed for supervision, case presentations, and managed care. The success or failure of all these other tasks will depend primarily on how well you have been able to process what you see and hear.

From our earliest years, we process all kinds of information outside of conscious awareness. We take in cues that tell us this person is friendly or that one is dangerous. We learn from these clues how to manage social situations, about how close to stand, how loud to talk, and what level of language to use. Without much thought, people change their tone, words, and manner when talking to a baby, a supervisor, a lover. The only difference is that as a therapist you'll make deliberate observations of behavior that you ordinarily take for granted in other settings.

As you observe, you make assumptions. Those assumptions can help you, but they can also be a source of error when they narrow your perspective. An essential attribute of learning to observe therapeutic interaction is the ability to remain open to alternative assumptions as you formulate a working hypothesis about what's really going on. Keeping your mind open to the many possibilities for interpretation lessens the likelihood of locking onto the wrong approach. As you and your client make progress in therapy, you will continually revise and reevaluate your initial impressions. But you will always want to remain alert in observing four basic factors:

1. Nonverbal cues
2. Verbal expression
3. The relationship between spoken language and body language
4. Your reactions

Observing Nonverbal Cues

We probably take in, and draw more conclusions from, what we observe of nonverbal behavior than from what is actually said. Our observations of clothing, grooming, eye contact, posture, and mannerisms provide us with valuable information about our clients.

Let's start with an example:

Juan made a telephone appointment after explaining to my secretary that his needs were urgent and that he wanted the first available time.

He was standing in the waiting room when I greeted him. He was about 5'11", with dark skin and dark hair, and he appeared to be of normal weight. Juan was dressed in a dark blue suit, a white shirt with a red tie, and was wearing glasses.

Before I could say anything, he reached out to shake my hand and introduce himself, stepping toward me. Without thinking, I stepped back—he seemed too close. I explained that my office was down the hall. Juan talked continually on the way to the office. He mentioned the weather and commented on furniture.

Once in my office, he looked out the window, then took a chair and moved it so as to be seated directly in front of me— again too close. He sat on the edge of the chair and took a folder out of his leather briefcase. He opened the folder, and I could see some letters and papers with handwritten notes. He handed me his intake forms.

On the intake form, Juan wrote about his reason for coming to therapy. He explained that he wanted to leave his wife and two children, but couldn't. He described himself as feeling anxious and depressed.

With this case in mind, let's go through the specific topics that require our attention.

General Appearance

We can often observe age and gender without much uncertainty. But not always. I guessed Juan was somewhere between thirty-five and forty-five. It turned out that he was fifty-five. Juan appeared to be in good health. He wasn't.

I assumed that Juan was healthy because his height and weight seemed normal, his ability to move seemed coordinated, and his complexion and eyes seemed clear. What I was not able to observe was that Juan suffered from an unstable form of diabetes, which I noticed later on his intake form under medical conditions.

Along these lines, you want to pay attention to anything that is physically noteworthy, such as race, complexion, height, and weight. I suspected that Juan was from a Spanish-speaking country because of his name, dark skin, and slight accent. I inquired, "It sounds to me like you might have grown up with another language. Is that so?" With that he launched into a lengthy explanation of his history.

"I am a *mestizo*," Juan said proudly. He went on to tell me that *mestizo* is a Spanish term used to describe people who are a mixture of Indian or African and European descent. His mother was Indian and his father European. He described being raised in Esmeraldes, Ecuador, by an aunt who was unable to conceive children. His parents gave him to her to raise when he was five. He said that he was aware of this arrangement and frequently saw his mother, father, and siblings. He explained that he attended school in Ecuador until he finished high school. At that time his aunt sent him to the United States for college. He remained in the United States with yearly visits to Ecuador to see his family. I noticed that he recited this explanation in what seemed like a well-rehearsed manner with no change in expression.

Clothing and Grooming

The cues you draw from clothing and grooming can provide information about affiliations and self-care. Juan's clothes suggested to me that he had a professional job, and I soon learned that in fact he was a physician. His grooming showed that he was indeed very careful about his dress. Furthermore, from his shoes to his suit, every item was not only high-quality but also immaculate.

I assumed that Juan enjoyed his occupation and appreciated being able to afford such expensive clothing. This turned out to be projection on my part. I learned later that Juan was uncomfortable with both his professional choice and his professional clothes. His aunt had always required that he dress with careful attention to detail, a requirement he hated but also had never really escaped. Juan detested obligations but also appeared to keep them—at least on the surface. His attention to his clothing stood out all the more after he described the self-contempt it produced. I was slow to pick this up because of my projection. But the initial observations were useful once we began working on ways to resist his aunt's prescriptions—he could stop wearing clothes he hated.

Sometimes what appears on the surface is more informative. For example, a client who comes to therapy in "grunge" can still have taken time and care to put it together. One young man showed up for successive appointments in my office with blue hair, then green, then purple, then red. He was twenty-one years old, less than five feet tall, and very slight in stature, with a pierced lower lip and left eyebrow. He was muscular, indicating that he most likely had worked out with weights. It was also clear that he liked to draw attention to his appearance.

On the other hand, a client can come to therapy in a suit that is stained, poorly cared for, and misbuttoned, indicating little regard for self-maintenance. Sometimes poor self-care is a result of not caring much about such matters. But it can also be an indication that something is interfering with normal self-care, such as depression, drug abuse, or psychosis.

Clothes also often reveal subculture associations. For example, skateboarders, football players, Deadheads, sorority women, and skinheads often dress in a distinctive manner. We might make assumptions about occupation or income level. In addition we might notice whether someone is trying to hide his figure or flaunt it. Even when we try to be cautious about making unwarranted assumptions, we all tend to react to our observations of dress according to the stereotypes we hold.

These guesses are important places to start, as long as we take care to remain open to other sources of information that may either confirm or disconfirm our original assumptions.

Facial Expression

Most of us look at a person's face to tell us about what's going on inside. We assume that facial expressions reveal thoughts and feelings that may not be expressed directly. Smiles, frowns, grimaces, and blank stares all convey meaning. Many clients reveal a great deal with each expression, whereas others show little about their feelings. Most display the expressions they think will be accepted. But efforts to control expression also convey meaning.

Sometimes you'll notice the absence of an expression that you might expect, considering what the client is saying. For example, when someone describes a great loss, a serious injustice, a calamity—we expect a facial reaction. When that reaction is not forthcoming, it's reasonable to wonder why. Some people almost appear frozen. You can see nothing. But the "nothing" is also important and should be noted.

We also need to remember that meaning will vary depending on the level of expressiveness within the client's culture. For example, Juan would have been considered very expressive for a male raised in Japan but not at all expressive for a female raised in Brazil. Regardless, as therapists our first impressions about the meaning of such expressions are important because we use that information to dictate our responses. When Juan burst into tears during his first appointment, it was reasonable for me to assume he was very upset. Under similar circumstances you will also make quick guesses that inform your other responses.

The important thing here is not ascertaining the exact meaning of facial expression. Your client will help you with that as therapy progresses. What is essential is that you notice not only the expressions your client presents initially but also changes as things move along. There will be many in most sessions. These changes in facial expression usually signal internal changes. As such they may indicate the need for more inquiry so that you can understand the meaning behind each change.

When Juan explained his interest in wanting to be in therapy he looked eager, almost expectant. He smiled frequently. But his eyes filled with tears when he talked about his mistress, Karen. He turned his head away from my gaze, as though not wanting me to see the emotions he experienced. Even though he seemed to be trying, he was not able to maintain composure.

When I inquired, "You seem to not want me to see how upsetting this is for you," it seemed even harder for him to contain his emotions. He bent over, hiding his face completely, and sobbed. He spoke into his hand. "I don't want this to bother me—it shouldn't. I don't understand why she did this to me. I love her." His nonverbal behavior made clear how uncomfortable Juan was. I was worried that it was too soon for him to reveal such emotion. His expressions made me aware that he wanted to maintain dignity.

But there was no stopping him. He went on to explain that three years ago he had become involved with Karen, who'd been employed to run his medical office. When she pursued him, he was flattered. She became his mistress and shortly thereafter gave birth to their daughter. "I love Karen's blond hair, the smell of her skin, and my baby daughter. I want them all in my life. But I was raised Catholic; I can't divorce."

Karen was outraged that he wouldn't leave his wife. She sued him for both harassment and paternity and won both suits. When Juan spoke about Karen his facial expressions were glowing, loving, and reflective of someone enamored.

As a result of Karen's lawsuits, Juan's wife learned about his affair. Nonetheless, she wanted to maintain their marriage. Juan told me, "My wife wants me to suffer; she knows I won't leave. I hate her because she knows I am a prisoner in this marriage—she's my jailer." The glare in his eyes, the purse of his lips, the tightness of his forehead all showed contempt. Juan continued to live with his wife and two sons but was overwhelmed by the intensity of his feelings and his continued obsession with Karen.

Eye Contact

Eye contact is an aspect of facial expression that often reveals comfort level: too much eye contact may indicate a desire to control or a need to intimidate; too little may indicate shyness, fear, or feelings of intimidation. Ease with the level of eye contact often goes unnoticed but reveals a synchronicity: what you are comfortable with is matched by your partner.

It's important to remember that eye contact is learned behavior and as such largely culturally determined.[1] Many people growing up in inner cities learn that it is dangerous to make eye contact. Only later, when they seek employment, do they learn that what was once a survival skill is now a professional liability.

Juan did not look at me directly. I wasn't sure if this was a cultural difference or if he was just uncomfortable with me. I wondered if not looking at me made it easier for him to minimize my importance. In fact, the cultural issue did not pertain here. Juan was very uncomfortable with this initial meeting. He was used to being seen in a positive light but was also aware that many would not understand his preoccupation with a twenty-eight-year-old woman. He wanted to talk about the loss of his lover but also wanted to avoid my judgment. He was aware of being watched and afraid of being judged. Thus he avoided eye contact.

Tears

As Jeffrey Kottler wisely points out, there is much to learned from "the language of tears." He challenges us all to become students of tears, learning not only to decipher meaning but also to respond empathically. But he also warns us that these emotionally laden symbols are bound by culture, gender, and motivation.[2] As therapists, we must first notice. Then, together with our clients, we must search for both meaning and motivation.

We can usually start with the assumption that tears require sensitivity, patience, and permission. It helps if there is a box of tissues in the room. Sometimes not drawing any attention to the flow of tears demonstrates a readiness to understand.

When Michelle cried, she tried to stop by breathing deeply, sighing, and blotting her eyes. She said it was "crazy to cry over losing

Pepper," her dog. I didn't think her response was crazy, and I told her so.

The gender differences related to crying are enormous. Women are expected to cry, men aren't. But women aren't supposed to cry during a business meeting, and men are supposed to be sensitive enough to show tears—sometimes. Nonetheless, we all cry. Many women cry when they are angry, not sad. The tears represent the frustration of unexpressed anger. Men cry after years of holding back, touched by something tender. These and many other social prescriptions complicate our ability to understand what's happening with our clients.

Even our responses to tears have social prescriptions. We are expected to notice, even though our noticing doesn't always help matters. Likewise, when therapist and client are male and female respectively, the therapist needs to take care. Some women expect men to take away their tears, to reassure, or to "make it better." Some men feel pressured and guilty when women cry and so move quickly to minimize. Likewise many men are more ashamed to cry in front of another man than with a woman. Yet many men experience great relief and acceptance when they cry together. Women may be more comfortable with each other when one cries, but not always.

The social and personal prescriptions for tears are vast. As therapists we often have to help our clients understand not only their personal reactions but also their own social standards. Because tears provide relief, they are more than just a signal—they can promote healing. But in order to receive the benefits of crying, clients must be relieved of their personal and social prohibitions.

Sharon never cried. And the absence of her tears had great meaning for me. She had witnessed horror. She was ridiculed and abused. But she didn't cry. Even when she wanted to, she couldn't. I could see that she missed the healing that came from releasing tears. Permission was given, she knew it was now safe, but she still couldn't cry. If she had been able to cry it would have been an important therapeutic sign that she was able to experience not only relief but also a fuller range of emotional response. Unfortunately, the safety of our therapeutic relationship was not enough to overcome the personal prohibition she acquired as a consequence of growing up with parents who ridiculed her for crying.

Tears can also mean "Back off, this hurts, stop!" or "Help me" or "I'm sad." Almost always the meaning is complex. If the context does not provide clarity, you will have to ask the client what the tears mean, because this important clue should never go unrecorded. We'll talk more about this in the chapter on handling difficult situations.

Kinesics

Taken together, overall posture, facial expressions, movement, gestures, breathing changes, and eye focus constitute body language or, more formally, kinesics. When we observe, we rarely separate eyes, mouth, and posture. More likely, we notice an overall presentation. When someone rocks back and forth, plays with her hair, looks at his watch, leans forward and stares, or crosses her arms and glares in contempt—we notice. Popular magazines are full of advice on how to interpret these signals from friends, bosses, and lovers, even though research has warned that personal and cultural bias prohibits us from deciphering body language accurately.[3]

Regardless of these cautions, therapists still search for meaning in body language. We have to use all available data, and that certainly includes these nonverbal clues. We accumulate impressions. When it seems appropriate and when their confusion dictates, most therapists heed the warnings of the researchers and present their observations to their clients as speculative. In order to ensure that we're on the right track, it's wise to ask our clients to clarify any ambiguity. For example, you might say, "This is what I'm seeing; does that match the way you see it?"

One of the reasons I enjoyed working with Juan was that his nonverbal signals were easy to read. And when I pointed out what I observed, he responded with increased understanding. Juan displayed his anxiety nonverbally by pacing in the waiting room, furrowing his brow, and sitting rigidly on the edge of his chair. His body language conveyed what he was too uncomfortable to say, "I'm scared." When I remarked, "You seem frightened," he was clear: "I didn't think I would be, but I am scared—just a little bit of you. Mostly I am scared of what I will learn by being here."

Proxemics

Proxemics, or the use of personal space, includes three important features: distance, position in the room, and touch. Meaning is conveyed by how close we stand, where we sit, and when we touch. Generally speaking, we only allow people we consider close into what we think of as "our space." In a therapeutic setting, most middle-class Americans find a distance of about three to four feet comfortable.[4]

A therapist who sits behind a large desk conveys something very different than does a therapist who sits on the floor. My office doesn't have a desk; there is a circular couch and two stuffed chairs. Most clients pick a space that they return to on successive visits. Claire always sits as far away from me as she can get. Even though all the seats allow for eye contact, she sits at an angle and looks away. Claire keeps her distance.

Perhaps one of the most important features of proxemics is touch. We all know that our professional codes prohibit any form of sexual touch; however, there is still a lot of room for interpretation. When a client reaches for your hand or opens her arms, it's reasonable to assume an invitation to touch. Later on we'll cover how to handle these complicated situations. For now it's important to note your client's signals.

Returning to our example, Juan's use of space was noticeable when we first met in the waiting room. He moved toward me, introducing himself. His body language had already signaled his discomfort. As I mentioned earlier, he wasn't the only one uncomfortable; I was uneasy with how close he stood. Once I understood this as a cultural difference I felt more at ease with how close he chose to stand and sit, but probably not before Juan noticed that I had backed up and looked uncomfortable, which he took as a subtle sign of rejection.

When he came into the office, Juan moved the furniture. He positioned the chair to be directly in front of me, assuring attention and taking control. Juan also tried to control the conversation by initiating topics and switching when he was uncomfortable. Taken together, these gestures indicated to me the possibility that this was Juan's style of dealing with people. When I asked, Juan explained, "Of course I must be in charge. I am a doctor."

Observing Verbal Expression

Nonverbal cues provide a significant contribution to understanding our clients. There is also much to observe in verbal behavior. At this point we are not really talking about what is said but rather how things are verbalized.

We rely on such characteristics as volume, inflection, rate of speech, fluency, laughter, pauses, and silence to enlarge the meaning of what is actually spoken. Furthermore, as already noted, paying attention to dialect, vocabulary, and phrasing helps us better understand a client's education, developmental level, and culture. In fact, the way someone speaks often tells us more than what is actually said.

Observations of Juan's verbal behavior added to the nonverbal cues. As you've probably noticed already, there was a lot to be learned from what he said. But there was also a lot to learn from how he spoke. In the middle of the second session, Juan paused for over a minute. Then he spoke slowly as though measuring each word. With no inflection, he said, "Karen won't let me see my baby daughter. She has cut herself off from my love. I don't understand." I could hardly hear him. The words explaining what happened were clear. His feelings, however, were revealed by how he spoke. He was angry.

Therapists add depth to visual cues by understanding something about sociolinguistics, the study of the social and cultural aspects of language. Our interest in understanding the full meaning of what our clients say is enriched by our following cues provided by how they speak. But again, we need to know where to focus our attention.

Manner of Speech

Some people speak rapidly, some slowly; some barely talk above a whisper, whereas others can be heard down the hall. Therapists often use these clues as indicators of other problems. In most cases it would be reasonable to identify a soft tone as an indication of shyness, embarrassment, discomfort with disclosure, or fear of ridicule. Likewise, a loud voice could be a sign of hearing loss, an attempt at intimidation, or a reflection of the intensity of emotion.

Sometimes the style of speech serves as an indicator for more serious mental health problems. In some cases a fast pace, a loud voice, and pressure to continue talking could be signs of a manic episode; a slower pace, soft tone, and lack of concentration may be symptoms of depression.

If you are from the same culture as your client, you can probably make some reasonably accurate guesses about what these clues mean. But when you are from a different subculture or culture, you need to be very careful making assumptions from a style of speech.[5] For example, Americans often are more comfortable with a louder voice than are people from other cultures.[6] Although counselors must be careful about drawing conclusions, they must also take care not to miss the obvious.

Returning to our example, I actually missed the obvious because of my desire to be culturally sensitive. Originally I was aware of Juan's soft voice and assumed it related to a cultural difference. Had I been more astute I would have noticed that Juan's voice was barely above a whisper only when he talked about his mistress. On other occasions he used a louder voice.

A more careful observation would also have revealed that Juan used a soft voice only when he talked about things he assumed would be met with harsh judgment. Even though Juan's verbal behavior matched his lack of eye contact, I missed these signs that Juan was particularly dependent on my approval.

Fluency

Fluency generally refers to the person's ease of articulation and the smooth flow of word and topic. Any tendency toward speech errors is exacerbated when people are nervous and anxious.[7] Because people are often anxious in therapy, it is likely that stuttering, stammering, and problems with some sounds will be worse when a client is discussing something that provokes strong feelings.

You should watch for fluency not only in speech but also in subject matter. Some clients jump from topic to topic, making it difficult to understand what is going on. It's important to ascertain why this happens. There is evidence that memories are stored in categories, one of which is likely to be painful feelings. A client's talking about one upsetting event can thus trigger memories of other things that are also upsetting.[8] When this happens your client may jump from talking about one upsetting thing to another.

On the other hand, clients sometimes shift to a new topic in order to avoid focusing on uncomfortable feelings. In this case the client is likely to shift to a topic that is less stressful. This pattern was evident with Juan. Even though his articulation and word flow were fluent, his transitions were not. Juan would often switch the topic when it came to discussions about his health. When asked, he explained only the bare facts about how he had recently passed out, suffered several seizures, and was beginning to have both visual and nerve damage as a result of his inability to balance insulin and sugar.

When I asked directly, "What has your doctor explained about how to better manage your diabetes?" Juan answered, "When I was at my doctor's all I could think about was how much I wanted to see Karen. She doesn't know how much I miss her, how much I need her." All my approaches led to the same superficial answers followed by elaborate explanations of his love for Karen.

I could certainly understand why he would want to minimize the impact of his disease. On the other hand, his avoidance also left him in danger of creating more trouble for himself. This lack of fluency made clearer one of Juan's major defensive strategies: focusing on romance when confronted with something painful. Later on, when the time came to provide Juan with examples of how this defensive tactic worked, my concrete descriptions of how he switched topics were essential to helping him comprehend his misguided strategy for avoiding discomfort.

Meaning and Choice of Words

It is easy to assume that we are speaking the same language. But there are many words that most likely have personal meanings for each user. Words like *love, hate, sex, passion, commitment, date, trust, hard work, late, messy, careful, dependent, concerned,* and *lazy* are delivered with the assumption that we are all on the same page. Rarely is that the case. Further, these words are usually laden with heavy meaning to the user. Who wants to be considered *lazy* or *messy*? Likewise, most of us want to be seen as *loving, caring,* and *reasonably organized.*

When someone complains that he has "failed" because he got a B, or "dependent" because her spouse was unfaithful, it would be reasonable to question the associated meanings. Unless the meaning is blatantly obvious or unimportant to what is being communicated, you'll want to make sure you understand what your client intends. In order to ascertain that meaning, it's helpful to ask her to describe which behaviors, thoughts, and feelings she associates with the words she chooses. For example, "When you say you love him, Jennifer, I need to know more about what you mean. I'd also like to understand your ideas about what the word *love* means to you. Can you tell me more about what those feelings are like for you?"

There is also an increased probability of confusion and misunderstanding when our clients use psychobabble—words and phrases that gain popular acceptance without corresponding clarity. People often use such terms and phrases as explanations for their behavior: "I am codependent," "I'm an adult child," "My inner child is lost," "Men are from Mars," or "Women are teasers." Usually such phrases resonate with something the client is trying to communicate, but it is also true that the meanings are unique rather than generic. You will want make sure that you understand what your client is trying to convey.

We all use vocabulary, grammar, and phrasing as indicators of education level, age, and sometimes intelligence. For example, most of us would rule out the possibility of retardation when someone is very articulate. Initial guesses about education and training are reasonable because vocabulary is one of the best predictors of academic success.[9]

Vocabulary and grammar often reveal more than just education and background. The choice of words may also demonstrate the client's internal focus. A client who describes feelings in great detail is indicating that her attention has most likely been on her emotions. Another client might describe a similar situation using concrete explanations that are devoid of feeling. This may indicate that the client is uncomfortable with or is avoiding a focus on affect.

With Juan I noticed that when he spoke about his wife and two teenage sons, he used simple, almost terse language. When he spoke about his mistress, however, he used very flowery phrases, such as "I am devoted to her in my deepest heart." He wanted me to read the notes he had written to Karen quoting Shakespeare with such lines as "Doubt that the stars are fire, doubt that the sun doth move; doubt truth to be a liar; but never doubt my love."

Furthermore, the choice of words and tone is most likely a reflection of the client's self-talk. What clients say to themselves is usually revealed by what they say to you. When someone uses derogatory language such as "I'm so stupid!" or "I hate the way I look; I'm ugly," it is likely that the person also uses a similar tone and words internally.

Laughter

Most often laughter goes with something funny. But laughter can also be used as a cover when someone is nervous, anxious, or worried. We need to notice when and how our clients laugh. Some laugh when nothing is humorous; it sounds strange and seems to come from nowhere.

One of my clients, Kate, would laugh when describing times she was frightened. I was thrown off at first but noticed that her laughter didn't sound normal; rather, it sounded forced, almost strained. She punctuated her sentences with this pained laughter. After several sessions, I was able to ask, "I notice you laugh, but it doesn't seem like you think this is funny." That helped. She was able to say, "People have told me that before. I don't even notice, but I am aware of not wanting to upset you. Maybe that's why."

This example illustrates how you can use your observations to ascertain meaning. If you point out what you have observed and then ask for clarification, you provide your clients not only the opportunity to get feedback but also the chance to explain their responses.

Pauses and Silence

Most people are uncomfortable with too much silence, although what is considered too long a pause certainly varies not only by culture but also by situation. Most of us assume that counseling and therapy involve talking, not silence. Also, most beginning therapists are so anxious about silence they jump in with words before they have adequately understood the reasons for the silence in the first place. Nevertheless, there will be many occasions when your client will sit quietly, even when it seems to you that it is his turn to talk. Some possible causes are that the client

Is thinking

Is overwhelmed with emotion

Doesn't want to talk about what is on her mind

Is scared of your reaction

Is fearful of being overheard

Wants to tell you something that will betray another's confidence

Can't find the right words

Is trying to regain composure

Your observations of the overall context of the silence will help you discover the reason for it. Facial expressions, the focus of your client's eyes, gestures, and movement can provide clues. If you really don't understand, you can ask: "You don't seem to know what to say, is that right?" or "Can you give me some feedback here? I don't understand why you are quiet."

In addition to understanding the reason for the lull in conversation, it is also important to ascertain whether or not your client is comfortable with the silence. Verbal and nonverbal cues may help you assess this issue as well. If the client is looking away, in a relaxed pose, you might assume comfort. On the other hand, if the client looks at you, then away, then back at you, you might safely assume that he expects you to do something about the silence. Incidentally, that does not mean you have to take care of the silence, but it does mean you must notice your client's expectations.

From the beginning I was aware that Juan was very uncomfortable with silence. Every time he came for a session, from first meeting to sitting down, he talked about details that were not relevant to his feelings or problems. After several sessions I was able to ask him about his intolerance for silence. Because he was unaware of this pattern, he was able to use my observations to understand how he avoided feelings: if he just kept talking, he didn't feel.

Taken together, nonverbal and verbal expression provide clues to the meaning and sometimes the underlying motivation for client behavior. When carefully observed, this information provides the data that can help therapists understand their client's concerns. Experienced therapists build on their awareness of both verbal and nonverbal behavior by noticing the interaction of these variables.

Observing the Interaction of Verbal and Nonverbal Behavior

Throughout each session all therapists use their observations of the interaction between spoken and body language as clues to client reactions.[10] If a client slouches and cries after explaining, "I lost my job," we assume grief. If a client slouches and cries after saying, "I've had it with this relationship," we assume exasperation. But when a client slouches and cries asserting, "I am so happy with my new marriage," we wonder. Is this ambivalence, joy, sadness, uncertainty, or some combination? Therapists need to understand more than what is readily apparent, and the interaction of nonverbal responses with what is actually said provides important clues to what's happening.

Consequently, therapists must view the interaction of body language with spoken language as a signal for our attention rather than as a definitive statement. Most often these interactions provide cues for inquiry.

Discrepancies

Nonverbal and verbal behavior are obviously related. Sometimes they complement each other, such as when a client cries when discussing a great loss, laughs when telling a funny story, or gets up when mentioning, "It's time to go." Other times verbal and nonverbal behavior can seem quite at odds, such as when a client shakes her head no but says yes; says, "It's time to go," but stays in her chair and begins a new topic; or expresses anger with a smile. Certainly, such discrepancies deserve careful attention and indicate not only the possibility of ambivalent feelings but also the need for further inquiry.

As we listen the meaning may be clarified. When it isn't, we need to investigate further with questions like "You're telling me you are pleased, but you're crying. Can you help me understand what's going on?" or "You tell me one thing, but show me something else. I'm confused. Are you?"

Turn Signals

The signals we deliver to indicate that it is the other person's turn to talk reveal another important aspect of verbal-nonverbal interaction. Turn-taking is something we largely take for granted. Many signals indicate that it is "your turn," such as when the speaker stops talking and moving, gazes at the listener, extends the palm of his hand, or raises pitch at the end of a sentence to indicate a question. All of these signals usually indicate that the speaker expects to stop talking and is looking for a reply.[11]

Nonverbal behavior is also used to indicate the desire to speak. Such gestures as raising an index finger, sitting forward, and, certainly, interrupting usually indicate the desire to speak.

Conversations that seem smooth and easy most assuredly involve the clear reading of turn signals. You will want to notice when either the client or you seem out of sync. At times when you feel pressure to speak but you have nothing to say, you may need to clarify with "You seem to want me to say something here, but I'm not sure what to say." Or when you want your client to continue a subject: "Can you tell me more about that?"

Movement Harmonics

Another important aspect of the interaction of body language and spoken language is movement harmonics.[12] This variable is the reciprocal motion created in all conversation. It can be noted as early as infancy when a young baby responds in rhythmic gestures to her caregiver's voice. As people age and develop, the tendency to move in rhythm remains.

When that movement is synchronous it generally leads to feelings of comfort, ease, and connection. As one person moves, the other responds, each in tune as though dancing. The lack of synchronicity creates the opposite effect and occurs when there is no rhythm between those in conversation. A lack of synchrony exists, for example, when the counselor sits on the edge of the chair with open stance and maintains steady eye contact while the client sits back in a relaxed pose with crossed arms, and looks away as if to avoid the constant gaze of the counselor. This situation is likely to make both client and therapist uncomfortable.

Another aspect of harmonics is called movement complementarity. We all know the easy feeling that comes when someone responds to our gestures in kind. Whether that gesture is a handshake, a smile, or an eye roll in response to something ridiculous, we usually expect a reciprocal reaction. On the other hand, when someone doesn't respond as expected we're thrown off. Think of times when you've smiled expecting a smile in return but instead received an icy stare. That discomfort is a result of the lack of complementarity or of an expected return response.

Our Interpretations

It is clear that you will be interpreting what you see and hear. Therapists often pride themselves on their insightful interpretations. But you want to be aware that sometimes an event is just that and not a symbol for something else. When asked about his love of cigars, even Freud admitted, "Sometimes a cigar is just a cigar."

On that note, I remember one young man who sat on the edge of his chair and leaned forward. Finally, I inquired. He explained that he was a drummer and that he had just come from a class where he was instructed on how to strengthen his stomach muscles. That was why he was sitting in such an unusual and rigid posture.

Body language may be a result of other physical conditions and therefore may not be a sign of underlying emotion. A client whose hand shakes as she writes a check may have a tremor that only occurs when grasping. It would be inappropriate in this case to assume anxiety. Another client explained to me that her inability to settle her eye movement was nystagmus, a physical condition. But it's also possible that shaking or tremors can be exacerbated by anxiety. So whenever you are in doubt, ask. If you ask gently and explain the question as an effort at understanding, it's likely to be appreciated. More will be explained later on how to do this kind of investigating.

Learning to observe the essential features of the interaction of verbal and nonverbal behavior involves practice with supervision.

As you learn to check out your observations, you will refine your skills. Asking clients to help you not only serves to keep you on track but also contributes to building rapport. You can say, "I want to make sure that I am understanding you. Do you think I have it right?" or "This is what I am understanding: [fill in the blank with what you understand]—is that it?"

Observing Yourself

Clients expect that a consultation with a therapist will provide an "objective" if not scientific view of their concerns. Certainly it is the intention of most therapists to meet that expectation. But most experienced therapists are also aware that clinical observations are neither neutral nor totally objective.

Freud used the term *countertransference* to describe "the patient's influence on the therapist's unconscious."[13] Freud recognized that the therapist's personal reactions could serve as both a hindrance to therapeutic progress and as a tool to advance treatment. The outcome depended on the therapist's ability to recognize and manage these reactions.

We all want our personal reactions to inform, not impede, therapeutic progress. Therefore we must take careful note of how we influence what we observe. Right from the start there are variables that most assuredly distort our observations.

Personal Reactions

We see through the filters of our childhoods, personal expectations, troubles, interests, fears. Likewise, we are influenced by our own culture, gender, and age. Most of us seek to confirm what we already believe, which in turn influences what we look for and therefore what we will see. Therapists who have been obsessed with food or who have been battered, raped, humiliated, oppressed, addicted, or in other ways harmed are obviously influenced by those experiences. Likewise, we are also influenced by positive events.

None of these experiences precludes your becoming a competent therapist as long as you are able to understand how those experiences affect your ability to see "objectively." It is imperative that you monitor the filters created by your own experience. Most often that is accomplished by a combination of personal therapy and careful supervision. By taking care to observe yourself, you minimize the possibility of making errors in clinical judgment.

Along with understanding the influence of your own personal history, you need to notice how each client affects you, what your impressions are, and how those impressions influence treatment choices. You should monitor these reactions carefully. It is crucial to notice when you feel pressured, manipulated, flattered, seduced, enchanted, scared, bored, confused, overwhelmed, anxious, tired, or any other way, for that matter.

You'll use these observations in two ways. First, these reactions may inform you about how other people in the client's world react. So when a man complains that his wife never listens, and you notice that you don't feel like paying attention to his pedantic diatribes, you may better understand why his wife is ignoring him. Second, you need to notice any reactions that may signal difficulty in establishing a therapeutic relationship. Because therapy must be primarily geared toward helping the client, you will need to take notice

If you have had a great deal of trouble with the same problem the client is presenting

If you find yourself irritated with your client

If you feel sexual attraction

If you're bored, tired, or feeling as though you'll fall asleep

Before you can handle any of these situations, you must first of all notice your reactions. Indeed, your reactions can help you help your clients. Boredom may signal that the client is avoiding talking about things that matter. Anxiety may signal the need for you to take more direct action. Fear may indicate that it is time for you to get a consultation. You will learn what your individual signals mean as you pay attention to your own reactions. In addition, your reactions may be useful in guiding your understanding of client dynamics and potential clinical interventions.

Going back to our example, I was aware of my concern about Juan's self-destructive behavior. After all, it was apparent that he wasn't hurting only himself—he was also hurting others. I wanted

Juan to understand that the methods he used to solve problems—finding another woman, drinking, and excessive work—all made his problems worse.

But Juan noticed that I sighed, looked away, and sometimes spoke with a tinge of irritation—all signs of frustration. Juan incorrectly assumed these responses stemmed from some sort of moral disapproval rather than from concern over not being able to help him resolve his problems.

Professional Filters

Theoretical orientations also prescribe a focus of attention. For example, a therapist who subscribes to object-relations theory will be very attentive to the client's early childhood, whereas a solution-focused therapist will pay particular attention to aspects of the client's coping ability. These filters are important sources of both guidance and error. We all need to take note of the adage that if the only tool you have is a hammer, everything looks like a nail.

Professional obligations, such as your being a provider in a capitated insurance program, or trying to keep a private practice going, or staying within a six-session limit, will also dictate focus. At this point in our discussion, what is important is a clear understanding of how these obligations influence what you are able to observe.

The Effect of Our Behavior

The final variable to discuss here is how your participation influences what you are seeing. In a therapy relationship both client and therapist participate, both observe. And both observe the other observing. Like mirrors facing each other, each image reacts to the other. The therapist sees the client, who is aware that the therapist is observing (and vice versa). A careful sensitivity is required to know how your behavior may influence a client, which in turn will influence what you observe.

As you have seen, my concern over not being able to help Juan understand his destructive qualities was interpreted by him to mean that I disapproved. He was aware that I was watching, and he assumed that I disapproved because he wasn't "loving." So he tried to show me just how loving he was by describing all his romantic fantasies of Karen. I, in turn, saw this as part of his destructive cycle, which produced more concern and frustration on my part.

After observing this not very therapeutic process take place, I was able to discuss my participation with Juan. After explaining what I thought was happening between us, I asked him what he thought. He explained, "I want to please you. I shouldn't want to, but I do. I really want to please lots of people that I let down; I hate that. Then I guess I just get lost with too much alcohol and too much work—I don't know what to do, but this isn't working." He got it. That was just the beginning of a lot of hard work that followed. But the work was now easier because we were working on the same problem. He could now see that I was frustrated with his avoidance, and he was too.

Chapter Eight provides more information on how to interpret and manage our own reactions. For now, we need to note that these variables have a profound influence on our interpretation of what we have observed.

———————

This chapter provides some suggestions about what to look for as you begin working with clients. As you learn to observe your clients you'll refine your observations by checking out what you have seen and heard. Likewise, you will need to check out the conclusions you draw, with both your clients and supervisors. The more you can see, the more you will learn. Your ability to describe what you have seen and heard will be a great asset. As we proceed through this book, we will return again and again to this basic skill.

As you gain practice, you will learn what works best for you. Some of us learn more from visual cues, others gain more from verbal, but most of us need all the information we can get from the combination of all we see and hear. Now we move to a special refinement of observational skill: essential assessments.

Notes
1. Arredono, P., Toporek, R., Brown, S., Jones, J., Locke, D., Sanchez, J., & Stadler, H. (1996). *Operationalization of the multicultural counseling competencies*. Alexandria, VA: Association for Multicultural Counseling and Development.

2.   Kottler, J. (1996). *The language of tears.* San Francisco: Jossey-Bass.
3.   See note 1.
4.   Lecomte, C., Berstein, B. L., & Dumont, F. (1981). Counseling inter-actions as a function of spatial-environmental conditions. *Journal of Counseling Psychology, 28,* 536–539.
5.   Ramirez, S. Z., Wassef, A., Paniagua, F., & Linskey, A. (1996). Men-tal health providers' perceptions of cultural variables in evaluating ethnically diverse clients. *Professional Psychology: Research and Practice, 27,* 284–288.
6.   Sue, D. W., & Sue, D. (1977). Barriers to effective cross-cultural counseling. *Journal of Counseling Psychology, 24,* 420–497.
7.   Knapp, M. L. (1978). *Nonverbal communication in human interaction* (2nd ed.). Austin, TX: Holt, Rinehart and Winston.
8.   Schacter, D., Verfeallie, M., & Pradere, D. (1996). The neuropsy-chology of memory illusions: False recall and recognition in amnesic patients. *Journal of Memory and Language, 35,* 319–334.
9.   Follman, J. (1990). Enhancing children's vocabularies. *Learning House, 63,* 329–332; Espin, C. A. (1996). Validity of general outcome measures for predicting secondary students' performance of content-area tasks. *Exceptional Children, 62,* 497–514; Ward, D., Wilson, T., & Ward, S. (1994). A common business and accounting vocabulary base: Are black students adequately prepared? *Journal of Education for Business, 69,* 267–272.
10. Cormier, W. H., & Cormier, S. L. (1991). *Interviewing strategies for helpers: Fundamental skills and cognitive behavioral interventions* (3rd ed.). Pacific Grove, CA: Brooks/Cole, pp. 66–71.
11. Duncan, S. P., Jr. (1972). Some signals and rules for taking speaking turns in conversations. *Journal of Personality and Social Psychology, 23,* 283–292; Duncan, S. P., Jr. (1974). On the structure of speaker-auditor interaction during speaking turns. *Language in Society, 2,* 161–180; Knapp, M. L. (1972). *Nonverbal communication in human interaction.* Austin, TX: Holt, Rinehart and Winston; also see note 7 above.
12. Ivey, A. E. (1994). *Intentional interviewing and counseling: Facilitating client development in a multicultural society* (3rd ed.). Pacific Grove, CA: Brooks/Cole, pp. 73–74.
13. Freud, S. (1961). The future prospects of psycho-analytic therapy. In J. Strachey (Ed. and Trans.), *The standard edition of the complete psychological works of Sigmund Freud* (Vol. 11, pp. 139–152). London: Hogarth Press, pp. 144–145. (Original work published 1910).

Chapter Two

Essential Evaluations and Assessments

Whether we have a single session or fifty, we are always observing and evaluating our client's presenting concerns, assessing the fundamental aspects of our client's psychological status, and determining what, if anything, needs to be done. In order to provide this service we must be able to focus our observational skills on essential evaluations and assessments.

When some of us think about therapeutic assessments we imagine many highly specialized tasks such as analyzing responses from a Rorschach Inkblot test or giving IQ tests. Likewise we would assume that on-the-job training is necessary for us to assess the need for protective services at a shelter from domestic violence or to evaluate a client's readiness for parole from prison. But these formal assessments requiring specialized training are not the focus of this chapter.

Rather, the skill we want to discuss here is the ability to evaluate those aspects of client functioning that always must be monitored regardless of whether the problem is domestic violence, an eating disorder, loss of an important relationship, marital discord, panic attacks, or addiction. During each and every session we must be prepared to evaluate and assess the following:

- The client's presenting problems
- The client's mental status
- The client's possible involvement with drugs
- The client's danger to self and others

In addition we must be prepared to use those assessments to provide ourselves, our supervisors, and managed care administrators with diagnostic information that includes a description of presenting and, later, maintaining symptoms.

Furthermore, we are aware that scientific method and professional tradition require a thorough period of data collection and observation before we draw conclusions. Yet we also know that therapeutic practice rarely provides that luxury. Although some clients are prepared for a lengthy assessment period, most are not. Moreover, 40 percent of psychotherapy clients come for only one appointment.[1] Therefore we must have the skill to make assessments accurately, quickly, and efficiently.

Our primary task as therapists is to work with our clients to find solutions to the problems that brought them to us in the first place. This means we must assess how clients understand their problems. Likewise with each successive appointment we must monitor our clients' understanding of their problems and progress.

Presenting Problems

Our first task is to understand why this person has decided to seek therapy at this time. It's our job to locate what commands the client's mental and emotional energy. This usually means finding out what's most on our client's mind, what preoccupies, what commands his attention, and what stimulates emotion. In order to figure this out it is usually best to let clients tell you why they decided to seek therapy, and you can provide the focus with the questions you ask.

Why Now?

Initially the best indicator of our client's motivation comes from the answer to the question, "What made you decide to seek therapy now?" In their book *Theory and Practice of Brief Therapy*, Simon Budman and Alan Gurman point out that Why now? is *the* central question for therapists to assess.[2] The answers to this question provide key information about the client's motivation and focus.

When I first started asking, "What made you decide to seek therapy now?" I was often surprised by the results.

My roommate is sick of listening to me complain.

My mother said that if I didn't come, she wouldn't give me my
allowance.

I cry all the time. I don't know why. I'm desperate. I'm afraid I'll
lose my job.

I'm not a hormonal person, and my husband wants me to change.

My health insurance just started to cover mental health and everyone tells me—you need help. I'm not sure why.

You can see from these answers that the reason for coming to
therapy may or may not be the stated problem. For example:

When Julie, a twenty-eight-year-old attorney, came for her first
appointment, she explained that her problem was low self-esteem.
She described in detail how she worried about her weight, was
belittled by her father, and failed to pass the bar exam on her
first try. But when I asked her why she chose to start therapy now,
she explained, "My jealousy is out of control—I promised Matt,
my fiancé, that I would get help because he can't tolerate my
possessiveness anymore."

You can see that Julie's answer to the Why now? question provided important information about her motivation and expectations for therapy. From her response, I learned that she was
worried more about losing her fiancé than about her stated problem of low self-esteem. We can also observe that she assumed her
jealousy resulted from her low self-esteem—not her fiancé's behavior. Julie's primary motivation for therapy came from her conclusion that therapy would help her get rid of her jealousy, thus
protecting her relationship.

It is our job to make sure we understand, from the client's
point of view, why she chose therapy as an option now. This understanding helps us engage our clients because we're focused on *their*
most pressing concerns. We also need to figure out how our
clients' problems affect their overall ability to function with their
daily responsibilities.

What Are the Symptoms?

There are two important areas we need to assess to determine how
the presenting problem(s) create trouble for the client. First, we

need to understand what symptoms are present, and second, we need to get a clear picture of how those symptoms affect daily functioning.

Most therapy settings, as well as all third-party payers, such as Medicare, managed care, and private insurance companies, require therapists to make a diagnosis using the fourth edition of the *Diagnostic and Statistical Manual of Mental Disorders* (*DSM-IV*).[3] For us to make a diagnosis, we need a clear picture of basic symptoms.

Take Julie's problem, for example. It would never work to tell her insurance company that she needed five sessions because her fiancé was threatening to break off their relationship. Instead, we must be able to provide a diagnosis based on symptoms. Consequently, we must observe or hear about each client's pattern of symptoms, or we need to ask questions that will reveal this pattern.

We should ask about any symptoms suggested by what our clients have already revealed. The following are some other questions that help clarify symptoms:

How is this a problem for you now?

How have you been feeling about this? What are these feelings like?

Does this problem affect your ability to function? How?

How does this problem play itself out during an average day?

Do you have any sleep problems? What kind?

Have you experienced any changes in eating patterns?

Do you have crying spells? How often?

What do you worry about?

Do you have any difficulty with irritability, concentration, fatigue, panic?

We also need to know how the problem functions. Like a journalist trying to understand a story, we need to ask clarifying questions: who, what, where, when, how. Furthermore we need an understanding of what's going on when the problem(s) aren't bothering the client.

For example, Julie explained that she felt shaky and fatigued, had difficulty sleeping despite excessive exercise, and also had problems eating. It may seem obvious why those symptoms would be problematic, but we have an obligation to make sure we understand each individual's pattern.

After I asked, "How does this cause you trouble?" at first Julie said, "At least, I'm losing weight. Thank goodness." I noticed that Julie was thin and seemed to have no observable weight problem. When I asked her about this, Julie explained that she didn't eat because she was afraid she would gain weight. She noted, "I worry about my weight all the time, except when I worry about what Matt is doing."

I asked if she saw a connection between her symptoms and the way she ate and exercised. Julie explained proudly, "I'm doing well with my eating. You know, for the last two weeks I've eaten practically nothing and then only fat-free foods. That's great." It was clear that she did not associate the symptoms she mentioned—fatigue, anxiety, or sleep disturbance—with her eating habits.

In answer to the who, what, when, where, and why questions, Julie spelled out that she had the most trouble controlling her jealousy when her fiancé was with his best friend, a woman. He spent long hours with her, fixed her car, and came whenever she called. Whenever Julie expressed concern about being left alone, he complained about her "incessant jealousy." The only time Julie wasn't bothered was when she was exercising. She ran, went to aerobics, or bicycled each day.

What happened with Julie is an important example of how we learn more when we ask about how problems function. In this case, we discovered that even though Matt's behavior was provocative, she blamed herself for having low self-esteem and being jealous; and when I asked about her symptoms, I learned of a possible eating disorder. Even though Julie had not defined her eating and exercising as a problem, her symptoms suggested otherwise.

Once we understand why the client has decided on therapy, what symptoms are present, and how those symptoms create trouble, we need to understand what the client is motivated to work on.

What Shall We Work On?

One of the most helpful assessments we can make is to determine our client's readiness to change. James Prochaska and Carlo Di Clemente have identified stages that clients move through during the process of change: precontemplation, contemplation, preparation, action, and then maintenance.[4] This paradigm for change fits most client concerns, cuts across all theoretical orientations, and provides very useful information about motivation.

It makes sense to do a preliminary assessment of where the client is located on the continuum of change with each individual problem. This determination helps you plan appropriate strategies. Because most clients cycle in and out of these stages several times before achieving their goals, it is helpful to gauge the current status of each problem during the initial session, and to continue to do so in each successive session to record signs of progress.

Prochaska and his colleagues outline these five stages as follows:

1. *Precontemplation.* In this stage tne client is only thinking about the possibility of change. The problem may not even be defined as a problem. Clients in this stage may be those mandated by the courts to come into therapy and who think there's no problem; they may come in because a family member (usually their wife or husband) insists; they may come in to complain about someone else, blaming them for the problem; or they may blame other contextual situations at home or work, still not thinking they have a problem or a need to change. In fact, when some clients enter therapy, they may only be seeking reassurance that there is, in fact, no "serious" problem.

Our role at this stage is to assess whether or not this client sees a problem. We may see it, such as when substance abuse or some other destructive behavior is involved, but that is not the same thing as the client's seeing the problem as one he wants to tackle.

2. *Contemplation.* At this stage, clients are aware that they have problems but are still considering the pros and cons of change. Most clients with relationship problems enter at this stage. Such clients are aware that change may be necessary but are also aware of reasons why making those changes will be difficult. At this stage the clients aren't clear about what kind of changes to make, so it's our role to help them weigh their options as well as the consequences of their choices.

3. *Preparation.* During this phase clients know that change is in order and are beginning to take steps to make those changes. At this stage most clients are collecting information about the best

way to proceed. They consider strategies, options, and plans.

We can help them evaluate their plans with such questions as, What have you done in the past? As things progress, what do you envision yourself doing? Is there anything holding you back? Who will notice these changes? How will that affect you? What are the advantages of making changes now? What can you imagine yourself doing?

4. *Action.* In this stage, the client is ready to act. The advantages of changing outweigh the advantages of not changing. The client is clear about some course of action and is actively engaged in trying out solutions.

Certainly, we can help by providing support, fine-tuning strategies, assessing the outcome, and offering encouragement. Most therapists function very well when clients are at this stage. Indeed, just coming to a therapist is a form of action, but we need to be aware that many clients aren't quite ready for concrete action at the very beginning.

5. *Maintenance.* Once clients have made changes, they must practice and manage any setbacks. This is the time for figuring out how to preserve what seems to be working and to revise whatever is not quite going as well as expected, but the overall goal is to keep the changes in place. Sometimes, after some time has elapsed, clients come back for a "tune-up." They may have made changes in the past but are now fearful of losing ground.

After two sessions, Julie was able to understand that her jealousy was not going to be fixed by maintaining her current pattern. She began to consider the possibility that her low self-esteem was related to two erroneous assumptions: first, that she had to be thin to be loved; and second, that she had to be loved by Matt to feel good about herself. Because she couldn't control Matt, she tried to control her weight. Once Julie could see that what she was doing wasn't going to change her jealous feelings and that this pattern was harmful to her, she was able to consider the possibility that she had developed an eating disorder. At that point she moved from the precontemplation stage to the contemplation stage with the eating disorder.

Julie was also beginning to see that her problem with "incessant jealousy" stemmed more from her fiancé's provocative behavior than from her lack of assertiveness. Once she saw her relationship as needing change, this problem moved from the preparation phase (it was originally at this point because she was prepared to change her jealousy with no clear plan of action) back to the contemplation phase. Julie now worried about the pros and cons of change. She didn't want to lose Matt but was also aware that she might not be able to feel good about herself if she stayed in this relationship.

Julie's progress in therapy illustrates two important features about readiness to change. First, clients move back and forth between stages as they work. And second, a client's readiness to change is not uniform across various problems. In other words, our clients may be one place with one problem and another place with a different problem.

To work effectively, we need to be prepared to stay with our clients' ambivalence and confusion while they're in the beginning stages of change, thus avoiding the very common error of embarking on an action plan before the client is actually ready. Once they're ready, we can plan and implement action strategies.

Studies show that client motivation is a key variable in the success of psychotherapy.[5] Our ability to assess what clients are concerned about is an essential part of providing quality care. This is particularly important during an initial session, but therapists must remain alert to changes from session to session. To assess this level of general functioning, we evaluate mental status.

Evaluating Mental Status

We evaluate mental status as part of our overall assessment of a client's functioning and ability to benefit from treatment. Most mental status assessments are geared toward locating factors that signal the need for immediate attention, for referral to another source, or for more detailed evaluation by a specialist.

Generally speaking, we evaluate mental status by making skilled observations of the client's appearance, attitude, motor activity, level of consciousness, affect, mood, speech, thought processes, thought content, self-perception, sensorium, memory, cognitive function, judgment, insight, use of drugs, and danger to self and others. We don't always evaluate all these variables, but we do assess those attributes pertinent to the problems of our clients and our own work setting. The following sections describe the most common attributes that deserve attention when we assess mental status.

General Presentation

Therapists form impressions of their client's general presentation by considering several variables.

Appearance

We need to take note of dress or appearance that is disheveled, bizarre, or inappropriate. People who are preoccupied with drugs or who have serious mental health problems are often unable to devote any attention to self-care. Someone who appears with clothes that reek, or wears a winter coat when the temperature outside is 105 degrees, or is carrying a lightning rod in her right hand—all are examples of how unusual appearance signals disturbance in mental status.

Attitude

We assume that those who come for therapy are willing to cooperate. When they aren't, this is noteworthy. Sylvia, a woman I saw in the university counseling center, provides an illustration of significant noncooperation. In fact, she was so suspicious that we were unable to proceed. Sylvia was a thirty-two-year-old medical student with excellent grades; her supervisor sent Sylvia for counseling because Sylvia was extremely ineffective with people. After seeing her, I understood her supervisor's impressions. As soon as she sat down for her first appointment she started to interrogate me. After fifteen minutes of intense questioning about whom I talked to, where records were kept, and places I went, it was clear that she was very suspicious and beyond reassurance. When I asked, "Sylvia, you seem to think I am going to hurt you. Is that how you feel?" she answered sarcastically, "Of course you will, everyone does, you may not even know yet how you will hurt me—but you will."

Sylvia was too guarded and suspicious to allow even a minimum of trust. I followed up with other questions: "Have you felt suspicious of other people?" "How long have you felt like this?" "Can you give me some other examples?" Her cryptic and cynical answers revealed a lifetime of isolation, hypervigilance, and disruption related to her suspicions. Unfortunately, her worst fears were enacted. People did hurt her. And sadly, she wasn't able to understand her role.

During mental status exams, we also should note belligerence and hostility. For example, I remember being caught off guard by Frank, a forty-year-old accountant. He had one of those interesting faces that made me want to know more about him. But right away, he seemed to have a chip on his shoulder. Even before he mentioned the problems that brought him, he told me that he was not to blame. He interrupted. He demanded that I destroy any record of this appointment or any other he might make. He threatened, "If you won't destroy this record, I'll sue you for slander." He seemed to want a fight. All this, without his ever explaining the reason he decided to come. When I wouldn't agree to his terms, he left. His hostility seemed to come from no place, and because he was not willing to explain, there wasn't much I could do.

Motor Activity

Most adults are able to sit through a one-hour interview without pacing, jumping up, moving excessively, or in some other manner demonstrating severe agitation. Likewise, we expect clients to have enough energy to remain upright, involved, and alert. If someone presents too much or too little psychomotor activity, we note that information as part of mental status.

Level of Consciousness

Without a doubt, if a client is not conscious, we can't conduct an interview. But I have been called on many occasions to deal with someone not fully conscious. When doctors or family members are concerned about a suicide attempt, a violent assault, a drug overdose, or some other acute trauma, they often request a mental health consultation. So when a client is recovering from a drug overdose or some other condition that hinders her ability to attend and cope, we need to record that information as part of mental status.

You can generally discover whether or not someone is conscious enough to participate in an interview by observing breathing, eye contact, emotionality, and ability to verbalize. If there is an attending physician, you can inquire about consciousness before attempting an interview. Furthermore, you can save yourself frustration when called to emergencies if you inquire ahead about the client's ability to respond and then arrange to meet when you know that the client is fully conscious. Likewise, as therapy proceeds you need to notice any signs of altered states of consciousness that might interfere with what you're trying to accomplish.

Sensorium

Sensorium refers to an individual's general awareness of, or orientation to, his surroundings. We say that a client's sensorium is "clear" if that client is oriented to person, place, and time.[6] Some clinicians say, "He is oriented times three," meaning the client is oriented to person (he knows who he is), place (he knows where he is), and time (he knows the date and approximate time), and is aware of other general information about what's going on. When a client is *disoriented* it is often a sign that he is suffering from psychosis, brain injury, or drug abuse.

Most often orientation can be observed without asking any direct questions. Just getting to an appointment, if that applies, usually indicates that a client is oriented. But you will certainly want to take note if your client doesn't know who you are, who she is, or why you are there; is totally unresponsive or extremely distracted; or confused by what is going on.

Affect and Mood

Affect is the outward expression of emotion. It's what others observe. We assess four primary attributes of affect: appropriateness, intensity, mobility, and range.[7]

When assessing *appropriateness,* we look for how a person's affect corresponds to what is discussed. For example, we would not think it appropriate for someone to laugh, smile, and seem energetic when discussing the death of someone loved. Consequently, we would describe this person's affect as inappropriate.

Intensity refers to the strength of reaction. When someone shows minimal response to situations that others would more typically react to with intense feeling, a clinician describes his affect as *blunted* or *flat.* When we note exaggerated reactions, we use the terms *excessive, heightened,* or *dramatic. Mobility* of affect refers to the manner in which a client moves from one emotion to another. People who respond slowly or unresponsively are described as *constricted* or *unresponsive.* Some people move up and down so quickly that they seem unpredictable—clinicians describe fluctuating affect as *labile,* and note the time between mood changes.

The *range* of emotion reflects the complexity and variety of emotional expression. We expect most people to be able to express a range of feeling. In other words, we expect people to react with a variety of feelings appropriate to varied situations. If the response is always anger, or sadness, or elation, we would note the lack of range. Further, we expect gradations. For example, when someone is angry, we might expect a range from mild annoyance, to irritation, to frustration, to aggravation, to exasperation, to rage. But when our client's responses don't correspond to the events that precipitate them, we describe the range as *limited.*

Mood is how someone feels, the personal experience of emotion. As therapists, we first look to what people tell us to assess mood. Then we watch for nonverbal cues. Normal mood is an appropriate reaction to events and thoughts. Mood can be described as *euphoric* if the feeling is too good to be true, and *dysphoric* when overly down or pessimistic.

Thought Content and Process

We evaluate three primary attributes of thought: (1) how closely content resembles reality, (2) assumptions about the control of thinking, and (3) how thoughts are organized.

Highly unusual thoughts signify the possibility of *delusions.* When ideas seem irrational but deeply entrenched and not consistent with the client's intelligence or cultural background, we assume the presence of delusions. Believing that God has anointed you to reconcile all of the world's good and evil, assuming that you must seduce the president because Congress has picked you to produce a master race, believing that your husband is inseminating you with particles from Jupiter—these are all delusions.

Most adults may be troubled by their thinking from time to time, but they usually experience a basic sense of control. Some people experience delusions about forces controlling their thinking. When we hear any expression from a client that makes us wonder about delusions of control, it may be necessary to ask for clarification:

Do you feel as though your thoughts are controlled by some force or power outside yourself?

Can people tell what you are thinking, even when you don't express yourself?

Do you ever feel as though your thoughts were put into your head, that they're not your own?

Are you distracted by intrusive thoughts that you find hard to control?

We must also notice how thoughts are organized. Sometimes the associations between thoughts are so loose that there appears to be no logic or order to what is said. For example:

> *Question:* Do you know where you are?
> *Answer:* Here, there, where I don't care. The
> police care. The thieves are working.

When clients put ideas and words together in such a disorganized fashion with only tangential connections (such as rhymes or loose associations with idiosyncratic meaning), we can assume that something is wrong with their ability to organize thoughts in a fashion that allows others to follow the meaning.

Sometimes thoughts are strung together so quickly that we notice a "flight of ideas." The client strings ideas together without regard for order or the listener's ability to follow. The client jumps from one thought to the next. There's no room to ask a question. If you try, the client proceeds without regard for what you said. This can be a sign of mania or amphetamine use, but it can also signal stroke and other complications.

These assessments of thought content and process are generally made through observation. If you need more information about the possibility of delusions or the way thoughts are organized, you can ask direct questions about what you need to know, such as the following:

May I ask you some more questions about that?

Can you tell me more about why you think aliens live in your backyard?

Do you feel confused by what you're saying?

Do you understand why I am having trouble following what you
have said?

Can you slow down?

Can you help me understand the connection between [one thought]
and [another]?

If your client is able to clarify his thinking or you believe the
unusual thought pattern is a rare occurrence, you can proceed by
taking note and getting on with other matters. If, on the other
hand, your observations indicate that there is considerable disruption to general functioning, that's a clear signal indicating the
need for further evaluation by a psychiatrist, neurologist, or other
qualified professional.

Perception

Although auditory or visual hallucinations are rare, we must remain
alert for such occurrences. The obvious clues are easy, such as when
a client tells you directly about hallucinations. "When I look up
I see daggers—three of them, dripping with blood." Or a client
tells you about voices: "The voice in my head told me to go to his
room. They told me not to wear clothes, only a coat. I was scared
because I wasn't sure if they were real, but they seemed to be."

Sometimes you will get hints that someone is hearing voices
from such statements as "They kept telling me to get up and do
something." Without a referent for "they," you would need to ask.
"Who are you referring to? Can you tell me who 'they' are?"

If you have any hints or questions in your mind about the possibility that your client is hallucinating, you can always inquire with
such questions as:

Do you ever hear voices?

Has there been anything unusual about the way things looked,
sounded, or smelled?

Do you see or hear things that other people don't see or hear?
Do you ever hear or see things that you suspect are not real?
Have you had any unusual experiences that other people might
not understand?

We need to keep in mind that some people can have thought
disturbances and still function in other, more normal ways. For this
reason, you should inquire about how their thoughts affect more
general functioning. Usually people are disturbed by these unusual
experiences, but not always.

Intellectual Functioning

A disturbance or deficit in intellectual functioning is important
because it may signify the presence of physical problems, such as
retardation, stroke, or some other type of brain damage. Impairments in intelligence may or may not affect the client's ability to
manage basic life skills. But therapists need an appreciation for
both intelligence and adaptive behavior because they affect treatment planning. Some therapists are skilled with low-functioning
clients. Others are not.

Many mental health clinics see clients who are low functioning
and who have very complicated sociological and economic needs.
Some of these needs may be better served by social workers, home
health aids, or others skilled in intervention and education techniques. Medication, direct training, and financial assistance may
be much more effective than psychotherapy or counseling for
some problems.

As we make assessments of intellectual functioning, we should
have some idea about the intellectual levels that we are prepared
to handle. Memory problems, inability to understand metaphors
or abstractions, and low vocabulary are all important signs of
impairment. The following are some questions used to assess basic
intellectual functioning:

Count backwards by sevens.

Please read this and do what it says. (Show a card that says, "Tell
me your name.")

Spell *WORLD* backwards.

Who is the president of the United States? Vice president?

What does this proverb mean: "A rolling stone gathers no moss."

The Vineland Adaptive Behavior Scales is an instrument designed to measure personal and social sufficiency.[8] This instrument reveals social skills, adequacy of self-care, work habits, and other general attributes of adaptive behavior. Clinicians familiar with this instrument will have an understanding of appropriate developmental expectations and norms. When you think that a client lacks such skills, it is imperative that you inquire using questions that get at what you need to know:

Are you able to take care of yourself?

Are you able to purchase food?

Do you have a place to stay?

Do you have friends or family you can count on?

Are your health needs taken care of?

Are you able to work? Attend school? Manage your children?

Self-Perception

For therapy to be effective, a client must have some sense of self-identity or self-awareness. Some clients feel so disconnected from themselves that they experience *depersonalization* or a feeling that even though they know their name and history, they aren't sure who they are. Susan, for example, reported that she felt like she wasn't herself; rather, she felt as though she was always watching herself. She was twenty-eight years old, single, and employed as a computer programmer. She explained, "I'm sitting here explaining these nightmares like they don't bother me, like I am up there in the corner watching us talk. I can't tell you about my feelings or opinions because I don't know what they are."

A similar problem is *derealization* or a feeling of not being connected to one's experience of things. John, a thirty-eight-year-old recent divorcé, explained that "everything seems unreal; I'm numb, almost like this problem belongs to someone else."

The best way to check out self-perception is to ask the client questions:

Do you sometimes feel like you don't know who you are?

Do your thoughts and feelings seem to belong to you?

Do you feel what you are describing? How?

Do your feelings seem real?

Do you feel numb?

Identity confusion is a normal part of adolescence or periods of crisis and change. Otherwise, we expect adults to know who they are, what roles they play, and what responsibilities they have. We notice signs of identity confusion when clients assume that they're controlled by someone or something else or that multiple personalities exist within them, or when they have a bizarre feeling of not belonging in the body they inhabit.

Insight and Judgment

Insight relates to how well clients understand themselves, their situations, and their responsibility for their own dilemmas. The ability to have self-understanding is an essential aspect of most psychological treatment. To assess this attribute, we must notice how comprehensively clients are able to explain their problems. Most important, we need to listen to the answers to such questions as "Do you understand your role in what happened?" or "Do you see how you got to this point?" or "What happened?" If the answers reflect complexity, appreciation for sequence, and sensitivity to others, we could assume the client is insightful. If, on the other hand, he answers, "Huh?" or "Gosh, I really haven't a clue," or "It was all her fault!" we might wonder about the depth of insight.

For example, Sarah repeatedly got involved with men who physically beat her. At forty-two, she still had no insight into how this happened. She overlooked obvious warning signs in the men she dated: having violent outbursts, breaking objects, and hurting animals. Then she was surprised when she was hit. Sadly, Sarah seemed blind to how she ended up with such men. It was safe to say that she had little insight into her problem.

Judgment is the process used to make choices. We make choices constantly: what to do, who to do it with, when to eat, how much to eat, when to sleep, with whom, under what circumstances, what to say, where to go. Some people weigh options endlessly, never able to decide, whereas others act on impulse. Most of us at least weigh the consequences of choices before we make important decisions. As therapists, we make assessments of our clients' judgment by listening to them describe their behavior and the reasons why they made certain choices. Sometimes clients have good judgment in one area but not another. Sarah, for example, demonstrated poor judgment about her intimate relationships, but she showed excellent judgment in her career choices and work habits. She enjoyed her job as the manager of a convenience store. She was always on time, and she attended to details, juggled the schedules of eighteen other employees, and always received good evaluations.

Mental status also involves assessing the role of substance use and abuse, the client's danger to self, and the client's danger to others. But these three aspects of client functioning are so important that separate sections have been set aside for these assessments.

Assessing Substance Abuse and Addiction

Psychoactive drugs influence all aspects of verbal and nonverbal behavior. Furthermore they influence consciousness, emotions, behavior, and cognitions. Because abuse patterns are often concealed, the problem of getting accurate information about psychoactive substances is staggeringly difficult. Consequently, we must always be alert to the possibility that what we observe may be influenced by reactions to such substances. There are many clues:

- Slowed or sped-up speech
- Dilated or constricted pupils
- The smell of alcohol or pot
- Sleep and appetite disturbance
- Poor coordination
- Excessive or blunted emotional reactions
- Dry mouth
- Not being able to hold still
- Distractibility
- Inappropriate behavior
- Compulsively picking blemishes on the face, legs, or arms
- Demanding drugs for relief of sleep problems or pain

- Fighting
- Accidents
- Repeated trauma and crises
- Relationship discord
- No motivation
- Poor work habits

For example, a man called and came to see me for what he described as "an emergency appointment." He was tall and thin and was dressed in casual but noticeably wrinkled clothes. His pace was rapid as he walked from the waiting room to the office. Once in the office, he sat down and started ranting in a loud and rapid manner about "injustice." He allowed no room for me to speak. Then he started taking off his shirt. When I asked what he was doing, he got out of his chair, sat on the floor at my feet and said angrily, "I'm hot!" These initial observations suggested that he was intoxicated. He didn't smell of alcohol. As it turned out, he was on methamphetamine, a form of speed.

Mimicking Other Symptoms

Many symptoms of psychological problems are also symptoms of drug abuse or withdrawal. For example, panic attacks, anxiety, fears, sleep disturbance, paranoia, and weight loss are often associated with amphetamine or cocaine use. Apathy, inability to get things done, confusion, convoluted explanations, impaired memory, panic, paranoia, depersonalization, and loss of insight are associated with marijuana.[9] Dissociative reactions, paranoid ideation, heightened emotional responses, convoluted explanations for normal events, and occasional flashbacks from bad experiences can be associated with psilocybin mushrooms and LSD.[10] Depression, crying spells, loss of important relationships, aggressive behavior, chronic fighting, low self-esteem, panic, and sleep disturbances are often associated with alcohol, benzodiazepines (Xanax, Librium, Ativan) and barbiturate dependence.

It's imperative that we be alert to the role drugs play in psychological symptoms. Most clients are likely to deny or minimize the connection between their symptoms and their use of psychoactive substances. In addition, most people use these substances for their positive effects. They therefore remain attached to these benefits and defensive when they perceive our inquiries to be challenging their use of drugs. Therefore, we must carefully but routinely inquire about substances: "Can you tell me about any substances (drugs) you use?" You may need to remind your clients that confidentiality will protect them from public exposure if they discuss their substance use during therapy.

Inquiring About Prescription Drugs

Keep in mind that many prescribed medications—such as the painkillers Dilaudid, Demerol, and codeine—also influence mood and behavior. These medications are also addictive. Some high blood pressure medication as well as some antidepressants affect libido and sexual functioning. Therefore, it is imperative that we ask about medications early on in therapy, not just about the ones clients take regularly but also those they take for temporary relief. And because most of us are not trained in pharmacology, we may need to check the *Physicians Desk Reference* for side effects.[11] In addition, it's important for us to know if our clients actually take their medications as prescribed, or as they decide.

Asking About Over-the-Counter Remedies

We should also ask about over-the-counter and herbal remedies. Some cold, allergy, and sinus medications as well as many diet aids contain high doses of caffeine, which when added to a daily dose of coffee and cola can certainly have an impact on anxiety problems.

Some trendy health aids seem harmless but aren't always. Marlene, a forty-year-old math teacher, came to therapy because she was worried about a problem her teenage son was having. After reading in *Time* magazine about the "wonders" of melatonin, Marlene decided to try it because she was having trouble sleeping. When she got more depressed even though her son's problem improved, we learned from her family doctor that this popular aid also increases symptoms of depression in some people. When she stopped taking the melatonin, her depression lifted.

A full review of drug effects is beyond the scope of this chapter, but we do need to be on the alert for the possibility that these products can have an effect on behavior, emotion, and cognitions.

Seeing Beyond Stereotypes

Many therapists miss the association of symptoms and drug use because of the stereotypes they hold about the kinds of people who use certain drugs. We all need to be alert to these stereotypes because they can blind us to noticing clients who don't fit our image of a substance abuser. If the client is seventeen, with a punk hairdo and a poor school record, it might be easy to guess about substance abuse. However, when the client is a physician in her fifties who dresses carefully, it might be easy to miss the impact of substance use on the presenting problems.

> Initially I wasn't aware that alcohol was a factor in Mary's problems. But on her third session, a morning appointment, I noticed the smell of alcohol. I asked about her alcohol use. She talked about how stressful her schedule was and then excused herself with, "My husband wants perfection. What can I do? I try. The kids are never satisfied. And then there are my patients: they never stop. Of course I need a few drinks to unwind."

Mary also drank when she was angry. Alcohol served as both a distraction and as a method of coping with anxiety. Mary's alcohol use also clouded her self-knowledge, memory, and judgment. And even though she was a doctor and clearly understood the consequences to her health, she denied the impact of her drinking. Both the positive appeal of minimizing stress as well as the danger of continuing this destructive method of coping were unmistakable.

Making Drug Assessments

When dealing with the use of drugs there are two primary types of evaluation that therapists need to make. First, we need an assessment of the problem. This means we must try to find out what drugs are used, how often, how much, and under what circumstances. Even though the CAGE test was designed to assess alcohol problems, this quick and easy instrument can be adapted to other drugs as well.[12] Traditionally, an affirmative answer to two items from the CAGE is an indication that a more thorough screening is required:[13]

- Have you ever felt the need to **CUT** down on your drinking?
- Have you ever felt **ANNOYED** by someone criticizing your drinking?
- Have you ever felt **GUILTY** about your drinking?
- Have you ever felt the need for an **EYE** opener (a drink soon after waking up)?

Many therapists also find it very informative to ask, "How old were you when you started drinking?" (The younger and the more involved the use, the higher the risk.) In addition, we need to know the consequences of the client's current usage. There are several instruments that can help us assess drug use: the Michigan Alcoholism Screening Test (MAST), the World Health Organization (AUDIT) structured interview, the Alcohol Dependence Scale (ADS), and the Minnesota Multiphasic Personality Inventory MacAndrew Alcoholism Scale.

If there is a problem, we also need an assessment of readiness to work on that problem. Our clinical assessment of readiness to change, discussed earlier, is an essential aspect of effective treatment planning when dealing with substance abuse and addictions.[14]

Danger to Self

As therapists, we are expected to know when someone may be dangerous to himself or to others.[15] Most clinicians are aware of the difficulties in making consistently reliable predictions about the possibility of harm.[16] When it comes to assessing risk of violence to self or others, clinicians are currently in a position of being damned if we do, damned if we don't. If we don't evaluate risks and spot those who are dangerous, we are negligent. If we do make assessments that predict danger, there are often serious repercussions resulting in the restriction of freedom for either the client or someone else. And because the actions taken are preventive, some of those who are inconvenienced are likely to be angered. The ethics involved are beyond the scope of this chapter; we must simply say here that as therapists we have a professional duty to evaluate risk factors.

We certainly need to use common sense when assessing danger. But because we know that systematic evaluations will improve our clinical judgment, we must also consider other facets when making such assessments: (1) known risk factors; (2) client ideation, intentions, and impulsiveness; and (3) lethality.

Risk Factors

If a client swallows a bottle of Tylenol, or sits outside in freezing weather, or cuts her wrists, we recognize this behavior as immediately life threatening. But there are many other ways our clients harm themselves: they drink too much, they smoke, they drive without a seat belt, they have unprotected sex, they don't eat for days. But these behaviors are not likely to cause death immediately. Generally speaking, when we are assessing risk we are talking about immediate and imminent risk. But we have a responsibility to recognize passive methods as well as techniques that are more actively dangerous.

Whenever someone's characteristics match the known risk factors for suicide, we must be prepared to evaluate that individual's risk. The following characteristics are known to increase the risk of suicide:

- Past suicide attempts[17]
- Pain or illness[18]
- Feelings of hopelessness[19]
- Being elderly or adolescent[20]
- Being male[21]
- Being unemployed[22]
- Being single[23]
- History of panic disorder, depression, addiction, or personality disorders[24]
- Stressful life events experienced as shameful or humiliating[25]
- Significant interpersonal disruption or conflict[26]
- Recent improvement after a period of severe depression[27]
- Recent or accumulated losses[28]

As you review this list, you can see that many clients will fall into these categories. But you can probably also see that this list has limited value if it doesn't fit the client you're assessing but he nevertheless tells you that he is thinking of suicide. Whenever we have any suspicion that a client may be suicidal, whatever the basis for our concern, we must be prepared to make an assessment of suicide potential.

Assessing Suicide Potential

To evaluate potential we assess three variables: ideation, intention, and impulsiveness (the three I's that help us determine lethality).

Ideation

Ideation refers to thoughts of suicide. You should take note when a client talks about wanting to be dead, wanting to end it all, seeking revenge, or not being able to stand it anymore.

The best way to find out if your client is thinking about suicide is to ask, "Sometimes when people feel like you do, they think of hurting themselves. Are you?" If the answer is yes, you need to follow up with questions about the kind of thoughts. Some examples of suicidal thinking are "I wish I was dead," "I wonder what it would be like to take all the pills in my house," "I can't stand this anymore," and "I think about myself at my funeral."

Because it is not uncommon for people who are upset or overwhelmed to be thinking about suicide, we must differentiate thinking from a readiness to act.

Intention

Intention has to do with determination and with plans for suicide. We know that the more lethal, the more detailed, and the more imminent the plans, the higher the risk. It is important for us to discover the nature of any plans as well as the details for carrying them out. When assessing intentions, we really need to pay particular attention to the answers to questions about what, when, where, and how. Furthermore, we need to know if the client actually has the means to implement his plans. Likewise, we know that strong emotions like anger, desperation, and the desire for revenge can fuel intention. Any suspicion means that we must check for *intentions* by asking such questions as:

Have you ever tried to hurt yourself before now?

(If yes) How? *and* What happened?

Have you thought of what you would do to hurt yourself?

Have you decided on a plan?

Do you really think you will do what you are planning?

(If yes) Have you decided on when?

Do you have the means to do this?

What do you think the consequences will be?

Impulsiveness

Impulsiveness is, of course, the most serious problem because we have little time for assessments beforehand. "I was driving and noticed I was headed for the tree; I didn't care." "I was on the top of the water tower and I just thought—jump!" "I picked up the gun and went to the bathroom. I was going to shoot myself, but the phone rang." Intense feelings, intrusive thoughts of suicide, drug use, and personality disorders all contribute to increasing the risk of an impulsive act. Our observations of prior reports about impulsive behavior are what will generally inform our assessments. But if we need information that we don't already have, we can ask directly about impulsive behavior with such questions as:

Do you ever feel impulses to hurt yourself?

What are your impulses like?

How hard is it to resist these feelings?

How do you usually cope with these [events or feelings]?

Do you know what you're doing when you feel these impulses?

Do you think you can control yourself under these circumstances?

Determining Lethality

Lethality is determined by combining factors. When assessing how likely someone is to commit suicide we consider risk factors and the content and frequency of suicidal thoughts. Clients who want to die are more dangerous to themselves than clients who want their problems to disappear. Whenever there's doubt, we can ask directly: "I'd like to understand this better. Do you really want to die, or do you just want these problems to go away?"

Risk is higher for those clients who have made a previous attempt, who are apt to be impulsive (such as substance abusers), or who have chaotic lifestyles and few meaningful relationships. Clients with more persistent and intrusive thoughts of suicide present more of a danger than those with occasional fantasies. Those clients who have definite intentions, clear and imminent plans, and the means to accomplish what is intended are at the greatest risk.

Whenever there is doubt, we are generally wise to err in the direction of assuming the risk is greater. When lethality is high, we must do something. Without reasonable reassurance from the client, and sometimes even with assurances, we must take steps to protect the client; we'll discuss how to handle such situations in Chapter Six.

Being at Risk for Violence

Being at risk for violence has not been traditionally considered a part of assessing danger to self. I decided to include it here, however, because the facts on violence are compelling, and many experts now call for such evaluations to be more routinely included in general assessments and history taking.[29] Mental health professionals should take the following facts about violence into consideration when assessing danger:[30]

- Both men and women can be physically and verbally aggressive; however, women are more likely to be injured.
- Between 21 and 34 percent of all women will be physically assaulted by an intimate male during adulthood.
- More than three out of every hundred—1.8 million—women were severely assaulted (that is, punched, kicked, choked, beaten, threatened with a knife or gun, or had a knife or gun used on them) during the period between 1989 and 1990.[31]
- Of married or formerly married women, 14 percent report being raped by a husband or ex-husband.
- Women who are assaulted by their partners experience higher than average rates of suicidal ideation, suicide attempts, depression, and helplessness.

- Physical aggression occurs in 40 percent of lesbian relationships; the percentage is higher in gay male relationships.[32]

These facts alone mean that we must be sensitive to the possibility of violence for our female and gay male clients. And because heterosexual men also experience assault we must not be numb to the possibility that they too can be at risk.

Whenever we are trying to determine potential danger, we must be sensitive to the fear that surrounds revelations of violence. Most women are aware that if they "tell" they may feel guilty of betrayal, afraid of being forced to take action they aren't ready to handle, hurt by the financial ramifications of divorce, or afraid of a retaliatory assault. Because many blame themselves for the violence they suffer, they also feel shame, which makes it hard for them to reveal the danger they experience. Nonetheless, therapists must be willing to ask about the client's being at risk for violence:

What happens when you fight with your partner?
Are you ever afraid that you will be harmed? How?
Have you ever been threatened or injured?
What happens when you resist?
What actions have you taken to protect yourself?
Are you willing to consider taking steps to better protect yourself?
Have you thought about the consequences for yourself and your children?

We must be careful to ask these questions when the perpetrator is not present. We must also be aware that a client may tell you that she is not in danger even when she is at considerable risk. As already mentioned, there are profound reasons to keep violence a secret. Nevertheless, if we ask, we open the door for a later disclosure when the client feels less fearful and has a need to discuss such matters. Our questions also indicate that we, as therapists, believe violence is an important variable to consider when assessing mental health. When we ask, we must be prepared to offer alternatives without insisting on a course of action the client is not prepared to take. We'll talk about this in Chapter Six.

Danger to Others

The prediction of violence is one of the most complex issues facing mental health professionals: We know we can't make these predictions with guaranteed accuracy, and yet we will be called upon to make determinations about the possibility of violence.[33] As we work with situations that could lead to violence, we need to be mindful of the consequences of our assessments. For example, calling the police because an angry spouse seems threatening may serve to exacerbate that feeling as well as fuel the conflict. Obviously, we'd prefer to defuse explosive situations. Still, it's probably better to err in the direction of predicting violence rather than to underestimate risk, because the consequences are less drastic. Certainly, common sense is vital. As such, we'll want our actions to lessen the risk of harm to our clients and those dependent on them.

Risk Factors

Experts in the study of violent behavior advise clinicians to be informed by research on risk factors, but these same experts acknowledge that the worlds of research and clinical practice "scarcely intersect."[34] Most clinicians are in a position of having to make quick assessments using clinical interviews. Therefore, the guidelines suggested here follow the same method used when assessing suicide. As long as we aren't doing forensic evaluations, for which formal procedures are required, therapists can make assessments during a clinical interview.

The risk factors vary somewhat for different groups. But lists of such factors are usually developed by sampling a population of those convicted of violent offenses; therefore they represent the most serious offenders. As clinicians we must often assess risk in those who may not have been convicted of a violent offense but who are nonetheless dangerous.[35] The following list contains factors that are correlated with high risk for violent behavior.[36] The more items that match your client's characteristics, the greater the risk of violent acting out.

- History of violent acts
- History of physical attacks or fear-inducing behavior in the last two weeks

- History of victim injury
- Absence of suicidal behavior in last two weeks
- Diagnosis of schizophrenia, mania, or personality disorder
- Lack of empathy
- Dwelling on feelings of revenge and anger
- Being male
- Separation from parents by age sixteen or younger
- Never married
- Elementary school maladjustment
- History of damaging property or harming animals
- History of drug abuse

Assessment of Violence

Some clients make such statements as "I wish I could shoot her," "I would love to lock my kids in the closet," or "I think about blowing up her house." Most often such self-reports are graphic descriptions of feelings or wishes that will never be acted out. Nevertheless, when we hear such reports we must investigate. We make these assessments in the same manner we discussed when assessing suicide risk—by evaluating ideation, intention, and impulsivity to determine lethality.

As mentioned before, violent *ideation* is thinking about harming another. When someone mentions the desire to harm, we need to inquire.

When you think about hurting her, what do you think about doing?

What stops you?

How often do you think about hurting [name]?

When do you think about [violent acts]?

Do your thoughts disturb you?

Have you ever felt like this before? What did you do then?

The *intention* to harm must be evaluated whenever a client mentions thoughts of violence and you are not 100 percent clear that no action will be taken. When Salman told me that he thought about committing a rape, it was imperative that I asked many questions to determine if he had any intention of acting on these fantasies. He was a married graduate engineering student from Pakistan and not yet accustomed to U.S. mores. (As a child he had been told that women who dress like those he saw were "looking to be raped.") He didn't really intend to rape; in fact, he was terrified of his thoughts. But I had to ask a lot of questions to make sure he was not dangerous.

Even though we ask questions, we must remain aware that most people with serious intentions to harm are usually reluctant to reveal their plans.

Do you plan to do [what client described wanting to do]?

What do you do to keep yourself from [doing what client described wanting to do]?

What would happen to you if you did this?

Why would you do [what client described wanting to do]?

Can you imagine any situation that would allow you to act on this idea?

In order to evaluate *impulsiveness* we need to know about three things: motivation, the conditions that release the impulses, and prior history. Most often we can inquire about motivation directly by asking, "Why do you want to hurt [name]?" "How strong is this feeling?" or "Do you think you will really do this?" Most people act impulsively under certain conditions and not others. We need to ask about those circumstances that allow for impulses to be acted out as well as those that create control. And certainly we need to check into the client's history: How did he manage feelings of anger, revenge, or humiliation in the past? We need to know about our client's history of dealing with other impulsive feelings as well as the consequences.

Lethality

Again, we determine lethality, or the likelihood of acting violently, by combining factors. A client must be considered dangerous when she threatens, has clear intentions to act, and has a history of violent acting out.

Therapists have been admonished to follow a three-stage model when dealing with potentially violent clients.[37] First, we must collect relevant information to make a determination of risk. Second, we must select a course of action. Third, we must implement that course of action. We'll talk about what to do about these situations in Chapter Six. I would add that we must be prepared to document how we made choices by keeping careful records of our assessments of ideation, intention, and impulsive behavior.

General Guidelines for Assessment

Most clients come with a story to tell. Our ability to respond to their problems on their terms is an essential aspect in building rapport. If we observe our clients as though we were scientists watching a bug under magnification or interrogate like a Mafia boss, we run the risk of alienating those we seek to understand. Therefore, we must make assessments in a manner that allows us to collect the information we need without destroying the relationship we are trying to establish.

The evaluations and assessments we are describing here can be conducted both formally and informally as part of a clinical interview. A standardized set of questions is a formal procedure if implemented and then evaluated by specific criteria. Although you will most often use a less structured format, the questions and standards used in more formal assessments help you understand what information is needed when you use a less structured format.

When you understand what you're looking for, you can proceed with other tasks. In other words, you can evaluate key aspects of client functioning while conducting an interview on other matters. For example, while Kyle was discussing his desire to leave his marriage, I was paying attention to what he said and to his mental status. I was aware that his mental status seemed normal except for a very flat affect and sad mood. This alerted me to check for suicidal ideation and for substance abuse. But I also knew that he wanted to discuss the history of his marital dissatisfaction. Therefore, I had to look for opportunities to ask questions about suicide potential and substance use without drastically shifting the topic or sounding like an interrogator.

I was able to ask about suicide when Kyle talked about how bad he felt. I summarized using empathy and then asked, "Kyle, you sound like your marriage has been really upsetting to you for a long time. Does it ever get so bad that you think about hurting yourself?"

He responded emphatically. "No chance. I want some time without her, not no time at all."

I thought it would be harder to ask about substance abuse. But when he talked about how the only time he felt good was when he sat down with a drink after his wife went to bed, I saw an opportunity to ask. "I'm glad you have some time during the day when things feel better for you. Can you tell me something about how many drinks it takes to feel some relief?"

Kyle explained, "After three scotches, I'm cruisin'."

I went on, "So how many do you usually have?"

He said, "I never know, I drink till I fall asleep—I guess I end up with a lot of empty bottles by the end of the week."

Assessments are always a part of treatment, so we must be aware of our methods. We need to be clear that we can jeopardize a client's trust if we are not careful. If we ask questions in a manner that offends or that seems to come out of left field, we run the risk of alienating our clients or making them defensive. If we are too timid and hesitant, we run the risk of going down the wrong road because we lack important information. Consequently, we must remain alert to finding a balance between probing for additional information and respecting our clients' privacy. Here are some general guidelines:

• *Be clear about what you need to know.* Therapists have a clear professional responsibility to know what information they need to gather in order to estimate risks and plan for treatment. The variables suggested in this chapter cover the basic things we need to know. In addition, each work site may require you to collect other specific information. For example, a therapist who works at a college will need to know about school performance, a therapist in a community crisis center will collect data so priorities can be set, and a marriage and family counselor will collect information to evaluate family relations.

• *Be sure the client knows who you are.* Before you begin, an introduction is in order. We always need to introduce ourselves, let the client know what she can call you, and inquire about what the client would like to be called. For example: "I am Dr. Heaton, from the sexual assault team; please call me Jeanne. It says here that your name is Elizabeth; is that what you would like me to call you?" I have been called in to do many assessments for suicide potential when the client didn't know me or why I was there. Some clients are even offended that a psychologist was called. It may also be necessary to explain your role: "I am a psychologist with emergency services," or "I am the counselor from hospice." Sometimes it helps to ask, "Do you know why I am here?"

• *Make sure you have permission.* Before you begin collecting any information, you need to be sure that your client is willing to answer your questions. For example, when I am assessing someone's alcohol use, I might first say, "Is it all right if I ask you some questions about your drinking?" Be aware that sometimes people say yes but their body language says no—they glare at you, look away, sigh, or sound fed up. It is usually pointless to proceed with most evaluations if the client does not want to participate.

• *Let your client know why you need the information.* If we explain why we need certain information, our clients can help us by being clearer with their responses. "Before we go any further, I need to ask you some questions about your suicidal thoughts. We need to do this so that we can decide how we want to handle the next few days."

• *Be aware of how much time is available.* If you have only an hour you will have to set priorities for obtaining information. Likewise, you won't have time for a detailed history. For example, if your client is seriously depressed, you will need to attend to suicide potential. If you have any concern about danger to others, that too must take priority. In other words, we must be prepared to take control of what is discussed so that we can adequately assess important matters during the available time.

• *Obtain enough information for responsible clinical decisions.* As therapists we will be routinely called to make decisions that involve the assessment of risk factors. It is our responsibility to know what information we need, to collect that information, to estimate risk factors, and to communicate those factors to the people involved in making clinical decisions. When you need more time or information to make responsible decisions, request it. If you don't have enough information to answer the questions of your supervisors or others, explain that clearly.

• *Maintain an awareness of cultural issues.* Formal and informal assessments have long been criticized for a lack of cultural sensitivity. It is imperative that we avoid making mistakes due to a lack of understanding of cultural differences. We must keep in mind that even abnormal behavior has a cultural context. Customs, languages, religions, values, and rituals all influence behavior. Further, we need to understand how we could be perceived as threatening if we are a member of the majority culture and have the power to affect our client's life circumstances. We shouldn't be surprised when minority clients react with defensiveness, apprehension, or nervousness. Consequently we need to take an accounting of our own contribution to the reactions we get.

• *Explain informed consent.* All clients should be informed about who will have access to the information they are revealing. If the supervisor or others will know, clients have to be informed. In addition, clients need to know that you will break confidence under two conditions: first, when there is a life-threatening situation involving either the client or someone else, and second, when there is abuse involving a minor (or, in some states, a dependent elder). That does not mean that you *will* break confidence—only that you might. You must also provide information on other matters such as costs, any limitation on the number of visits, and other agency or insurance guidelines. This subject will be covered further in other chapters.

––––––––––

These basic guidelines are certainly not inclusive; each setting and each client will require special sensitivity. Basically these fundamental evaluations allow us to evaluate risk and plan for appropriate therapeutic strategies. Because we're frequently asked to write evaluative reports as well as prepare case presentations, it might be helpful to organize this material by the headings used in this chapter. Rarely would each and every segment be included, but at least this chapter could be used as a basic outline for possible topics to consider as part of an overall evaluation.

Most often we'll begin by making the observations and assessments we've been discussing within the context of an intake interview. We'll now discuss how such interviews are conducted as we move forward with diagnosis and treatment planning. Certainly, the overall intent is to maintain rapport with our clients while managing these basic tasks. And because all therapeutic skills are cumulative, it's important to remember that our assessment and observation skills will inform everything else we do in therapy.

Notes

1. Kleinke, C. L. (1994). *Common principles of psychotherapy.* Pacific Grove, CA: Brooks/Cole, p. 176.
2. Budman, S. H., & Gurman, A. S. (1988). *Theory and practice of brief therapy.* New York: Guilford Press, pp. 28–32.
3. American Psychiatric Association. (1994). *Diagnostic and statistical manual of mental disorders* (4th ed.). Washington, DC: Author.
4. Prochaska, J. O., & Di Clemente, C. C. (1982). Transtheoretical therapy: Toward a more integrative model of change. *Psychotherapy Theory, Research and Practice, 19,* 276–288.
5. Gomes-Schwartz, B. (1978). Effective ingredients in psychotherapy: Prediction of outcome from process variables. *Journal of Consulting and Clinical Psychology, 46,* 1023–1035. O'Malley, S. S., Suh, C. S. S., & Strupp, H. H. (1982). The Vanderbilt Psychotherapy Process Scale: A report on the scale development and a process-outcome study. *Journal of Consulting and Clinical Psychology, 51,* 581–586.
6. Barlow, D. H., & Durand, V. M. (1995). *Abnormal psychology: An integrative approach.* Pacific Grove, CA: Brooks/Cole, p. 82.
7. Trzepacz, P. T., & Baker, R. W. (1993). *The psychiatric mental status examination.* New York: Oxford University Press.
8. Stevens, F. (1986). Testing the test: Vineland Adaptive Behavior Scales: Classroom Edition. *Journal of Counseling and Development, 65,* 112–113.
9. Julien, R. M. (1995). *A primer of drug action.* New York: Freeman.
10. See note 9.
11. Medical Economics Company. (1996). *Physicians' desk reference* (50th ed.). Montvale, NJ: Author.
12. Hasin, D. S. (1991). Diagnostic interviews for assessment: Background, reliability, and validity. *Alcohol Health & Research World, 15,* 293–302.
13. Weed, N. C. (1994). Development of MMPI-A Alcohol/Drug Problem Scale. *Journal of Studies on Alcohol, 55,* 296–302; Ross, H. E. (1990). Diagnostic validity of the MAST and the Alcohol Dependence Scale in assessment of *DSM-III* alcohol disorders. *Journal of Studies on Alcohol, 51,* 506–513; Sobel, L. C. (1994). Behavioral assessment and treatment planning for alcohol, tobacco, and other drug

problems: Current status with emphasis on clinical applications. *Behavior Therapy, 25,* 533–580.

14. Prochaska, J. O., Di Clemente, C. C., & Norcross, J. C. (1992). In search of how people change: Applications to addictive behaviors. *American Psychologist, 47,* 1102–1114.

15. Grisso, T., & Tomkins, A. J. (1996). Communicating violence risk assessments. *American Psychologist, 51,* 928–930.

16. Monahan, J. (1992). Mental disorders and violent behavior: Perceptions and evidence. *American Psychologist, 47,* 511–521.

17. Patterson, W. M., Dohn, H. H., Bird, J., & Patterson, G. A. (1983). Evaluation of suicidal patients: The SAD PERSON scale. *Psychosomatics, 24,* 343–349.

18. DiBianco, J. T. (1979). The hemodialysis patient. In L. D. Hankoff & B. Einsidler (Eds.), *Suicide: Theory and clinical aspects* (pp. 291–297). Littleton, MA: PSG Publishing.

19. Dixon, W. A., Heppner, P. P., & Rudd, M. D. (1994). Problem-solving appraisal, hopelessness, and suicide ideation: Evidence for a mediational model. *Journal of Counseling Psychology, 41,* 91–98.

20. National Center for Health Statistics. (1990). *Health United States, 1989* (DHHS Publication No. PHS 90–1232). Hyattsville, MD: Public Health Service.

21. U.S. Department of Health and Human Services. (1995). Mortality surveillance system. *Monthly Vital Statistics Report, 43,* 4–7.

22. Dooley, D., Catalano, R., Rook, K., & Serner, S. (1989). Economic stress and suicide: Multilevel analyses. Part 1: Aggregate time-series analyses of economic stress and suicide. *Suicide and Life Threatening Behavior, 19,* 321–336.

23. Winokur, G., Black, D. W., & Nasrallah, A. (1988). Depressions secondary to other psychiatric disorders and medical illnesses. *American Journal of Psychiatry, 142,* 233–237; Anthony, J. D., & Petronis, K. R. (1991). Panic attacks and suicide attempts. *Archives of General Psychiatry, 48,* 1114; Cornelius, R. R., Salloum, I. M., Nezzich, J., M. D., Fabreaga, H., Ehler, J. G., Ulrich, R. F., Thase, M. E., & Mann, J. J. (1995). Disproportionate suicidality in patients with comorbid major depression and alcoholism. *American Journal of Psychiatry, 152,* 358–364.

24. Klerman, G. L. (1987). Clinical epidemiology of suicide. *Journal of Clinical Psychiatry, 48,* 33–38.

25. Blumenthal, S. J. (1990). An overview and synopsis of risk factors, assessment, and treatment of suicidal patients over the life cycle. In S. J. Blumenthal & D. J. Kupfer (Eds.), *Suicide over the life cycle: Risk factors assessment and treatment of suicidal patients* (pp. 685–733). Wash-

ington, DC: American Psychiatric Press.

26. Hatton, C. L., Valente, S. M., & Rink, A. (1977). Assessment of suicidal risk. In C. L. Hatton, S. M. Valente, & A. Rink (Eds.), *Suicide: Assessment and intervention* (pp. 39–61). Englewood Cliffs, NJ: Appleton-Century-Crofts.

27. Roy, A. (1989). Suicide. In H. Kaplan & B. Sadock (Eds.), *Comprehensive textbook of psychiatry* (3rd ed., vol. 2, pp. 1414–1426). Baltimore: Williams & Wilkins.

28. Hatton, C. L., Valente, S. M., & Rink, A. (Eds.). *Suicide: Assessment and intervention.* Englewood Cliffs, NJ: Appleton-Century-Crofts.

29. Browne, A. (1993). Violence against women by male partners: Prevalence, outcomes, and policy implications. *American Psychologist, 48,* 1077–1087.

30. See note 29.

31. Straus, M. A., & Gelles, R. J. (1990). *Physical violence in American families: Risk factors and adaptions to violence in 8,145 families.* New Brunswick, NJ: Transaction.

32. Brownworth, V. A. (1993, November 16). Domestic blitz. *Advocate: The National Gay & Lesbian Newsmagazine, 642,* 96.

33. Borum, R. (1996). Improving the clinical practice of violence risk assessment: Technology, guidelines, and training. *American Psychologist, 51,* 945–956.

34. Webster, C. D., Eaves, D., Douglas, K., & Wintrup, A. (1995). *The HCR–20 Schem: The assessment of dangerousness and risk.* Burnaby, British Columbia, Canada: Simon Fraser University and Forensic Psychiatric Services Commission of British Columbia.

35. See note 33.

36. McNeil, D. E., & Binder, R. L. (1994). Screening for risk of inpatient violence: Validation of an actuarial tool. *Law and Human Behavior, 18,* 579–586; Gardner, W., Lidz, D. W., Mulvey, E. P., & Shaw, E. C. (1996). A comparison of actuarial methods for identifying repetitively-violent patients. *Law and Human Behavior, 20,* 35–48.

37. Appelbaum, P. S. (1985). *Tarasoff* and the clinician: Problems in fulfilling the duty to protect. *American Journal of Psychiatry, 142,* 425–429; Monahan, J. (1993). Limiting therapist exposure to *Tarasoff* liability: Guidelines for risk containment. *American Psychologist, 48,* 242–250.

Chapter Three

First Session
Diagnosis and Treatment Planning

There's a lot to accomplish in a first session. Sometimes this initial contact alone may resolve our client's concerns, but more often than not additional sessions are required. If you and your client agree to continue, you will need a diagnosis and treatment plan. We have already discussed using observational and assessment skills to find out why someone has decided on therapy and what is wrong. Now we need to focus on how to conduct an initial session and formulate a diagnosis and treatment plan. To accomplish these tasks we'll use the skills we have already discussed plus some essential new strategies for conducting an initial interview.

Because there's a lot to do during this session, we need to provide structure. However, we'll want to do this in a manner that encourages positive interaction. We know that our clients have the best outcome when they view the therapeutic relationship as helpful.[1] Therefore we must develop a style that allows us to collect information and to communicate about diagnosis and treatment plans while at the same time expediting a good working relationship.

We'll begin with suggestions on how to organize the initial consultation. Next we'll move on to a description of the fourth edition of the *Diagnostic and Statistical Manual of Mental Disorders* (*DSM-IV*) and how to use it. Then we'll see how to put together treatment plans.

Organizing the First Session

As I mentioned elsewhere, research tells us that 40 percent of all therapeutic encounters last for only one visit, so it's wise to have a single-session plan in mind. Because this contact may very well be the one and only, we must make the most out of this opportunity. So during this session we need to

1. Establish the tone.
2. Set expectations.
3. Focus the problem(s).
4. Explore emotions.
5. Reach mutual agreement on what needs to be done.
6. Explore options for solution. One of the alternatives may be to continue therapy.

Establishing the Tone

Imagine yourself in your client's place. You are

Overwhelmed with feelings
Not clear about what's wrong
Scared things won't improve
Worried about bothering friends or family
Confused about what to do
Apprehensive about talking to someone you don't know

In short, most of our clients are in a very awkward position. As Jerome Frank says, our clients come to therapy because they are "demoralized." He uses this term to describe "the subjective experience of incompetence, coupled with distress" that people feel when they're aware that they have not been able to solve their problem(s) on their own.[2] Our clients are likely to be very anxious because they know they'll be talking about personal matters to someone they hardly know, and they are often apprehensive about being judged. Yet they take these risks in the hope that therapy will help.

These vulnerabilities make people defensive. Rightly so. Our clients are looking for clues that signal it's safe to proceed. We therefore need to establish a relationship that will allow our clients to put aside their hesitations enough to reveal what's necessary for their therapy.

The first meeting sets the tone: nonjudgmental, compassionate, empathic, open, warm yet professional. The question is how do we create these conditions? It's easy enough to feel empathic, nonjudgmental, and concerned; it's much more difficult to make sure those feelings are communicated to our clients. Furthermore, there are times when demonstrating these compassionate traits is difficult—such as when we're preoccupied with all that needs to be accomplished during an initial session. Regardless of these obstacles, communicating compassion and acceptance is precisely what we need to do. We need to be consistently attentive to how what we say and do affects the therapeutic climate. And we need to be particularly attuned to the communication of empathy, warmth, and acceptance in the beginning.

Our clients need hope.[3] Right from the start, we must perform our duties in an optimistic and hopeful manner. So far, however, we've talked about focusing our observations and assessments primarily on what's wrong, uncomfortable, and upsetting. Nonetheless, we should assume our clients want us to be hopeful that their problems can be resolved and that they have the resources to reach solutions.

It isn't so hard to be optimistic when we realize that for most people therapy does help and that each client has most likely chosen this course of action because she wants things to improve. So from the beginning we have genuine reasons to be hopeful. But we need to remember to communicate that optimistic attitude directly: "I am glad you decided to try therapy (because I believe it will be helpful, you want to solve your problems, and I want to help you with that process)." "I can see that you seem nervous about being here, but therapy is usually helpful, and we'll see what we can do to help you out."

The initial meetings also establish our professional boundaries. It's our professional obligation to establish and maintain what James Masterson has labeled "therapeutic neutrality."[4] This means we must maintain a neutral attitude—professionally interested and concerned but not personally and emotionally involved with the circumstances of our client's lives. In other words, we aren't going to step into the role of friend, lover, mother or father. From this perspective, it's our responsibility to facilitate the *process* of therapy while our clients are responsible for the *work*.

Handling Initial Greetings

First impressions count. When people are upset, as our clients often are, these initial greetings set the stage. Our clients begin formulating ideas about us and what to expect right from the onset. From the first introduction, phone call, meeting in the waiting room, or conversation in the office we need to convey a professional willingness to be involved.

When we are students, our first contact with clients often occurs largely from referrals in an agency set up for practicum experiences. Under these circumstances, the way introductions are handled is critical. Let's start with an example of how a very bad impression was created:

> Susan, a twenty-year-old pre-law student, came to the college counseling center because she was concerned about her parents' divorce. After an initial session, we established her diagnosis as Adjustment Disorder with Mixed Emotional Features. Even though she was very upset, she had basically good overall coping skills. I thought she would be a good training case and so decided to refer her to Lauren, one of our advanced graduate student trainees.
>
> When Susan and I went to the appointment desk to make her appointment, Lauren happened to be standing there. I explained that I was going to refer Susan to her and asked if she could set up a time. Without ever looking at Susan or even me, Lauren curtly said, "I have a class in five minutes, get back to you later." Then she walked off. Susan and I looked at each other, and I could see that Susan was apprehensive. Lauren conveyed no interest, willingness to be involved, or concern. After Lauren left, Susan asked me, "Could I maybe see someone else?" I understood.

I use this example because it illustrates how important it is to get off to a good start. Needless to say this could have been handled differently. When I spoke with Lauren about this episode, she explained that she was in a hurry and hadn't really thought of that introduction as part of the therapeutic relationship.

We went on to discuss how Lauren could have looked directly at Susan and said, "Susan, I'm glad to meet you. I would be happy to set up a time, but right now I need to get to a class. Would it be all right if I called [or, will you call back this afternoon when I'll be here], so we can schedule a time? I'll look forward to talking with you then."

In general, regardless of our personal style and where and how the first contact occurs, we need to take care to communicate: "Your concerns matter, I am willing to consult with you, and we will

gether what we might do to proceed." Likewise our non-
havior should match what we say, with such signals as
appropriate eye contact, a smile, a handshake—gestures that signal "I am here, your concerns are important to me, and I am ready
to work with you."

Setting Expectations

Most clients come to us naive about what we do and how we do it.
They may have seen therapists in the movies or heard Oprah Win-
frey explain how important it is to get "help." But these popular
sources may confuse more than prepare our clients for real-life
therapy.[5] That's why we need to help our clients understand what
to expect at the beginning of the first appointment.

You can best accomplish this important therapeutic task by
explaining right away what you plan to do during this interview.
For example, once seated in your office, you might start with something like this: "I'm glad you decided to try therapy. Let me start
by explaining what we'll do together today. We have about fifty
minutes. I want to review our agency's policies (we have a five-
session limit, fees are expected at the end of the hour, we will file
insurance forms, and so on). [Review the policies with the client.]
Before we begin, do you have any questions about procedures or
agency policy?"

Next you might say something like this: "I know this can be difficult, but I'd like you to tell me about what you need help with;
then we can figure out the best way to take care of your concerns.
Now you need to try to let me know what's going on. Do you feel
ready to do that?" Sometimes I add things that help clients understand my style, such as "I'll be trying to understand how you feel
and what's going on; please let me know if you feel like I'm missing something or not understanding, because it is my intention to
understand you and your concerns."

When we tell our clients what we expect them to do during our
first session, we reduce their stress by taking the guesswork out of
the equation. If we sit and stare expectantly, our clients can't pos-
sibly know what we want.

Each of us develops our own version of how to prepare our
clients for therapy, depending on our own personal style and

work setting. As we learn new skills, our colleagues and supervisors can provide essential information about how well our style is working. When we leave ourselves open to feedback, we'll discover how others perceive and receive our behavior. (Incidentally, getting feedback is useful for all of us even when we have lots of experience.)

Focusing on Presenting Problems

We have already talked about how to assess presenting problems. As you recall, we need to understand why this client has decided to come to therapy now, what symptoms are present, and what the client wants to work on.

During a first session, we're trying to bring some focus to the problems. This means we need to communicate that we understand the client's point of view. Our client will usually describe lots of details, other related material, and even tangential associations. We need to provide focus for problems by generalizing and reframing what the client has explained into some workable concepts. In other words, we want to pull together the details of what has been said into something we can work with. And we need to do this in language that will resonate with the client's understanding of her problems. For example:

Joanne, a forty-five-year-old special education administrator, came to see me in private practice at the suggestion of her physician, who felt her stress level was too high. She agreed, and during the first half hour explained a whole series of complicated occupational pressures mixed in with expressions of dissatisfaction about her marriage, concern about a brother who was seriously depressed, sadness about her seventeen-year-old son who was "growing up too fast," and a desire to go to Alaska and camp in the wilderness, if she could only get the time.

Joanne worked twelve-hour days with long meetings. She had the major responsibility for curriculum planning for a three-county area. When she got home, she worried about her husband who "always seemed distant," and her son who "just doesn't really need me anymore." She was aware that she wasn't like her father, who had suffered from depression, so she assumed she was all right. She accepted the anxiety as part of the overall picture and never really questioned what this was doing to her until her doctor raised the issue. Then she realized that she didn't feel very good about herself or her situation.

To provide some focus for Joanne, I said, "It sounds like your doctor thinks your life is out of hand, and you agree. It also sounds like you have a lot of pressure and there isn't much time for pleasure." The point was to accomplish two tasks: provide a platform for treatment goals and an opportunity for further clarification.

Furthermore, our summaries of content shouldn't leave out how the client feels. The content of the problems and the client's feelings about those problems are separated here for clarity. In actual practice, when we talk with our clients, we're trying to understand and help them understand both the events that occur and the feelings that are associated with those experiences.

Exploring Emotion

During this first contact it's important to give clients an opportunity to express their feelings. Some individuals come in ready to do that and start right off with vivid explanations of how they feel. Others have a more difficult time, so we need to draw out their feelings by asking, "How do you feel about that?" or guessing, "It seems like that makes you angry."

Joanne explained that she felt anxious: she had difficulty sleeping and frequently felt irritable, she was often fatigued and easily moved to tears, and she had increasing difficulty concentrating. She exercised strenuously and sometimes smoked marijuana. But ironically she didn't see these symptoms as connected to her stressful life. Rather, she believed they resulted from "constitutional weakness." She worried that she would be like her brother, who she described as "chronically depressed." She saw her own feelings as blemishes to be hidden, yet she noticed that the harder she tried the more anxious she became.

We need to handle any exploration of a client's painful feelings and events with empathy and compassion. It's never enough to feel empathy; we must also be prepared to express that understanding. As suggested before, we accomplish this expression by summarizing our understanding of the client's feelings, and we do it for two primary reasons: to facilitate rapport and to create the opportunity for clarification.

Research has shown that the communication of empathy is associated with therapeutic progress.[6] So as we listen, we need to communicate that we understand our clients' concerns from their point of view. We can do this best by summarizing and reflecting their ideas and feelings using words and phrases that pick up on key aspects of what they have said.

Perhaps even more important, we need to communicate what we're understanding so that our clients have an opportunity to correct us if we're missing the essence of what they're trying to describe. We need to provide lots of opportunities for correction, using statements like these: "Am I getting this right?" "Correct me if I'm wrong [or, not understanding]," or "Do you think I am understanding this?" These kinds of statements provide our clients with the opportunity to get us on the right wavelength.

Agreeing on the Main Issue

It is important to keep track of time (or be able to see the clock) because we need to leave enough time to agree on the problems and to plan for what will happen next. Most often it takes at least ten to fifteen minutes to take care of the last part of the first session. This can be handled by saying, "You've described so much today, but before we run out of time I need to give you some feedback, and you need to give me some reactions so that together we can figure out what to do next."

At this point it's helpful to summarize the problem as you see it. For Joanne it went something like this: "Joanne, before we go any further, I'd like to give you some feedback. Then I'd like to get your impressions."

She nodded, and I went on, "As I mentioned earlier, it seems to me like you're more anxious than either you or your doctor think you should be. You've mentioned work pressure and dissatisfaction with your marriage, but you've also pointed out that if you let these things bother you, you'll end up even more upset and worried—like your brother. Does what I'm saying match your understanding of your problems?"

Then we need to get feedback from the client on her views. Joanne reacted with, "Yes, I'd like to feel less pressured, and I certainly want to feel better about my personal life—I don't enjoy myself much. But I don't know what to do."

At that point I said, "You have several options . . ."

Reviewing Alternatives

Sometimes the exploration of a client's concerns, coupled with opportunities for the client to express the feelings associated with what's going on, is all that is needed. Other times the solutions are obvious, and the client feels that he can tackle the problem without additional support from therapy. If this is the case we can close the session with a review of the problem and a summary of what has been decided on as a course of action. We can finish by asking if there are any questions and leave the door open for further assistance if necessary.

More often, we need to discuss therapeutic options. With Joanne it went like this: "You have several options here, Joanne. First, you could continue as you are. Second, you could take the medication (imipramine) suggested by your doctor and continue trying to improve things on your own. Or third, you could take the medication and work with me on understanding your pressures and how to alter things so you feel better and enjoy your life more. Would you like to think about it, or do you feel ready to decide?"

These choices are broad and general. If we start with global suggestions we can get a clearer idea of how the client wants to proceed. Joanne was clear that she wanted the third option. This paved the way for the next steps. On the other hand, when our clients need more time to decide or prefer medication to psychotherapy, we need to provide support for those options as well. Arguing with clients to take the therapy option is rarely a good idea; it is usually unsuccessful, but it also can backfire if clients comply but resent the choice.

Joanne wanted her circumstances to improve, and she was embarrassed about not having things in better control. Because we both agreed this would take more than one session, we were now ready to talk about diagnosis and treatment plans.

Making a Diagnosis

Before we discuss how a diagnosis is made, it makes sense to digress slightly into a brief history of the diagnosis of mental health problems. Psychotherapy and counseling are medical traditions that require a diagnosis before treatment is implemented. Doctors and their patients assumed certain diagnoses inevitably led to prescribed treatment protocols. Most medical doctors and the World Health Organization use the *International Classification of Diseases and Related Health Problems (ICD-10)* to classify medical problems. But in its earlier versions, the *ICD* did not include "mental disorders."

In an effort to compile statistical data and to facilitate communication about mental health problems, the American Psychiatric Association developed its own nomenclature. By 1952 this classification system was published as the first *Diagnostic and Statistical Manual of Mental Disorders (DSM-I)*. Since 1952 both the *ICD* and the *DSM* contain parallel descriptions and numbers to identify mental disorders. Likewise both manuals are continually revised to reflect the needs of the population and the most up-to-date thinking of the professionals who use the manuals.

Nowhere do we see more evidence of change than in what is and isn't classified as a mental disorder in the *DSM*. There are many examples: the term *Neurosis* is no longer used because of its tie to psychoanalytic theory—now behavioral descriptors are used to classify disorders; Hysterical Personality was changed to Histrionic Personality Disorder because of the former term's negative connotation.

Homosexuality as a classification has undergone an even greater transformation. In the 1952 and 1968 editions of the *DSM*, homosexuality was classified as a mental illness. In 1980 the panel of experts responsible for the *DSM-III* responded to pressure from activist groups and accepted the social observation that sexual preference is not in and of itself a diagnosable condition. In consequence, homosexuality was not listed as a mental disorder unless the individual was distressed with that characteristic (Ego-Dystonic Homosexuality). By 1987, the classification was dropped altogether in the *DSM-III-R*, reflecting the professional understanding that homosexuality is not a mental disorder under any condition.

These changes demonstrate that the *DSM* is a work in progress. The *DSM-IV*, released in 1994, contains seventeen new sets of criteria for further study. These include Mixed Anxiety-Depressive Disorder, Dissociative Trance Disorder, Premenstrual Disorder, Binge Eating Disorder, and Passive Aggressive Personality Disorder. The political and social issues surrounding the inclusion of a disorder in the *DSM* are substantial but beyond the scope of this chapter. (We'd really digress if we followed this fascinating topic.) It suffices to say that once we're involved in the process of making diagnoses, we need to remain sensitive to the attendant social and political issues.

Worldwide, the *ICD-9* remains the primary manual used to identify all diseases, including mental disorders. (Although the *ICD-10* was published in 1992, it won't come into official use in the United States until the late 1990s.[7]) In the United States, both *DSM-IV* and *ICD-9* diagnoses are generally accepted by insurance companies,[8] but most mental health agencies and professional associations advocate the use of the *DSM-IV* because of the refinement and utility of the multiaxial system.

The *DSM-IV* was not developed to specify a course of treatment. Rather this multiaxial system is specifically designed to identify symptom clusters and provide additional data about medical problems, stressors, and general functioning.

Many mental health professionals see official diagnosis as being of limited value. Some argue that it's unimportant because the labels do not suggest a course of treatment.[9] Others complain that labels may in fact lead to identifying clients by their pathology rather than as people with problems in living.[10] One survey of mental health professionals discovered that a majority of the respondents used the *DSM* diagnoses for insurance and legal purposes but for not much else.[11]

Regardless of the validity of these complaints, we must acknowledge that all third-party payers—most mental health agencies, researchers, funding organizations, training programs, and, in some cases, legal authorities—insist on the use of a diagnostic label. In other words, if you want to get paid, you must submit a diagnosis. In most states, moreover, it's only those professionals with appropriate degrees and licensing who are allowed to diagnose and treat mental illness. This means that if we are going to be licensed we must be prepared to fulfill this important function.

For these reasons we must learn how to make a diagnosis using the *DSM-IV,* and it only makes sense to accomplish this task in a manner that is useful as well as pragmatic. There are many formats for "structured clinical interviews" that outline specific questions in a preset order designed for assessment geared toward reaching a diagnosis. These systems are particularly helpful for research purposes but also show promise as assessment tools. Although these formats are relatively reliable, their clinical value is limited by their lack of flexibility.[12] Regardless of the method we use, we need to know how to make a *DSM-IV* diagnosis and then how to use that diagnosis to help our clients.

Using a Multiaxial System

One feature that makes the *DSM-IV* useful is the multiaxial system. Each axis describes different aspects of client functioning.

Axis I

- Clinical disorders descriptive of the client's current presentation, such as Schizophrenia, Panic, Hypoactive Sexual Desire, or Alcohol Intoxication
- May include more than one diagnosis
- Prioritized with presenting problem listed first

Axis II

- Personality disorders, mental retardation

Axis III

- General medical conditions

Axis IV

- Psychosocial and environmental problems listed by category, such as problems with primary support group, social environment, housing, occupation, education, or access to health care services, and interaction with the legal system

Axis V

- Global Assessment of Functioning (GAF)
- Listed on a continuum of 1 to 100 (the lower the number, the more dysfunctional the person is)
- Parentheses following the number indicate whether the assessment is (current), (highest level in past year), or (at discharge)

In order to use this manual, we must be familiar with the section of the *DSM* entitled "Use of the Manual." Pages one through thirteen outline the coding and reporting system as well as procedures for classification. Once you're familiar with the large edition, you may find the *Quick Reference* very handy. It's a little paperback that can be easily carried around or placed on a crowded desk, and it contains the basic criteria needed to make a diagnosis.

Establishing a Diagnosis

In order to establish a diagnosis, we must identify clusters of symptoms that are considered "clinically significant." The *DSM-IV* informs us that clinically significant symptoms cause distress, disability, or dysfunction (the three D's). They also increase the risk of death or loss of freedom. Further, we're told that such symptoms are *not* normally expected, nor are they a culturally sanctioned response to an event such as the bereavement over the death of a loved one.[13] We've already discussed assessing those exceptional symptoms related to daily functioning such as sleep, eating, sexual activity, drug use, thinking patterns, mood, and self-esteem. We then look for the diagnostic category that best describes the cluster of symptoms presented by the client.

So during each session, but particularly the first, we're on the lookout for symptoms. During the session with Joanne, I noted these statements (and symptoms):

"I'm jittery even when I don't drink coffee." (anxiety)

"I always think I'll make mistakes, even with things I do all the time." (worry)

"I dread trying anything because I think I'll screw it up." (low self-esteem)

"I cry too much, too often, for no reason." (crying spells)

"I can't sleep at night because I worry so much." (sleep disturbance)

"I'm always feeling like I can't pay attention to what's going on."
(difficulty concentrating)

"I can't take this much longer. My husband is already distant, and
now he is saying that he's fed up with my crying. I worry all the
time. Pretty soon I won't be able to go to work." (symptoms
interfering significantly with her present level of functioning)

As mentioned before, these observations led to questions that clarified the significance of each symptom (how often, how much, how
long, when, where, why).

Some clients expect a diagnostic label and understand the
necessity of providing insurance companies with information.
Other clients may be caught off guard by this process. It's best to
assume our clients need an explanation of both the diagnosis and
how it will be used.

Sometimes you can work out the diagnosis with the client, as I
did with Joanne: "Your insurance company requires a diagnosis,
but it's also wise for us to discuss what we're going to focus on in
therapy. I'd like to hear your opinions." We might ask what label
she would use to describe her problems. This might also be a good
time to explain that a diagnosis is a work in progress and that we
expect it to change.

I explained to Joanne that her insurance company required a
DSM-IV multiaxial diagnosis, and we discussed what would go on
her form. "From what you have described, Joanne, it sounds like a
diagnosis of Generalized Anxiety Disorder fits your symptoms.
You've pointed out that you feel anxious, have trouble concentrating and sleeping, and worry a lot." I also pointed out that her
low self-esteem and crying spells might indicate depression. Then
I asked her what she thought: "How do you see this?" At first, she
was apprehensive about seeing herself as someone with *any* diagnosable problem, but she also wanted her insurance company to
pay for her treatment.

Joanne responded, "I'm anxious and keyed up all the time; the
stress is what's killing me." Reaching agreement on the diagnosis

is one more way of cementing the contract to work on certain areas. It was clear that Joanne wanted relief from the anxiety she felt. She was certainly aware that her symptoms were personally *distressing*, at times *disabling*, and in addition had lasted for years. The *duration* was significant to both her and her physician.

The more familiar we are with the *DSM-IV* classification system, the more comfortable we'll be arriving at a diagnosis. Let's discuss the rationale for Joanne's diagnosis.

Axis I

• Generalized Anxiety Disorder 300.2 (Joanne fit the criteria because she had a significant disruption in her ability to function in her job and relationships. She was anxious and frequently worried, and she had difficulty sleeping. Her self-esteem was low, and she experienced frequent crying spells. I did not include a diagnosis of Cannabis Dependence, Abuse or Intoxication because her use was sporadic and did not seem to interfere with social or occupational functioning. I was aware that the family history of depression and Joanne's low self-esteem and crying spells could be a further sign that a diagnosis of Dysthymic Disorder might also fit, but because she was most concerned about her anxiety—her presenting problem—Generalized Anxiety Disorder became the "working" diagnosis.)

Axis II

• Condition Deferred on Axis II (Her family's history of mental health problems and the long-standing nature of Joanne's problems could have indicated a personality disorder: an Axis II diagnosis. But at this point, I didn't have enough evidence of either current dysfunctional behavior or significant events in her history to warrant an Axis II diagnosis.)

Axis III

• Hypertension (not on medication)
• Ovarian cyst (listed on intake form)

Axis IV

- Her psychosocial stressors were the following: problems in her marriage, the stress of having her son leave their home, and feeling unable to meet the demands of her job

Axis V

- GAF = 55 (current) (I chose this number because she had some moderate symptoms that resulted in significant personal distress and some moderate social and occupational difficulty.)
- GAF = 65 (past year) (Joanne had explained that the pressure of her son getting older, her husband's distant behavior, and her job stress had all increased during the last four months. As a result there was slightly more disruption to her current functioning than in the previous year.)

Taking Steps to Reach a Diagnosis

In summary, to complete a multiaxial diagnosis, you take the following general steps:

1. *List all the symptoms you notice.* It is helpful in the beginning to note all the symptoms you have observed. And it's useful to be familiar with the criteria for each diagnosis; but even with experience, it helps to check the *DSM.* Then consider the diagnosis that best describes what you have assessed.

2. *Study criteria in the* DSM-IV *with attention to differential diagnosis and distinguishing characteristics.* The *DSM-IV* encourages clinicians to consider the criteria for differential diagnosis rather than to assign multiple diagnoses whenever possible. In addition, we need to be attentive to any diagnosis that requires a *specifier* or data to clarify the current or past course of the disorder. We may need to specify the *subtype* of the disorder, as with anorexia: Restricting type or Binge-Eating/Purging type. Or we may need to specify when the disorder occurs (for example, with onset during intoxication or with onset during withdrawal), or whether the disorder is acute or chronic. The *DSM-IV* is really quite helpful and easy to use because it tells us when a specifier is required, and then it clarifies exactly what to mention and how to record those specifications.

3. *Use the prescribed suggestions for indicating diagnostic uncertainty when necessary.* We have the option to defer a diagnosis when we aren't sure. When we have enough data to know that the client has a mental disorder but we don't have enough data to specify the type, we can indicate what we know with a specification such as Unspecified Mental Disorder (not psychotic) 300.9 or (psychotic) 298.9. We also have the option to use the term *provisional* in parentheses to indicate that we only have enough information to confirm a "working" diagnosis.[14]

4. *Decide on the diagnosis.* At a later time, when you have enough data, you can remove the parentheses from the label and indicate your opinion. The requirements of your client's insurance company and your work setting, service, or funding organization will determine whether you use a full *DSM* multiaxial diagnosis, just an Axis I classification, or an *ICD-9* code.

5. *Fill in the information for the other axes.* In addition to the five standard scales already mentioned, the *DSM-IV* proposes three optional scales: defensive functioning scale, global assessment of relational functioning (GARF), and social and occupational functioning assessment scale (SOFAS). This information may be particularly interesting when preparing a case presentation. The defensive functioning scale provides good information on coping strategies that are both adaptive and maladaptive and may be very helpful in some work settings.

6. *Consider the consequences.* If you have reason to believe that the diagnosis will create problems for the client, you need to consider the consequences. As therapists we need to be sensitive to our ethical responsibility to accurately report what we see. But we should also be aware of how these labels can be used. Serious consequences can also occur when a client does not want his employer to have access to his diagnosis. Because we can't guarantee the confidentiality of a diagnostic label once that information is given to a managed care organization or an insurance company, we'll need to make sure our clients are aware that negative consequences could occur. For example, I saw a man who was eligible for therapy as part of an employee assistance program, but because he was a police officer and his diagnosis was Compulsive Gambling, he opted to avoid letting his employer know the label and so paid for treatment himself.

In most cases an insurance company uses the label to assess the medical necessity of financing treatment. But the client will not be reimbursed if the diagnosis is not accepted as treatable, which is often the case with an Axis II diagnosis (Borderline, Histrionic, or Antisocial Personality Disorder), or as medically necessary, as in the case of marital conflict (Partner Relational Problem). Ironically, insurance companies do not seem willing to define *medical necessity*.

7. *Review with your supervisor.* These ethical considerations as well as other diagnostic dilemmas make it imperative that we draw on the advice and expertise of our colleagues. It's good practice.

When you're not licensed, you'll have to review with your supervisor to comply with the law as well as to learn from experience. And you'll need your supervisor to sign off on any written documents. But even when we have years of experience, there are times when we need a consultation about quandaries or complications.

8. *Inform your client.* As mentioned earlier, we want our clients to be informed about how we view their problems and treatment. As part of our duty to provide informed consent, we'll need to help our clients understand diagnostic information. Our clients have a right to know what their diagnosis is as well as the possible consequences of that label being on record. In addition, many agencies require clients to sign off on diagnosis and treatment plans as an indication of their consent.

9. *Let your client know about diagnostic records.* Our clients have a legal right to request access to all records. We need to be aware that our clients can request information about their diagnosis and treatment at any time. They may also want to know how records are kept and who has access to them. In most cases the confidentiality of professional records is protected by state laws, which means that no information can be released without written permission from the client. However, our clients usually sign a waiver so that diagnostic information can be released to their insurance company in order to receive benefits. And once the information is released, we have no control over what is done with it. We need to inform our clients clearly about who will have access to diagnostic information about them now and in the future.

10. *Consider how the label will affect the client.* Often our clients don't ask about the labels we assign, and some aren't very interested.

But many benefit from knowing their diagnosis. Such knowledge contributes to their overall self-understanding and insight. Likewise a diagnosis can focus their attention and motivation on symptoms that need to be challenged. But we do need to keep in mind that some clients use their diagnostic label as an excuse: "I am a manic-depressive, so of course my charge cards are over the limit." Others are devastated to learn they fit the criteria for a diagnosable condition. It's our professional obligation to remain sensitive to how our clients respond to the knowledge that they've been assigned a diagnosis.

When we talk with our clients about the diagnosis, we need to make sure we cover all these areas. Certainly, we want them to understand how we plan to help them remove the symptoms, which brings us to treatment planning.

Developing Treatment Plans

When a house is remodeled, blueprints guide the transformation. In therapy, it's the treatment plans that provide the blueprint for progress. Architectural blueprints must be created by professionals, but always at the request of, in consultation with, and in response to the needs of the homeowner. So too in therapy.

There are a variety of ways to construct treatment plans depending on how they will be used. Most often this is a three-step process: (1) creating treatment goals, (2) specifying plans to achieve treatment goals, and (3) answering managed care requirements.

Creating Treatment Goals and Plans

We have already discussed the importance of establishing agreement on the problems to be addressed in therapy. Now we need to consider our goals and treatment plans.

Some clients have goals that aren't realistic. For example, Adrian, a forty-year-old librarian, said that her goal was to develop meditation techniques that would allow her to contact deceased relatives. Jason, a twenty-six-year-old store clerk who was studying to become a pilot, said his goal was to "be happy," not just sometimes but all the time. When we are confronted with unrealistic goals, we need either to reframe those goals or explain why we can't help.

It's our job to help our clients establish constructive and workable goals for therapy. In addition, many agencies and most insurance companies require treatment plans for accomplishing those goals. The following are some useful guidelines:

• *Goals should indicate the expected outcome.* We need to know where we're going, and we want our goals to identify the end point: termination of therapy. Therefore we may need to ask at the beginning of therapy, "How will you know when you are ready to end therapy?" The answers can help shape our goals. For example, we'll assume it's time for termination when our client is able to ask girls for dates without getting sick to his stomach, or is able to manage the anxiety of leaving the house without a panic attack, or can end her affair.

• *Goals should be reached by mutual agreement.* We need to be working toward the same end point. Usually we can easily agree, but sometimes our goals are inconsistent with those of our clients. This is often the case when a client has a problem with substance abuse or an eating disorder. For example, one of my clients, who had a problem with bulimia, maintained that her primary goal was to be thin. But her obsession with this goal jeopardized her health.

It's difficult to proceed unless we can reach mutual understanding, which may require some negotiation: we tell our clients what we think, we reflect what we hear them say, and we look for compromise. For example, my client was able to explain to me that her goal of thinness was originally established to accomplish other goals, such as getting more attention, having higher self-esteem, having more friends, and finding a boyfriend. Consequently, these "secondary" goals became the ones that we could both agree to work on in therapy.

• *Goals should be realistic.* The process of discussing our client's goals is therapeutic in and of itself. As we help our clients frame their goals in realistic ways, we set the stage for developing expectations about what can actually be accomplished in the time available. Our role is to provide the reality check: "Do you think it's a good idea to try to stop smoking while you're going through this divorce?" Our observations and experience can help our clients create reasonable goals. We need to be prepared to offer advice based on what we know about the process of change.

• *Goals should be attainable.* As one of my colleagues likes to point out, "You can't flunk therapy." Because we want our clients to succeed, we need to establish an atmosphere in which there can be no failure. It helps to follow our client's motivations, so ask, "What do you feel like doing?" or "What can you imagine yourself trying at this point?" To make sure our clients accomplish their goals, we need to assist them in establishing goals that are achievable: "We'll learn from each experiment regardless of the outcome, so you can't fail."

Now let's go back to our example, with a focus on how we develop goals and plans. Joanne had already explained that she felt most anxious when she was lonely. She was bored by her husband of seventeen years but was still committed to her marriage. She was aware that her husband and son didn't share her interests in outdoor activities. Consequently Joanne had isolated herself during the years her son was growing up and her husband was developing his business. (He ran a bagel buggy and was tied up from mid afternoon to late at night.) Joanne wanted friends who would be able to participate in activities that were fun for her. Because she was shy, she had alienated herself by working long hours and then dropping in front of the TV in the evening. The lack of balance between work and pleasure in addition to her lack of "playmates" made her irritable and restless. Joanne and I agreed to the following goals:

• To increase social supports. Joanne will have four different people she can call on to participate in outdoor activities.
• To lessen her anxiety. Joanne will no longer need to take Tums and will be able to get through the day without feeling fearful.
• To worry less. Joanne will develop cognitive-behavioral strategies to manage the things she worries about: her son, her job, and her anger.
• To change her occupational pressures. Joanne will develop assertive techniques so that she can say no when she needs to.

Now we'll need plans to accomplish these goals. The type and specificity of treatment plans will vary depending on the time available for therapy, the client's problem, and your theoretical orientation and style. In addition, each work setting will probably have a preferred format for how plans are actually written up and communicated to the client. Nonetheless, all treatment plans have some things in common; they should

- Engage the client
- Tap into the client's motivation
- Be manageable
- Lend themselves to identifiable steps

Treatment plans should inspire our clients and engage their experimental creativity. The way we go about creating plans will in large part determine how successful we are in engaging our clients in the process of therapy. As mentioned earlier, we want to be hopeful and optimistic. If we can also create a climate of experimentation, we'll enlist our client's curiosity: "Let's try something different." "How can we make these plans provocative, entertaining, or exciting?" "Let's see what might happen if you tried [something we have in mind that might help]." We'll want to add that "we can learn from whatever you're willing to try. So what would you like to experiment with here?"

We'll want to tap into our client's motivations. Make it fun: "Let's figure out what *really* gives you pleasure." Make it rewarding: "Would you like to experiment with finding more opportunities to enjoy your family?" Create an atmosphere of challenge: "Let's brainstorm about what needs to be done to get that promotion."

We'll also want to make our plans manageable. We do that by using specific and measurable steps: talk to one person at work before the next session; reduce the number of angry outbursts from three to one per week; spend thirty minutes every day alone reading or listening to music. These steps are the tasks we work on during therapy as well as the homework we assign between sessions.

When you write up a treatment plan, the goals are specified individually, as are the plans for accomplishing each goal. The steps are listed in parentheses because they are devised as you go along and may not be clear from the onset. For Joanne, the plans (and steps) for her first goal looked like this:

Goal 1. To increase social supports

- Have Joanne identify four new outdoor activities. (Because Joanne entered therapy still contemplating the pros and cons of change, it's important to have her weigh the consequences of trying to participate in activities. She needs to discuss both her desire to participate in more outdoor activities and her resistance to moving ahead. Have her clarify how much time would be necessary to create relief from her isolation.)
- Select four people she could involve with her in activities she likes. (Help Joanne identify people she would enjoy. Explore any resistance related to her shyness.)
- Create clear plans for outdoor activities. (Discuss her plans for cross-country skiing in winter and river rafting in summer and walking with friends on a more regular basis. Review with Joanne how she'll involve others in ways that are meaningful to her.)
- Experiment with the activity.
- Review the outcome.
- Plan for other opportunities.

You'll notice that I started out with specific plans and steps. The strategy was to establish a foundation of behavioral successes built from a series of challenging tasks. We'll want to be flexible enough to alter plans whenever new data make it seem wise to do so. Later on in the progression, you'll notice there is less specific detail and more room to devise steps that seem appropriate after information has been gathered about how well our earlier experiments worked.

Wrapping Up

At the end of this first session, we'll want to review what we have done, plan for our first steps, and ask for questions. In that way we accomplish two important therapeutic tasks: we provide more opportunity for clarity, and we reduce our client's feelings of "demoralization." We hope that we've helped our clients see that they can in fact do something about their problems. As they plan for their first steps, we create anticipation that even greater resolution will be forthcoming as we tackle our overall treatment objectives.

For example, with Joanne I suggested, "I can see that you're eager to get going, and I'm pleased with our overall plans, but now we need to decide where you'd like to begin." Joanne was eager to get started and wanted to attack all the goals at once. Her enthusiasm was beneficial in that it created the energy she needed to take on her problems. On the other hand, it also had the potential to cause trouble, because attacking all her problems at once wasn't realistic and set up opportunities for failure. So I asked her to pick the short-term goal she wanted to start with and assured her that we'd take on more of her overall objectives as we continued in therapy.

Joanne explained, "I want to feel better, and I think that the easiest way for that to happen is by trying to have more friends." Then I asked her, "During the next week, could you think about four people you'd like to get to know better? Also, can you think about two activities where you might meet new people?" After she answered, I posed another opportunity for questions: "Do these plans make sense?" "Do you have any questions?"

The attention to questions at the end is essential because it gives you and your client opportunities to fine-tune any ambiguity or to take care of any apprehension about proceeding. At the very end, you'll want to reinforce the client's decision to reach resolution by saying something like

I think we've made good progress today. I'm optimistic that eventually this won't be so painful.

I can see it's been hard to reveal these problems. I think we've outlined some good plans to get you started.

I'm aware of how confused you still feel. I think we have some good strategies to help you gain more clarity.

Creating Treatment Plans for Managed Care

In this era of managed care, providing insurance companies, Medicare, or other funding sources with treatment plans is a fact of life. Whereas some companies are satisfied with plans in outline form, others require answers to their own questions. Here is a list adapted from one insurance company's questions:

1. Provide a multiaxial diagnosis.
2. Describe previous psychiatric, chemical dependency, inpatient, and outpatient treatment.
3. List family psychiatric and chemical dependency history.
4. List marital, legal, financial, and employment history as it pertains to patient's current condition.
5. Describe current symptoms and their severity, behaviors, and functional impairments.
6. Describe current living situation and support systems. Is the patient utilizing available support?
7. List current medications, dosages, and any planned medication interventions.
8. Describe targeted treatment and behavioral goals.
9. List current frequency of sessions, type of sessions (individual, group, marital), and cost per session.
10. What is the estimated length of treatment to achieve goals?
11. Note the date you began.
12. To your knowledge, is the patient currently being treated by any other mental health care provider?
13. Note the number of canceled sessions.
14. Note the number of no-show sessions.

Each company has their own specifications. If you have any questions about what information will be necessary, there's usually an 800 number that you can call for clarification. Very often, regardless of the target questions, an insurance company will accept brief but clear treatment plans that delineate the diagnosis and therapeutic goals.

You can easily see that the skills we have discussed so far (observation, assessment, first-session strategies, diagnosis, and treatment planning) overlap and interrelate. No skill can be acquired in isolation from other therapeutic skills. Nowhere are these interrelationships clearer than with the skill we now turn to: building rapport.

Notes

1. Luborsky, L., Crits-Cristoph, P., Mintz, J., & Auerback, A. (1988). *Who will benefit from psychotherapy? Predicting therapeutic outcomes.* New York: Basic Books.
2. Frank, J. D.(1982). Therapeutic components shared by all psychotherapies. In J. H. Harvey & M. M. Parks (Eds.), *Psychotherapy research and behavior change* (vol. 1, pp. 7–37). Washington, DC: American Psychological Association.
3. Garfield, S. L. (1980). *Psychotherapy: An eclectic approach.* New York: Wiley; Frank, J. D. (1971). Therapeutic factors in psychotherapy. *American Journal of Psychotherapy, 25,* 350–361.
4. Klein, R. (1995). *Closet Narcissistic Disorder: The Masterson approach.* New York: Newbridge Communications.
5. Heaton, J. A., & Wilson, N. L. (1995). *Tuning in trouble: Talk TV's destructive impact on mental health.* San Francisco: Jossey-Bass.
6. Burns, D. D. (1992). Therapeutic empathy and recovery from depression in cognitive-behavioral therapy: A structural equation model. *Journal of Consulting and Clinical Psychology, 60,* 441–449; Duan, C. (1996). The current state of empathy research. *Journal of Counseling Psychology, 43,* 261–274.
7. American Psychiatric Association. (1994). *Diagnostic and statistical manual of mental disorders* (4th ed.). Washington, DC: Author.
8. See note 7.
9. Frances, A., Clarken, J. F., & Perry, S. (1984). *Differential therapeutics in psychotherapy.* New York: Brunner/Mazel.
10. Szasz, T. S. (1961). *The myth of mental illness: Foundations of a theory of personal conduct.* New York: Hoeber-Harper. (Rev. ed. New York: HarperCollins, 1974); Szasz, T. S. (1987). *Insanity: The idea and its consequences.* New York: Wiley; Persons, J. B. (1986). The advantages of studying psychological phenomena rather than psychiatric diagnoses. *American Psychologist, 41,* 1252–1260.
11. Kutchins, H., & Kirk, S. A. (1988). The business of diagnosis: *DSM-III* and clinical social work. *Social Work, 33,* 215–220.
12. Vace, N. A., & Juhnke, G. A. (1997). The use of structured clinical interviews for assessment in counseling. *Journal of Counseling and Development, 75,* 470–480.
13. See note 7, p. 7.
14. See note 7, p. 5.

Chapter Four

| Establishing Rapport

Think for a moment about the person you want to talk with most when you are confused, upset, or angry. More than likely, when you're with that person you can say what you need to say, without fear of being judged. You feel respected, understood, accepted— challenged yet safe. He knows when to push for more. She knows when to use humor and how to change the topic tactfully when the time is right. All this happens without explanation or irritation. If you think about it, it's like dancing gracefully with a partner: you move, she moves; he steps left, you respond; she dips, you bend. There is dynamic action and reaction creating a fluid exchange. This vibrant, engaging sensitivity to each other is rapport.

Now let's think about what happens when rapport is missing and you're out of sync. You explain—he doesn't get it. You try again. She changes the topic. You're left feeling alone. It's too much work. You're frustrated, overexposed, and undervalued. You move—she steps on your foot. He steps left, and you stand still. She bristles, saying, "What now?" You're irritated, thinking, "Here we go again: if I say what I'm thinking, we'll fight, but if I keep my mouth shut, I'll explode." You don't feel at ease. There's no comfort and no understanding, and more tension is the inevitable result.

Most bad relationships are bad because there's no rapport. And most good ones are characterized by rapport. But of course we all realize that most relationships, and this certainly includes psychotherapy relationships, are not an either-or (you have rapport or you don't) proposition. Rather, there's a blend—sometimes we're in tune, sometimes not.

As we search for the blend of factors that allows our clients to reveal personal difficulties, experience painful emotions, and take necessary risks, rapport seems a logical goal. When you have rapport, you have the glue, the camaraderie, the synergy to hold a psychotherapy relationship together. And because relationships fluctuate with subtle changes in interaction, mood, and behavior, we count on rapport to help us repair ruptures. In most cases we assume that rapport requires a reciprocal interaction, with both participants contributing to the quality, but in therapy the responsibility for creating and maintaining rapport isn't equal.

Most therapists agree that it is their responsibility to create the conditions necessary for their clients to resolve their difficulties.[1] Indeed, creating the conditions that enhance rapport is an awesome assignment, especially when we consider the variety of people and problems we must handle. When we take on this assignment, as we must with each appointment, we need to answer a fundamental question: What do I need to do to cultivate rapport with the client who is now sitting in front of me? For example:

Elva, who at sixty has just had her purse stolen and who's lonely and worried that there will be no more intimacy in her life.

Eric, a twenty-year-old pre-med student, who's convinced he will never love again after his girlfriend ended their relationship.

Carolyn, who explains as well as demonstrates her attitude problem. "People tell me I've got an attitude. What do they know, a bunch of dumb shits who expect me to care. You can't tell me it's worth it, can you?"

John, who can't believe he got drunk and had a sexual experience with a man.

In each situation, we must find a way to use who we are to facilitate our clients' work. Most likely our methods will be guided by study, experience, and our own common sense.

Basic Facilitative Conditions

There is no better place to look for advice on establishing rapport than the writing of Carl Rogers. His fascination with the curative powers of psychotherapy inspired his research and practice. His long and distinguished career was devoted to understanding the

therapeutic variables that facilitate "healing." He identified therapists' attributes that he believed were sufficient, in and of themselves, to be "growth promoting": empathic understanding,
unconditional positive regard, and congruence.[2]

Although studies have shown that these conditions alone do
not guarantee progress, researchers generally agree that these
qualities expedite the formation of therapeutic relationships. In
fact, research has repeatedly proven that the quality of the relationship is the single most important factor to the overall outcome
of therapy.[3] Moreover, research tells us that the relationship either
is well formed or fails to form in the first three sessions.[4]

Our clients' willingness to become involved in therapy is
another predictor of a positive outcome.[5] However, we can't usually rely on our clients' initial enthusiasm, because many of our
clients have relationship problems that predispose them to difficulties in establishing an alliance. Others are scared, and most are
nervous about talking to a stranger—so they test us.

Studies have shown that the level of disturbance in the client
is also likely to be a significant factor affecting the therapeutic relationship.[6] The more disturbance, the harder it is to establish a relationship. The important thing to keep in mind, though, is that
regardless of how serious our clients' problems are, the ones who
have successful experiences in therapy describe their therapists as
warm, attentive, understanding, respectful, experienced, and
active[7]—terms that parallel those Carl Rogers identified years ago.

This means we need to take on two basic tasks. First, we'll have
to understand what it means to be empathic, respectful, and congruent. Second, we'll need to figure out how to tap these qualities
in ourselves so that we cultivate positive rapport with our clients.

Figuring out what these terms mean to us individually is complicated by the vagueness of the words used to describe these conditions; we are left lots of room for interpretation. (In one graphic
example, Galdstein and his associates defined eighteen types of
empathy.[8]) In fact, we often identify these qualities by their absence.
For example, it's easier to identify a lack of respect than it is to
know how to be respectful. When there's ambiguity in terminol-
ogy, there are inevitable consequences for us as therapists: it's hard
to implement what we haven't clearly defined.

"Unconditional" Positive Regard?

Rogers describes unconditional positive regard as acceptance, prizing, or caring. It's demonstrated when "the therapist is willing for the client to be whatever immediate feeling is going on—confusion, resentment, fear, anger, courage, love, or pride. Such caring on the part of the therapist is nonpossessive. The therapist prizes the client in a total rather than conditional way."[9] But Rogers's conception of "unconditional" regard has generated considerable controversy.

Most therapists acknowledge the importance of positive regard or respect to the development of a good therapeutic relationship. But the notion of *unconditional* positive regard is generally viewed as unnecessarily confounding. First, there are problems generated when our values conflict with those of the client. Then there's the problem of how to handle disrespectful behavior directed at the therapist from the client. Finally, unconditional positive regard is compromised when we make choices that violate autonomy, which we sometimes have to do in order to protect our clients and other people.

For example, on those occasions when we set limits—"No, I won't come to your house," or "We can't do therapy when you're drunk," or "I'll need to inform your wife that you have a gun and intend to shoot her"—we aren't respecting our clients "unconditionally." Of course, we could argue that it's not respectful to allow someone to harm himself or others; we hospitalize someone who is psychotic but prefers to walk the streets unable to care for herself. These semantic struggles, which obviously reflect real issues, make it easier and clearer to stick with basic respect rather than with "unconditional positive regard."

In deference to these issues, it makes sense for therapists to start with the Golden Rule: to treat others as we'd like to be treated under similar circumstances. It's hard to imagine good rapport without including this kind of respect. It is safe to assume that therapeutic respect also includes:

- *Caring about our clients' concerns.* Our clients need to know that we have a genuine interest in helping them deal with their problems. Our clients' feelings of helplessness, social isolation, failure, and lack of self-worth result from not being able to manage personal problems on their own. Knowing that someone else is willing both to accept them with their imperfections and to be involved in a process to help them improve lets them know they don't have to struggle alone.

• *Suspending personal reactions.* We lay the foundation for therapeutic work when we convey that we're willing to listen without passing judgment. By suspending criticism, we create safety for therapeutic exploration. People in trouble aren't at their best, and consequently they're easily irritated, frustrated, and disappointed. By understanding rather than reacting, we demonstrate respect.

• *Appreciating our clients' autonomy.* We most clearly maintain respect by honoring our clients' rights to choose their own course of action. This means we must scrutinize our own biases, stereotypes, and assumptions so that we don't impose them on our clients.

• *Honoring cultural differences.* Respect most definitely includes an appreciation for cultural difference. What's respectful in one culture may be seen as disrespectful in another (bowing, eye contact, saving face, using personal pronouns, giving gifts, using surnames, avoiding surnames, using slang, swearing, touching, not touching, standing at a distance).

• *Valuing our clients' responsibilities.* We convey basic respect by expecting our clients to assume personal responsibility for the choices they make. Doing so implies a respect for the potential of the client to get better, act more appropriately, and feel better. James Masterson describes the importance of treating clients (in this instance, he was discussing clients who have a diagnosis of Borderline Personality Disorder) "as if" they do in fact have the capacity to act normally.[10] When we reinforce our clients' capacity to behave responsibly, we support the development of their own self-respect.

• *Maintaining our self-respect.* It's easier to respect others when we respect our own humanity (our basic needs, emotional reactions, wishes, values, and standards). At the most basic levels, our self-respect means we won't allow our clients to be disrespectful by not paying bills, consuming too much time, or speaking and behaving in ways that are inappropriate for therapy.

On a much less superficial level, we must acknowledge our own values, standards, and choices. This may mean we might avoid some counseling situations—such as working with sexually active teenagers, substance abusers, women seeking abortions, men convicted of a sexual offense, or people accused of child abuse—if our values will compromise our ability to communicate respect. On the other hand, many therapists are able to feel and communicate respect and still maintain an allegiance to opposing values and standards. These therapists accept "wrong" action while maintaining respect for the basic humanity of the client.

Basic respect requires an acceptance of our clients as they are but includes a willingness to be involved in helping them improve. This is an inherent part of empathic understanding. At no time is this need greater than when we're working with addicts. Suzanne was fifty-six when I first saw her. She'd been hiding her drinking for years, and her problems had really stacked up: a failed marriage, strained relationships with her children, no contact with her grandchildren, lost jobs. Nevertheless, I respected her for her willingness to tackle all these problems without drinking. Admonishing her for having made such a mess of things certainly wouldn't have been helpful. Suzanne was relieved to know that someone was willing to work with her, accept her mistakes, and help her experiment as she looked for solutions.

Empathic Understanding

Rogers was clear that empathic behavior is the most powerful way of using ourselves: "Listening, of this very special kind, is one of the most potent forces for change that I know."[11] Empathic understanding matters most in the beginning because it provides the therapist with a foundation for rapport.[12] This attribute is perhaps best described by Rogers himself: "The therapist senses accurately the feelings and personal meanings that the client is experiencing and communicates this understanding to the client. When functioning best, the therapist is so much inside the private world of the other that he or she can clarify not only the meanings of which the client is aware but even those just below the level of awareness."[13]

Empathic understanding is different than walking a mile in our clients' shoes or seeing through their eyes—it is knowing that it's always impossible to feel exactly what someone else feels. And it is recognizing that even though we participate in the same events, we never experience these situations in precisely the same way.

Rogers put it this way: "The state of empathy, or being empathic, is to perceive the internal frame of reference of another with accuracy and with the emotional components and meanings which pertain thereto as if one were the person, but without ever losing the 'as if' condition."[14] Recognizing the "as if" condition doesn't mean that we have to sacrifice our own views; nor does it mean that we necessarily have to provide sympathy or approval. But it does mean that we need to validate what is true for this client (at this time).

In fact, we're probably on safer ground if we approach all clients "as if" they come from another culture. In other words, if we assume less and want to find out more, we'll be more likely to avoid stereotypes and unwarranted assumptions. The worst thing is to pretend we're understanding things we can't comprehend. When something is unclear to us, it's better to let our clients know, emphasizing how important it is for us to comprehend their feelings.

For example, Claire, a forty-year-old dietitian, came for help after a separation from her alcoholic husband. She wanted relief and validation as she planned for her divorce. But she also wanted a pound of flesh—she was furious after years of neglect. And even though I'd been divorced and even though I had seen hundreds of couples struggle with the dilemmas of divorce, it was still important for me to assume that I didn't know exactly how she felt. I needed to start with the assumption that she was unique and special and that her particular brand of ambivalence needed understanding. From this position it was best to assume ignorance in an honest attempt to comprehend her special circumstances.

When you do have the opportunity to work with someone from a different culture or subculture, it's a good idea to mention that you'll need additional help because you aren't familiar with the client's background, customs, or standards. Ask questions about cultural norms. For example, Gene, a student from Thailand, came to the counseling center because she wanted to live as a man. She was ambivalent about everything: her gender, her relationships, her future plans. Empathic understanding required care, and extra time was necessary to appreciate both her background in Thailand and her perceptions of the American subculture of transsexuals.

Congruence

Rogers describes congruence as occurring when "the therapist is openly being the feelings and attitudes that are flowing within at the moment. The term 'transparent' catches the flavor of this condition."[15] When we're congruent we're easy to read; we are expressing what's genuinely thought and felt. When we're congruent, we spontaneously express our most authentic and honest reactions—with words, laughter, a frown, a sigh; and we allow the reactions to show because we assume they won't be harmful.

Another way of understanding congruence is to observe the reaction produced by its absence: "Why don't you just say what you mean?" or "How come you never seem to mean what you say?" When there's inconsistency among tone of voice, body language, and the content of what's said, it usually signals ambivalence.

I'm reminded of Anna, who during a marriage counseling session scowled but said she wasn't angry about her husband's affair. When I asked about her anger, Anna screeched back, "I'm not angry!" She was surprised when her husband, my cotherapist, and I laughed (it was hard not to). She was so incongruent, it seemed ludicrous. That was a very awkward moment, and certainly her feelings needed to be respected with an apology. But the cat was out of the bag, so to speak, and I needed to use considerable care in addressing this inconsistency: "Anna, you may not think you're angry, but your expression and tone of voice would say otherwise. Does that make any sense to you?" She went on to describe how she wished she wasn't angry but really was.

We can all think of examples of hearing one thing in someone's voice, seeing something else in his body language, and hearing a rationale for that behavior that further obfuscated understanding. We're mixed up because we don't know what to respond to: the voice, the tone, the facial expression, or what the person has said. In our role as therapists, confusing our clients this way is certainly not what we want to do.

I remember an incredible example of incongruence. Daryl, one of our graduate trainees, was conducting a therapy session in the early spring. It was one of those days when everyone was eager for fresh air. Daryl decided to open the window. Unfortunately, when Daryl did this the air conditioner, which was kept in place by the closed window, fell three stories to the ground below. This made an amazing amount of noise as the air conditioner hit the side of the building and the cars parked below.

I was next door and was startled by the racket. I leapt out of my chair, followed by my client, and was joined by others in the hall who were also trying to discover the source of the noise.

Daryl's door remained closed. Finally, we knocked on his door to ensure that he and his client were actually safe. Evidently, Daryl had just sat down and continued the interview as though this event hadn't happened. This situation was akin to sitting through a fire alarm as though it didn't demand attention.

Needless to say, Daryl's reaction wasn't congruent. It was a denial of what had just happened. He thought it would be disrespectful to pay attention to anything other than his client. Unfortunately, Daryl's ability to tune out interruption made him seem inhuman, disembodied, hard to read. And although his ability to attend was a virtue when Daryl was playing chess (at which he was a master, incidentally), I wondered how his client could trust Daryl's reactions if he wasn't genuine enough to respond to such a disturbance.

Our most important reactions, however, are not to outside events, even if we cause them (as Daryl did). Instead, what is crucial are the genuine responses to our clients, their problems and ideas, and the events they report to us. Therefore, to prevent shooting from the hip, without forethought, we'll need to be effective observers of our own reactions (as pointed out in Chapter One). This means not running away from our feelings but rather regarding them as important sources of information to be used in constructive ways.

In *Love's Executioner,* Irvin Yalom describes his reactions to ten clients. These stories embody the therapeutic skill of congruence. For example, here is his response to his client Elva: "She was a stubby, unattractive woman, part gnome, part sprite, part toad, and each of those parts ill tempered." Elva was sixty, 4'11", and 160 pounds. Yalom went on to explain, "But what I really disliked about Elva was her anger. She dripped with rage and in our first few hours together, had something vicious to say about everyone she knew—save of course, Albert [her deceased husband]."

Yalom quickly sized up the source of his annoyance: "I had spent too many hours in my youth silently hating my mother's vicious tongue. I played as a child trying to invent the existence of someone she did not hate." But during therapy, he had to manage these feelings. "All I could do with Elva was to hold on, hear her out, somehow endure the hour, and use all my ingenuity to find something supportive to say—usually some vapid comment about how hard it must be for her to carry around that much anger."

Yalom explains that his feelings gradually thawed as he separated his reactions to his own mother from his reactions to Elva. But a turning point occurred when Elva described having played eighteen holes of golf with her twenty-year-old nephew. When Yalom asked her how she did, Elva answered, "I whomped the shit out of him!"

Yalom laughed. Elva appreciated his authentic, human reaction and was relieved that he had finally stopped acting like "Herr Doctor Professor." The spontaneity of shared laughter is infectious and a real sign of rapport. This shared moment led to others, culminating later in what Yalom described as "the best hour of therapy I ever gave."

At the beginning of this story we learned that Elva had come to therapy because she was upset over having her purse stolen. This loss was particularly painful for Elva because the loss of her purse triggered the expression of grief over the death of her husband. Later on in this story, Yalom informed readers that his best therapy hour began with tears over the loss of Elva's husband. Yalom explains that he then used an "inspired gambit." On that day, Yalom noticed Elva's overstuffed purse and commented that it seemed to be asking for trouble to carry around such a large purse. Elva claimed it was necessary.

Teasing each other, they investigated. They unearthed three packets of Kleenex and twelve pens (plus three pencil stubs), two bottles of cologne and three hairbrushes, a large flashlight, bulky notepads, and huge pile of photographs. Yalom explained:

We quarreled over everything. The roll of dimes. Three bags of candies (low calorie, of course). She giggled at my question: "Do you believe, Elva, that the more of these you eat, the thinner you will become?" A plastic sack of old orange peels ("You never know, Elva, when these will come in handy"). A bunch of knitting needles ("Six needles in search of a sweater," I thought). A bag of sourdough starter. Half of a paperback Steven King novel (Elva threw away sections of pages as she read them: "They weren't worth keeping," she explained). A small stapler ("Elva, this is crazy!"). Three pairs of sunglasses. And tucked away into the innermost corners, assorted coins, paper clips, nail clippers, pieces of emery board, and some substance that looked suspiciously like lint.

When it was over, Yalom explained: "We were sorry the bag was empty and that the emptying was over. She turned and smiled, and we looked tenderly at each other." Now this is congruence—he was real, enjoying the moment. He allowed himself to be open, honest, intimate. Yalom explained the benefit to his client: "In that one hour, Elva moved from a position of forsakeness to one of trust. She came alive and was persuaded, once more, of her capacity for intimacy."[16]

You can see Yalom's exquisite skill. He knew which reactions to reveal and which ones to hide. This is true art—congruence at its best. And it illustrates that therapeutic intuition is really the result of very careful observation, assessment, empathy, and regard for the client's welfare. Likewise, it is a reflection of careful attention to the ongoing process of building and maintaining rapport.

Building and Maintaining Rapport

Even though most training emphasizes knowledge of problems and the strategies used to solve them, we now know that our personal traits make a significant contribution to the quality of therapeutic relationships. After all, these are the skills that grease the wheels, guide intuition, and ultimately provide the foundation for a therapeutic relationship. Consequently, we'll need to pay special attention to how we

- Listen
- Demonstrate empathy and respect

- Attend to the alliance
- Judge the quality of rapport
- Repair ruptures

Listening

It makes sense to anticipate what gets in the way of effective listening so that we can simultaneously hear better, understand more, and enhance rapport. Mind you, those of us with experience have made all of these mistakes many, many times. But therapy certainly proceeds better if we can avoid:

- *Acting on our biases, stereotypes, and assumptions.* The biggest obstacle to effective listening is our assuming that we already know enough and therefore don't need to listen. These suppositions originate from our family background and personal experiences. They're so much a part of us that we respond without recognizing the consequences. If I assume men can't talk about feelings, or that people who are Jewish don't have financial problems, or that all people who come from Japan are intelligent, I'm not listening with an open mind.

In fact, we'll listen better when we assume we're uninstructed. In this way we can learn. Whether we're working with people from other cultures, our own culture, with problems we've never seen, or with problems we've seen hundreds of times, we want to remain alert to the uniqueness of each new client. We'll want to listen for that individuality.

- *Being preoccupied with other matters.* It's hard to focus on the client's concerns when other things seem pressing. These distractions can run the gamut from grocery lists to personal turmoil, not to mention a preoccupation with doing therapy "right." It takes practice and lots of reminders to tune out our personal concerns.

- *Seeing your problems in everyone else's.* When you get pregnant you notice pregnant women everywhere; when you have an auto wreck, it seems like everyone else has one too; when your husband drinks too much, everyone seems affected by drug problems—that's normal. But when we're doing therapy, we need to be careful that we aren't generalizing inappropriately.

Moreover, it's harder to resist the temptation to talk about our own trouble when we're in turmoil. This is especially true when our clients' problems remind us of personal experiences of our own. When tempted to relate personal histories, you might ask yourself, Why do I want to disclose this now? Will this help my client? What's motivating me? It might make more sense to make a mental note about wanting to talk (about whatever it is) and then finding someone more appropriate.

- *Minimizing your client's situation.* After hearing about a vicious divorce, your next client's squabble with his roommate can seem pretty insignificant. Although someone else's trouble can bring problems into perspective, a "you don't have it so bad" attitude from the therapist rarely helps the client; if anything, it interferes with the therapist's ability to hear the client's perspective.

- *Identifying with others in the story.* It is particularly easy to minimize client concerns when you identify with someone else in the "story." I work in a college counseling center, and I'm the same age as most of my clients' parents. As one might expect, many of these students have problems with their parents, and sometimes my urge to justify what a parent has done or said can be hard to resist. When I'm saying to myself, "I can sure see why your mom doesn't want to send you any more money," I'm on the way to not hearing the student, and rapport is well on its way to being derailed.

Some of the difficulties just described were clearly brought to my attention as I sat in on a session with a graduate student, Amy. She was doing an intake interview with Eric, a twenty-year-old pre-med student who couldn't come to terms with his girlfriend's decision to terminate their relationship. Amy began well: she looked interested, seemed friendly, explained agency policy, and expressed optimism about working on his problems. She asked questions about why he came for counseling and what he hoped to accomplish, then made some other assessments about his health, family, and school progress. Then she turned to me, with an expression that conveyed "Help!" She knew she had to give something back, that she should summarize and explore alternatives. But Amy was scared. She was so busy checking and asking that she forgot to listen.

It was as though Amy hadn't heard (or didn't know how to react to) how Eric fought back tears when he explained, "I've got to get over this"; how he blushed, but smiled, when he said, "We used to have a wonderful sexual relationship, now we just study together" (ironically, they were taking the same human sexuality course); how he glared as he described his friends' impatience—"My friends think I'm a fool"; and how he sighed and looked downcast when he said, "I don't think I'll ever love like that again, but I guess I have to move on."

Because Eric was looking for a response and Amy was groping for words with a rescue-me look, I said, "It seems like she really means a lot to you and you don't seem to be ready to give up on this relationship." Eric smiled, nodded in agreement, then added, "I'm so relieved—you're not telling me to just get over this too." He wasn't ready to mourn this important relationship yet; he hadn't given up hope for reconciliation. Eric was relieved that I understood. And I was able to understand because I listened to more than just his words.

After the session, Amy said to me, "How did you know that? I was ready to give advice on how to get over this woman. I'm glad I didn't." She saw by Eric's reaction to what I said that her plan wouldn't have been helpful. I might add that, Amy's lack of empathic understanding for Eric's attachment would have been harmful to their rapport.

When we listen empathically, we learn a lot about how to help. For example, Eric told us that he was put off by his friends telling him to "get over this relationship." (If it was that easy, he would have done it.) By listening for what our clients have already tried and found helpful along with what hasn't worked, we can avoid repeating the same errors.

This kind of listening involves more than hearing words. It includes a kind of concentration that most of us don't use in our everyday encounters. At first, it's exhausting. Most of us aren't used to paying attention in this way. It feels unnatural to suspend performing logical analysis, looking for answers, making plans, or relating our own feelings and experiences. Moreover, it's really difficult (particularly when we're learning) to ignore judgments, tolerate our own anxiety, and avoid self-criticism. But that's just what we need to do.

A wonderful resource on this topic was written by Hannah Merker, who has a profound hearing loss. In her book, entitled *Listening*, she explains it this way: "To listen means to be aware, to watch, to wait patiently for the next communication clue. And as anyone with a speech or hearing disability can tell you, listening is not always auditory communication." She reminds us that "Listening becomes visual, tactile, intuitive. Listening . . . perhaps . . . is just a mind aware."[17]

Demonstrating Respect and Empathy

One of the best ways to communicate empathy is to let your client know what you're understanding. In the beginning you want what you say to match what your client has expressed in tone, feeling, and content. This conveys that you understand what's going on. A good exercise is to ask yourself (at any point in the interview), What am I understanding about this person? and then try to explain your impressions to the client.

Your clients need to hear what you're getting. As mentioned before, indicating that you want to get it right—"Correct me if I'm wrong here . . ." or "Have I got it?"—not only provides the best opportunity to find out if we're off the mark but also moves the general understanding of the problem ahead.

We need to do more than summarize what we've heard. We must *want to understand*. We must not be afraid to follow our confusion. Ask for examples. Search for clarification, significance, intention. Tell your client that you want to understand. Ask for help. Be willing to say, "Help me out here, I'm not sure I'm getting this," when you don't understand. When I don't understand or I feel confused, I'm anxious, and because I want to understand, it's my job to help my clients make themselves intelligible.

For example, Carolyn, a college junior with a 3.6 GPA, long brown hair, and a bad complexion, explained, "I'm here because I have an attitude problem. I have no friends and I fight with my mother. Even she says I'm a bitch." When I asked Carolyn questions, she demonstrated her attitude. She laughed when she explained that her parents divorced when she was four. She said, "Who cares about him anyway?" when I asked about her father. Her tone was flip and sarcastic. Carolyn's crossed eyes made eye contact difficult, and she was right—her attitude made rapport seem impossible.

But I wanted to understand why this manner of relating seemed like a good idea to her. So I asked, "You've said your attitude is a problem, particularly for your mother, but I would guess you have reasons why acting like this makes sense to you." In this way, I let her know that I wasn't going to just join forces with those who criticized her; I let her know that I wanted to understand her frame of reference, her reasons, even if they didn't make sense to her.

Because we need to do more than just ask questions and repeat what our clients have told us, it's helpful to demonstrate our concern and respect by being involved. Here are some suggestions on how to do this.

• *Be active.* Several studies suggest that clients prefer (and therapists rate as appropriate) situations in which the therapist speaks about a third of the time.[18]

• *Be expressive.* For rapport our tone should reflect the mood and manner of the client. But we also want our clients to be able to read our reactions so that they can respond appropriately without having to guess about our cues. Therapists who are animated and able to express their own feelings clearly are appreciated and more easily understood by their clients.

• *Be fluent.* Avoid using "you know," "uh-huh," and "kind of." Tape-recording a few sessions will help you pick up these errors quickly—they stand out when we listen to ourselves. Avoid using big words, or give synonyms if you have any reason to think your client doesn't understand. We want our vocabulary to match that of our clients. I have been surprised by how many clients don't know what the word *ambivalent* means. So now when I use this word, I say, "It sounds like you're ambivalent—like you have very different, maybe even contradictory feelings about that. Do you know what I mean?" That way clients don't have to say they don't know what the word means. Instead they can just indicate that they don't understand what I'm trying to get at.

• *Respond to your client's pace.* This means actively keeping up but also staying calm with wound-up or agitated clients. Likewise this means remaining patient with slow, depressed clients.

• *Respond nonverbally.* It is generally agreed that maintaining an open body posture, leaning forward, making eye contact, and smiling indicate interest and caring. There is also evidence that therapists who are judged as being well liked, expert, empathic, and trustworthy communicate with the use of these nonverbal gestures.[19] I'm reminded, however, of a graduate student I supervised who had obviously read this material. He was tense and seemed mechanical, but he sat, leaning forward, legs open. He smiled and maintained eye contact but nevertheless still communicated tension. He wasn't in rhythm, wasn't responsive to the client's body language, and was so nervous that these gestures looked out of place and incongruent.

Attending to the Alliance

We want the rapport we develop with our clients to approach what we have in our close friendships. However, therapy is different than friendship because it is goal oriented, contractual, time limited, and unilateral. These constraints alter the relationship and provide the framework for accomplishing the therapeutic work of achieving goals, reaching understanding, and reducing distress. Certainly rapport is the crux of that working alliance. And in a reciprocal manner, attending to the work of therapy fosters the development of rapport.

When our clients function better and accomplish their goals, we enhance rapport. We therefore need to recognize and reinforce strengths. Along these same lines, it's wise to bolster clients' adaptive coping skills, such as maintaining good self-care by sleeping, eating, exercising, and being responsible. We'll also want to pace ourselves by refraining from confronting our clients' vital defenses (even though they seem maladaptive) until our clients are ready.

For example, John, a twenty-year-old college junior, came to counseling because he was shocked that he had a homosexual experience one night after drinking too much. He explained that he had no sexual experience with women and only fantasized about men. Horrified with himself, John explained that he planned on a political career and that "being gay" would be ruinous.

I tried to communicate empathic understanding by saying, "John, I can see you're really upset and that you don't want your sexual fantasies about men to be important." Trying to move our understanding along, I added, "You might want to consider the reasons why this upsets you so much."

"No," he said.

I tried another angle. "Well then, you might want to think about how this experience affects you."

"No, I think if I just get busy enough, I'll forget all about this," John answered.

He looked anxious, bit his nails, and squirmed around in his chair. The only clue I had that he wanted to explore this issue was his insistence on more appointments.

I said, "I can see that you want therapy time scheduled, but I'm confused when you make clear that you don't want to talk. You seem to find staying busy and not thinking to be the best way to handle this. I'm unclear why you still want to come in."

John replied, "So am I, but I know that I do."

"So can we assume you are of two minds about talking?"

"Yes, I guess—I don't know."

I could best convey empathic understanding by focusing on the "here and now" feelings and reactions that were present during the session. The important thing for me to do was to stay with his ambivalence about talking rather than his ambivalence about his sexual activity. It would have been too intrusive to add more until he was clear about wanting to explore these feelings. In this manner, we build therapeutic trust because we haven't asked our clients to explore material their defenses can't handle.

In this particular case, it was very important to respect John's need to see himself as heterosexual as he ventured into gaining the courage to investigate his real feelings. A sensitivity to his defenses was essential to maintaining rapport, so I didn't want to contradict his intentions, add new understanding that might be too painful, or point out perceived flaws until there was enough rapport to do so. Therefore, I summarized, "I can see that it's very important for you to see yourself as heterosexual even though your sexual feelings and fantasies are for men." He agreed, and insisted that he wanted to continue talking, but now he wanted to talk about why he needed to see himself as heterosexual.

This led to a discussion of John's early fears of being different. He was afraid of his father's wrath and God's condemnation, and he remembered early criticisms of being labeled a "sissy" in grade school. No wonder he was apprehensive. He needed reassurance that he could make decisions about his sexual behavior and that he would feel more control over those choices if he wasn't drunk.

Another way we can strengthen the therapeutic alliance is to recognize progress. Our clients need to hear from us very specifically and clearly about our observations on what they've done well. I'm often surprised when I see my clients' eyes light up when I say things like "I'm really impressed with [something the client has done]," or "I like the way you [handled something hard]," or "You've really accomplished something important [regarding progress on a therapeutic goal]." These reinforcements not only bolster therapeutic progress but also enhance rapport.

Judging Rapport (How Good Is It?)

One of the most important aspects of building rapport is being able to assess the quality of the therapeutic relationship. Psychotherapy research makes clear that therapists both know how important the alliance is and misjudge the state of their particular alliance with a given client.[20] This finding suggests that therapists should learn to assess rapport. It's certainly nice when rapport feels positive to us, but that feeling can be deceptive and not necessarily informative. Many clients are socially gifted and able to provide a pleasant experience for us by entertaining or praising, but they are still not attending to their own work. We want rapport to be positive enough for the clients to accomplish their goals. Here's how we can track therapeutic rapport:

• *The client tells us.* It is easy to know that things are going well when the clients says, "I really feel like I'm getting what I need from therapy." But we should also frequently ask our clients, "How do you think therapy is going?" or "What was it like for you after our last session?"

• *The client isn't defensive.* One sign of good rapport is that you feel you can say what's important without worrying excessively about how the client will take it. If my client doesn't understand, adds "buts" to suggestions, and offers up excuses, I assume she is feeling defensive. I also assume that she wouldn't be defensive if it wasn't necessary; that is, her self-protection is still required.

• *The client reacts spontaneously.* He sighs, laughs, cries, moves comfortably, and appears congruent. The client is able to express himself on matters that are relevant to his problems.

• *The client reads our intentions clearly.* She isn't confused by what's going on. He doesn't misread my cues to stop, talk more, or listen. Under these circumstances I'm able to challenge and confront because the client knows these responses are grounded in a desire to help make things better, not to harm.

• *The client can argue, express a difference of opinion, or show annoyance.* In other words, the client feels safe enough to risk the expression of negative feelings and ideas, or to bring up things that might be threatening to us.

When rapport is positive there is affinity, empathy, respect, understanding, and cooperation. Staying in tune requires work, patience, and a sensitivity to ruptures.

Repairing Ruptures

No matter how sincere, well intentioned, and talented we are, we're still bound to make mistakes. Sometimes, too, we have to say things that are necessary but that hurt our clients' feelings. When we make mistakes or say something hurtful, we need to attend to the impact on the therapeutic relationship. Here are some ways to do this:

• *Provide support.* Sometimes our clients have to consider things that are painful. It helps to point out, "I can see this is very hard for you to talk about, but it also seems to be helpful. What do you think?" Acknowledging that some discussions are "traumatic," "annoying," "irksome," or "scary" reassures our clients that we appreciate what they're going through. When talking about death, for example, it helps to let our clients know that we'll take our time, move at their pace, make efforts to understand, and review when necessary.

• *Show empathy.* We'll need to convey that we understand that our responses might be hurtful. I once laughed after a client listed a series of tragedies; I just couldn't imagine enduring the death of a mother, a serious car wreck, migraine headaches, a dog dying, and a child needing help on a middle school project about managing stress—somehow it all seemed ridiculous. But if we laugh as I did we also need to express awareness that we might offend. I said, "Oh, I'm sorry, it just seems like so much." My client agreed and laughed as well. We both felt relief.

• *Seek clarification.* We'll need to ask, "How are you doing with what is going on, now?" or "How did what I just said affect you?" If the client explains that you've hurt his feelings, or confused or annoyed him, he opens the way for you to explain your intentions.

• *Apologize.* If you've made a mistake (for example, scheduled two appointments for one time, tangled up billing, said something insensitive, yawned, misunderstood, taken phone calls, or been called away), you can and probably should apologize. It's probably better to do this before the client complains, but sometimes we're unaware until our client lets us know.

These actions lessen the strain of hurtful responses and give us recourse should we make spontaneous slips and hurt someone's feelings. Knowing we can recover by addressing the rupture directly lets us relax.

Training for Rapport

We'll want our training to help us establish rapport. There's a lot to learn in this area, and it's particularly challenging because it involves integrating who we are with what we know. Aware that we can't rely on formulas, prescribed phrases, or strict adherence to theoretical models, we'll need to nurture our basic relationship skills. We'll want to think about how to apply techniques and theories and yet remain congruent enough to make sense. We know we'll need practice and supervision.

Getting Along with People

These are the everyday "people skills." This know-how includes manners, friendliness, responsiveness, and other skills that can facilitate rapport or hinder it. Our social skills evolve from observation of and reaction to family and culture, usually outside our conscious awareness. And because we absorb without thinking, we often don't question the impact of our social skills. But when we're doing psychotherapy and counseling, such questioning is essential. Because we know our style of relating can influence our clients' therapeutic process, we must scrutinize our approach, manner, and technique.

Needless to say, this scrutiny takes courage. We might start by considering how well we establish rapport in our nontherapy relationships. Chris Kleinke suggests the use of the Opener Scale.[21] It comprises ten items and is scored using a 5-point scale (4 = strongly agree, 0 = strongly disagree):[22]

1. People frequently tell me about themselves.
2. I've been told that I'm a good listener.
3. I'm very accepting of others.
4. People trust me with their secrets.
5. I easily get people to "open up."
6. People feel relaxed around me.
7. I enjoy listening to people.
8. I'm sympathetic to people's problems.
9. I encourage people to tell me how they are feeling.
10. I can keep people talking about themselves.

People who score higher on this scale are more successful in eliciting self-disclosure than are people with low scores.

If you look closely at these ten items, you can see that these skills can be practiced. For example, you can think about what you do that helps people feel relaxed, what makes you easy to talk to. Most likely, you can transfer those skills into a therapeutic relationship. Moreover, you can further develop your skill by watching others who seem particularly gifted in making others comfortable. Similarly, supervision and training are opportunities for us to develop an awareness of how our personal foibles influence our work.

Avoiding Rigid Techniques

Hans Strupp and his colleagues at Vanderbilt University reasonably assumed they could train therapists to reproduce factors known to be correlated with a positive therapeutic outcome. Ironically, when they gave therapists specific instruction in how to develop an alliance, outcome measures didn't improve. In fact, they got worse.[23]

Although these trained therapists were able to adhere to time-limited dynamic psychotherapy (TLDP), they were also less supportive, less optimistic, more authoritarian, more negative, and more defensive. The researchers concluded that a technical adherence to methods of responding without a corresponding attention to "the underlying interpersonal processes" resulted in this negative outcome. As a consequence, these researchers advocated that therapists be trained to monitor an alliance as it develops.[24] In other words, these researchers seem to be advocating for training and supervision that are very attentive to a rigorous assessment of the quality of the therapeutic connection.

These findings make good common sense for several reasons. First, there isn't one way to create rapport. And although we might agree on those qualities that enhance rapport, therapists tend to communicate empathy, respect, and understanding in unique ways. Second, relationships develop from the interaction of client and therapist, so what works well with one client in one setting may not work with another. Finally, rapport requires our "learning to dance"—or to put it another way, being congruent—while we also develop a keen sensitivity to our clients.

Consequently, therapists do well when they cultivate those characteristics shown to contribute to a positive relationship without becoming artificial or "technique bound." Even Carl Rogers was appalled by the emphasis on "nondirective" techniques. Reacting to the technique of paraphrasing what a client has just said, Rogers explained, "I was so shocked by these complete distortions of our approach that for a number of years I said almost nothing about empathic listening, and when I did it was to stress an empathic attitude, with little comment as to how this might be implemented in the relationship. I preferred to discuss the qualities of positive regard and therapist congruence, which, together with empathy, I hypothesized as promoting the therapeutic process. They too, were often misunderstood, but at least they were not caricatured."[25] Our challenge, then, is to find a way to create rapport in a manner that is both natural to us and matched to the current situation.

Looking for "Throw-Ins"

Most practicing clinicians readily acknowledge that there are significant variables and characteristics that contribute to rapport that aren't accounted for in research or in practice manuals. Irvin Yalom describes these special ingredients of therapy as "throw-ins."[26] He uses the analogy of a master chef who creates a delightful meal. Students stand back in awe, aware they have tasted something special. But these same students are left wondering when they can't duplicate the recipe by following the directions supplied by the master chef. Our students are often in a similar position.

I remember watching Donald Michenbaum, a cognitive-behavioral specialist, work with a client. Afterward, he described his attention to her symptoms and the behavioral interventions he employed. He attributed his client's progress to those methods (and perhaps he was right). But I wondered if this client would have made as much progress with a therapist (using those same methods) who hadn't established rapport the way Michenbaum had. Somehow, I couldn't imagine this same client being inspired to risk changes with a therapist who spoke in a monotone, made no eye contact, and paid little attention to her feelings. Although Michenbaum didn't mention it, I was impressed with the way he and his client moved together in rhythm. His sensitivity was exquisite; the rapport was obvious. The point is not that he wasn't aware of rapport or that his techniques didn't have merit, but rather that his efforts to establish rapport weren't mentioned to us, his students.

Developing our sensitivity to the moment-by-moment interpersonal process of therapy should be the foundation of training.[27] Although of course learning established techniques and methods (the recipes, if you will) is necessary, the corresponding need to integrate our own style is an ongoing challenge. In fact, everything we do in therapy must be done with a careful attention to rapport.

We could say that our rapport with clients provides the platform for all therapeutic work. Without observational, assessment, and diagnostic skills, however, the rapport we develop would only be that of a concerned friend. As we will see when we move on to discuss the essential aspects of clinical interviewing, the skills we've already addressed enhance our ability to take on these more complicated therapeutic tasks.

Notes
1. Strupp, H. H. (1986). Psychotherapy: Research, practice, and public policy (how to avoid dead ends). *American Psychologist, 41,* 120–130.

2. Rogers, C. R. (1980). *A way of being.* Boston: Houghton Mifflin, pp. 115–116.

3. Luborsky, L. (1994). Therapeutic alliances as predictors of psychotherapy outcomes: Factors explaining the predictive process. In A. Horvath & L. Greenberg (Eds.), *The working alliance: Theory, research and practice.* New York: Wiley, pp. 45–46; Henry, W. P., Strupp, H. H., Schacht, T. E., & Gaston, L. (1994). Psychodynamic approaches. In A. E. Bergin & S. L. Garfield (Eds.), *Handbook of psychotherapy and behavior change* (4th ed., pp. 467–508). New York: Wiley; Mallinckrodt, B., & Nelson, M. L. (1991). Counselor training level and the formation of the psychotherapeutic working alliance. *Journal of Counseling Psychology, 38,* 133–138.

4. O'Malley, S. S., Suh, C. S., & Strupp, H. H. (1983). The Vanderbilt Psychotherapy Process Scale: A report on the scale development and process-outcome study. *Journal of Consulting and Clinical Psychology, 51,* 581–586; Moras, K., & Strupp, H. H. (1982). Pretherapy interpersonal relations, patients' alliance, and outcome in brief therapy. *Archives of General Psychiatry, 39,* 405–409; Horvath, A., & Greenberg, L. (Eds.). *The working alliance: Theory, research and practice.* New York: Wiley.

5. O'Malley, S. S., Suh, C. S., & Strupp, H. H. (1983). The Vanderbilt Psychotherapy Process Scale: A report on the scale development and process-outcome study. *Journal of Counsulting and Clinical Psychology, 51,* 581–586.

6. Bordin, E. S. (1994). Theory and research on the therapeutic working alliance: New directions. In A. Horvath & L. Greenberg (Eds.), *The working alliance: Theory, research and practice* (pp. 13–38). New York: Wiley.

7. Strupp, H. H., Fox, R. E., & Lessler, K. (1969). *Patients view their psychotherapy.* Baltimore: Johns Hopkins University Press.

8. Greenberg, L., Elliott, R., & Lietaer, G. (1994). Research on experiential psychotherapies. In A. E. Bergin & S. L. Garfield (Eds.), *Handbook of psychotherapy and behavior change* (4th ed., pp. 509–543). New York: Wiley, p. 522.

9. See note 2, p. 116.

10. Masterson, J. F. (1981). *The narcissistic and borderline disorders.* New York: Brunner/Mazel.

11. See note 2, p. 116.

12. Egan, G. (1990). *The skilled helper* (4th ed.). Pacific Grove, CA: Brooks/Cole.

13. See note 2, p. 140.

14. See note 2, p. 116.

15.   See note 2, p. 116.
16.   Yalom, I. D. (1989). *Love's executioner and other tales of psychotherapy.* New York: Basic Books, pp. 144–152.
17.   Merker, H. (1994). *Listening.* New York: HarperCollins, p. 17.
18.   Friedlander, M. L., Thibodeau, J. R., & Ward, L. G. (1985). Discriminating the "good" from the "bad" therapy hour: A study of dyadic interaction. *Psychotherapy, 22,* 631–642; Klienke, C. L., & Tully, T. B. (1979). Influence of talking level on perception of counselors. *Journal of Counseling Psychology, 26,* 23–29.
19.   Weiner, M., Budney, S., Wood, L., & Russell, R. L. (1989). Nonverbal events in psychotherapy. *Clinical Psychology Review, 9,* 487–504.
20.   Horvath, A., & Greenberg, L. (Eds.). *The working alliance: Theory, research and practice.* New York: Wiley.
21.   Kleinke, C. L. (1994). *Common principles of psychotherapy.* Pacific Grove, CA: Brooks/Cole, p. 56.
22.   Miller, L., Berg, J. H., & Archer, R. L. (1983). Openers: Individuals who elicit intimate self-disclosure. *Journal of Personality and Social Psychology, 44,* 1234–1244.
23.   Henry, W. P., & Strupp, H. H., Schacht, T. E., & Gaston, L. (1994). The therapeutic alliance as interpersonal process. In A. Horvath & L. Greenberg (Eds.), *The working alliance: Theory, research and practice* (pp. 51–84). New York: Wiley.
24.   See note 22.
25.   See note 2, p. 139.
26.   Yalom, I. D. (1980). *Existential psychotherapy.* New York: Basic Books, p. 3.
27.   See note 22, p. 68.

Chapter Five

Therapeutic Interviewing

Of the 168 hours in a week, our clients will have only one hour, more or less, with us. Given all the other influences in their lives, that's not much time for us to make a difference. And because we don't possess magic wands, crystal balls, or divining rods, we must capitalize on what we do have: the therapeutic interview.

Harry Stack Sullivan points to the wizardry of that hour: it "occurs in the interpersonal relations, and the real magic is done by the patient, not by the therapist. The therapist's skill and art lie in keeping things simple enough so that something can happen; in other words, he clears the field for favorable change, and then tries to avoid getting in the way of its development."[1]

Following Sullivan's advice requires real proficiency in translating what we've learned about human behavior into interviewing strategies that induce change. To put it another way, we'll use the therapeutic relationship to serve many purposes: as a catalyst for change, as a stimulus for thought, as comfort for distress, and as an inducement to recoup and plan. In order to provide these services we'll need to master two basic tasks: first, designing a framework for therapeutic goals, and second, learning to use conversation to accomplish these objectives.

Establishing a Frame

To make each session productive, we'll have to assume the responsibility of setting and then maintaining the conditions that allow constructive work to occur. If we're not attentive to the framework for therapy, our sessions are likely to be drifting and aimless, leaving both therapist and client feeling as though nothing has been accomplished. Most of the time, therapists establish that framework by assuming the primary responsibility for (1) clarifying expectations, (2) pacing the therapeutic work, and (3) maintaining focus.

Attention to these basic tasks enables us to work together in a collaborative way, regardless of whether we're in the second or the tenth session.

Clarifying Expectations

We've already discussed how important it is to have clear expectations during an initial session. But it's also important in successive sessions. We often handle the first session by asking a lot of very specific questions; during subsequent sessions we might expect our clients to assume the responsibility for the choice of topics. Therefore, it makes sense to make that change clear by explaining, "I'm not going to be asking so many questions. In fact, I've found that therapy works better if you think about what you would like to talk about before you get here."

In fact, setting expectations often includes clarifying who will take the responsibility for picking the topics for discussion. Some therapists, and some clients, assume that it's the therapist's responsibility to decide what to talk about. If you want your clients to assume the responsibility for deciding on the topic, explain why. ("I want to make sure we're talking about what's important to you. I'll help you talk about what you choose, but I think it's better if you make that choice.") The important point to keep in mind is that both formats are workable, but only if we're clear about our expectations. We'll want to explain, directly, how therapy works and how our clients can help us help them. And we'll need to do this in a manner that makes sense to our clients.

We'll want to make our explanations both informative and simple. If I explain that "I'm an object-relations therapist and will be confronting maladaptive transference acting out of clinging and helplessness," I'm likely to get a look that implies, "What in the world are you talking about!" In fact, offering jargon-ridden explanations is one of the surest ways of undoing rapport. On the other hand, we're more likely to engage clients if we say, "You're interested in understanding why your relationships don't work, so from time to time I'll point out things I notice from our relationship."

We'll want to be particularly attentive to expectations about roles—both the client's and the therapist's. For instance, we may want our clients to report on dreams; or we might want to hear about the antecedents for crying spells experienced during the past week; or we may want them to tell us about the progress of their marital trouble; then again, we might want them to decide what they want to discuss. The primary point is to be clear about our methods and expectations whenever that seems necessary.

In addition, we'll want to clarify expectations about the personal dimensions of our clients' relationship to us. Clients are often unsure about what to expect. They may wonder what name to call us or if they can ask questions about our lives, call us at home, or be our friend. But on a broader scale, clarifying expectations has to do with being clear about therapeutic boundaries. Sometimes it's necessary to clarify the therapeutic framework by maintaining boundaries, such as by restricting physical contact or by not meeting outside of the office.

Whenever we point out boundaries, we need to be careful not to be rejecting; the best approach is to be clear about why these conditions are necessary for therapeutic work. For example, "I can appreciate that you're lonely and want physical contact. I hope you can also understand that my hugging you will not help solve this problem and could also complicate our relationship by making me a source of comfort rather than a resource for discovering how to better manage your needs for closeness. I think it would be more helpful for you if we could talk about what you can do to create more intimacy in your life."

Most important, we'll want to be clear about our role as their therapist, which will enable us to feel clear about what we're doing as well as allow us to answer questions posed by our clients. It's sometimes helpful to explain what you intend to do; for example: "As we move forward I'll help you track progress and plan additional steps. I think that it's my role to [facilitate discussions, or help you practice new behaviors, or help you understand other ways to think about your problems] so that we can reach your goals." Because every session presents new information that must be incorporated into what we do, we need to remain clear about any changes in expectations as therapy progresses.

For example, a suicidal client might require that the therapist be very active and directive, whereas later on, when the crisis is over, that same client might benefit from less direction and more support. Sometimes clients are caught off guard by changes in our approach. Usually it helps if we explain the reasons for changes in style. For instance, "I was more active in asking you questions and giving you advice when you were in crisis. Now I think you'll benefit more from trying to come up with alternatives for what to do yourself. I'll help you, but I'd like to hear what you think you should do first."

Pacing the Session

Our responsibility for pacing a session includes monitoring how sessions are choreographed. Like dance, therapy requires sequencing and attention to timing. This skill requires knowing where we're going, tracking the impact of our clients' problems on their daily life, and then coordinating that information with what takes place during the session.

More specifically, adequate pacing includes keeping track of how much time has elapsed during a given session so that issues are given sufficient time. We don't want our clients to embark on a discussion of something traumatic when we've only a few minutes left in which to manage the emotions the discussion will elicit. It's often helpful to call the client's attention to time constraints:

I can see that you want to talk about your fathers' suicide, but with only a few minutes left I don't think we can do that very well. Perhaps we should talk about this next time.

We've only ten more minutes—maybe we shouldn't get into this now.

If we spend all our time on this, I'm afraid we won't get to the other things you wanted to discuss today.

In order to avoid sounding like a drill sergeant, it's wise to include our clients by adding, "How does that sound to you?" or "What do you think?"

Being adept at pacing an interview includes remaining attentive to our clients' readiness to work on original goals, but it also requires enough flexibility to change gears if that seems appropriate. Arlene, for example, originally sought counseling to leave her marriage of twenty-two years. But during the third session, she explained that she was very concerned about both a recurring nightmare about her alcoholic mother coming after her with an ice pick and an actual memory of the refrigerator falling on her sister after her mother yanked the door open in the midst of a drunken brawl.

The intrusions of Arlene's nightmare and memories as she took steps to get out of her marriage were significant. Her present dilemma was bringing up her childhood feelings of helplessness. When we took therapy time to explore this issue, Arlene not only stopped having the nightmares but also realized she was no longer powerless and could choose another course of action. Maintaining sensitivity to the current pressures and symptoms our clients face strengthens progress on the original therapy goals.

Influencing the order in which our clients address issues and problems lessens the risk of their being overwhelmed (the reason most people seek therapy in the first place). For example, if a client with a history of sexual abuse starts talking about that abuse during therapy but then ends up cutting herself and not being able to get out of bed in the morning to go to her job, she's not ready to talk about her abuse yet. In short, these maladaptive symptoms demonstrate that she is overwhelmed by the emotions brought on during therapy. Therefore, it's wise to work on coping strategies first. We might believe that we're helping our clients by talking about painful events and feelings, but it's not helpful if their ability to function in their daily lives is seriously compromised.

For example, during my first session with Janine, a thirty-six-year-old single mother, she explained that she was overwhelmed with two children, two jobs, and two boyfriends. She described herself as "hyper," and added, "I've always been like this." Her blue eyes and dark lashes were engaging, but when she tried to smile, it seemed forced, as though her expression was an afterthought.

By the second session she was still sitting on the edge of the stuffed chair, holding her coffee cup, laughing awkwardly, and blotting her eyes as if to keep back tears.

She explained, "I didn't think about our first session. I was much too busy. But I'm relieved that I decided to come to therapy." She went on to describe crying spells, suicidal thoughts (no intentions), and difficulty sleeping. She said, "I still feel just horrible."

Her explanation led me to assume several things. First, Janine avoided her problems and feelings by keeping busy, but the more she avoided, the worse her situation became. Second, by working during the session I hoped she could think about her problems without becoming completely overwhelmed emotionally. Third, I hoped that with my help during therapy she could make a sequential plan for working on her concerns, not only in session but outside as well.

When determining how to pace and sequence therapeutic work with a client like Janine, there are some important points to keep in mind:

1. *Check on the problem(s).* Each and every session, we'll want to know about any changes in the status of the problems we're working on. We'll also need to note any major developments in our clients' life situation. We'll want to be aware of tensions and pressures that are affecting our clients because our original assessments and working hypotheses may require revision.

2. *Sequence work according to risk factors.* Issues or situations that pose a threat to the health and safety of our clients always have to be attended to first. Whenever our clients develop new symptoms or maintain symptoms that interfere with daily functioning, we'll need to make alleviation and comfort our priorities. For example, when we have a client who is not sleeping or eating, or who is working too much (common reactions to stress), we'll have to address those issues first. And because substance abuse threatens both health and safety, that too will need to be a treatment priority. For instance, we'll need to investigate and help our clients manage when they make such statements as these: "I can't seem to get started. I'm checking the doors, the lights, the smoke alarm" (teach stress management techniques, consider a referral for medication); "I'm drinking and driving" (ask why, how often, whether the client can consider stopping this); or "I haven't slept in days" (teach deep breathing and relaxation strategies, perhaps make a referral for medication).

3. *Synchronize work with clients' defenses.* When defenses are adequate, our clients can work on the problems without being overwhelmed by emotion, rendered numb, or seduced into acting out. If our clients can't function in their daily lives and still work on problems, we'll need to work on coping strategies first. In effect, it's our responsibility to help our clients judge what they can handle and to explain the rationale for why adequate coping must come first.

4. *Take advantage of clients' motivations.* When these basic needs are attended to, we can move on to other issues that motivate our clients, giving the highest priority to those items that most concern our clients. We'll want to be ready to react when our clients are most receptive, such as when they're in crisis or when they're doubting themselves.

5. *Be flexible.* We want to maintain a sensitivity to the pressures our clients face outside of therapy. For instance, a particular session may not be the ideal time for the client to work on certain issues because it takes place before an exam or just after learning that the client's mother has been diagnosed with cancer.

When I thought about pacing Janine's sessions, it seemed that we needed to focus first on strategies to manage her crying spells and suicidal thoughts. Once she was functioning better and had a chance to understand herself and her motivations, she could make better decisions about her boyfriends. So I pointed this out: "Janine, it doesn't seem like pushing yourself to decide about these men is getting you anywhere. Would it be OK to put these decisions on the back burner, until you're clearer about what's going on?"

Janine sighed, "You mean I don't have to decide now."

"That's up to you, isn't it?"

She smiled; this time her smile seemed genuine, and I could see her relief. We'll talk more about how we worked on these issues later in this chapter.

Keeping the Focus

Harry Stack Sullivan points out that "the interviewer is also entitled to exercise his skill in discouraging trivia, irrelevancies, graceful gestures for his amusement, and petitions of things he has heard. In other words, the expert does not permit people to tell him things so beside the point that only God could guess how they happened to get into the account."[2] There are many reasons why our clients resort to these maneuvers; most often they do so because the current discussion is

- Too hard
- Too painful
- Going to bring on tears
- Too embarrassing
- Irrelevant to what seems most pressing
- Challenging to their self-image
- Too boring

Handling these diversions in a constructive fashion requires that we understand why our clients avoid therapeutic work. When we're frustrated with these tactics, it's all too easy to accuse our clients of being evasive or resistant, leaving us likely to react in a manner that triggers more defensiveness from the client.

Sara, for example, was embarrassed to tell me that she called her boyfriend, Devin, to apologize after he had shattered the windshield on her car with a hammer. She assumed that she owed him an apology because he saw her coming out of a restaurant with another man at noon. The man was only a casual acquaintance, but Sara still felt guilty. She always assumed it was her fault when Devin was angry. She also assumed I would think that it was a bad idea for her to apologize. (She was right.)

When she came to her session, however, Sara told me nothing of this. She only sounded weary; she said she'd had a hard week and that her job was boring. Then she sat and stared into space.

"So it seems like you're avoiding working today?"

"I'm not; I've just been busy. I'm sorry. I should've been more prepared."

I could see she was defensive; I realized I'd made a mistake (putting her in a position to be both defensive and apologetic). There had to be a better way of handling this. If I had persisted without attending to my error, I would have confirmed my erroneous assumption that she didn't want to work on her problems. Likewise I would have missed the opportunity to point out that she was apologizing to me, when in reality she wanted to avoid criticism.

Instead, I needed to acknowledge that I'd made her defensive, and to regain the focus. So I said, "Sara, I realize what I said sounded harsh; I'm sorry. I'm concerned that you have some good reasons for not talking about what really matters to you."

"I'm just so stupid. I called him. I know you'll think that's dumb—I think it's dumb!"

Now we were working. I could explain that I didn't want to judge her, that I wanted to understand, and that together we could figure what was going on, if she was willing to explain. But first we needed to talk about what made it so hard to discuss with me what she had done.

"When I tell you about these dumb things I do, it makes me feel like I deserve to have my windows smashed. I don't care. I just want him to care, so I called."

Responding to diversions without jeopardizing rapport requires a lot of patience and persistence. It also means watching out for signs of discomfort when we refocus to make sure that we haven't created too much anxiety or been too abrupt. Usually, it's just best to say, "I'm getting lost here," or "We seem sidetracked," or "Let's go back to [the hot topic]."

Certainly, we can't force clients to talk about things when they're not ready. Forcing never works. Moreover, we want to make their hesitation a "discussable" issue. If we use some clinical tact, we can make such apprehension part of the conversation: "It seems like this makes you uncomfortable. Is that so?" or "If you'd rather not talk about this now we can wait, but first, I'd like to understand what makes this so hard." Talking about obstacles paves the way for other therapeutic work.

Therapeutic Work

It is our talent with interviewing that allows us to accomplish therapeutic objectives. We'll want to develop a dialogue with our clients that incorporates what we've learned from theory, training, our professional background, and life experience. Although we use different names for what we do, good therapists generally share the same common objectives:[3]

- Generating hope
- Providing an opportunity for emotional release

- Offering explanations and interpretations of problems
- Modifying cognitions
- Giving support and advice; trying out new behavior

These objectives are the essence of therapy. As therapists, our challenge is to use intervening strategies that make therapy simple, compassionate, engaging, and efficient.

Listening

We've already discussed how good listening fosters the development of rapport. Listening also provides our clients both the opportunity to work on problems and the support to tolerate that work. The key is being able to attend to what we're hearing without succumbing to the temptation to jump in. In other words, we want to provide space and time for our clients to hear themselves talk about what they think and how they feel. Our allowing this time gives clients the opportunity to voice their concerns and also the chance to express their feelings. One way we can facilitate this process is by asking our clients to tell us more about their thoughts and feelings, making such comments as the following:

I can't tell how you feel about that. Can you explain more?

A minute ago you said, . . . Can you tell me more about that?

What was that like?

What do you make out of that [referring to what they've just explained]?

What do you suppose was behind that?

I'd like to understand this better. Can you help me out?

Can you recall anything else?

Another way we can encourage further exploration and demonstrate that we're actively involved is to use *minimal encouragers* ("uh-huh,""Yes, I see") or *nonverbal signals* (head nodding, or beckoning with your hand to mean "Say more"). I've been embarrassed watching myself on videotape because I nod my head so much (it looks odd, at least from my perspective), but my clients inform me that it lets them know I'm listening.

Furthering Exploration

Accomplishing basic therapeutic objectives usually requires us to explore certain issues and feelings in depth. Our methods should pave the way for clients to deepen their initial understanding of problems. Likewise, our strategies should reinforce points that need more emphasis as well as alert our clients to areas they need to investigate further.

Paraphrasing, or repeating in different words the essence of what a client has said, is an especially productive way of developing more clarity. Paraphrasing should encourage more detail and clarity. Doing this well means more than just repeating what's been said: we'll need to say concisely what's most important. Using general terms, we'll want to pinpoint the central feature of what the client has explained, adding the hint of a question so that we encourage the client to furnish more detail and explanation. We can say things like "It seems like you're [paraphrase]. Is that it?" or "In other words, you feel [restatement]. Have I got it?" or "Then your plan is to [whatever you think it is]."

Cutting to the heart of the matter with Janine, the client described earlier in this chapter, involved clarifying her suicidal intentions: "You think about suicide as a relief from this stress, even though you don't intend to do anything, is that it?"

Janine was clear: "I just want to stop crying all the time; I want this pressure to stop. But I wouldn't really hurt myself; I have my kids to think about." Her response made clear that she was very unhappy and uncomfortable, but not suicidal.

"Let's see if I've got this right: when you get these thoughts about hurting yourself, you panic; and then it seems like you stop trying to understand what's going on with you, is that right?" This *summary statement* included a reflection of her intentions and added what I thought was going on.

The use of *questions* is another way we can stimulate our clients to explore their feelings, behavior, and thoughts. We can raise our own or follow along with those questions our clients raise. Very often, they raise the most germane questions: "I wonder why I'm always so sad," or "I don't understand how I can want to be with him when he drives me crazy," or "If my mother makes me so mad, why do I keep going over there?" It's helpful to get our clients to *answer their own questions* by asking them to consider what they've just posed: "That's really an important question. What do you think?"

Different types of questions are appropriate; our choice depends on what we want our clients to do. Sometimes we'll want our clients to be *specific* ("When do you lose your temper?" or "How often do you have crying spells?"), and other times we'll ask our clients to expand on what's meaningful to them. In that case, it's useful to use *open-ended* questions ("How did you feel about that?"). We'll want our questions to encourage the type of exploration we're looking for. Our questions are really directions or invitations for exploration: look into this, consider that, experience this. For example, we might want our client to think about how his symptoms affect his family, so we ask, "Are you aware of how your depression is affecting your family?"

As we encourage exploration, we'll discover issues and feelings that need to be worked on, or understood better. Very often, that work involves understanding, tolerating, and managing painful feelings.

Understanding, Tolerating, and Managing Painful Feelings

One of the most useful functions of therapy is to provide an opportunity for clients to express painful, confused, or conflicted feelings. Certainly many clients experience relief just by expressing themselves. In addition, clients' self-acceptance develops from realizing that their feelings make sense to someone else. Most assuredly, there is tremendous relief in feeling "acknowledged." In order to foster that acceptance, we'll need to make sure, first, that our clients understand their emotions, and second, that they can tolerate those feelings without harming themselves or others.

Many clients have trouble understanding feelings. We can help by *asking some questions* that help clarify their reactions and moods. For example:

How did you feel when that happened?
How do you feel, now, explaining this to me?
Can you help me understand how that made you feel?
I'm not sure I understand how you feel about that . . .
Can you describe what that's like for you?

It's validating when we *reflect clients' feelings* with such comments as "You seem [whatever you notice]," or "It sounds like you're [describe the feelings you notice]." It's wise to remember that most situations involve more than one feeling and often include contradictory emotions. When we *reflect that complexity or ambivalence,* it helps our clients understand themselves better. For example: "It seems like you're angry at him but also missing him, is that it?" or "I can see that you're disgusted with her but feel guilty about still wanting her attention; am I getting this right?"

For example, I was aware that Janine felt overwhelmed and didn't understand her feelings beyond the fact that she experienced crying spells. I tried during the second session to use some of the strategies we've discussed to help explore her feelings.

I started by saying, "I can see that talking about why you're crying so much is scary; you seem very uncomfortable."

When she responded, "I am, I'm always like this, all keyed up and tight," I tried to *encourage more explanation with a simple open-ended question:* "What else can you tell me about this?"

"What do you mean? I just feel terrible." (This is a very typical response—it meant she needed more prompting.)

Trying to help her gain more clarity, I asked, "Janine, I'd like to understand this better. What seems so terrible?" (*open-ended question*).

"I can't make up my mind between these two guys, and I know I'm going to hurt somebody. I can't give up Ted; he's older, stronger, more secure. But then I love being with Jason; he's fun. I'm such a mess." Then she started to cry.

I tried to *provide some empathy* for her feelings, so I paraphrased: "I can see this really hurts you. But you seem pretty worried about hurting others."

I was able to assure Janine that she was crying for a reason; most likely, because she was pressuring herself to make a decision that involved the loss of one of these men, and she wasn't ready. Once Janine was able to articulate her ambivalence, she was more able to tolerate her conflicted feelings. Consequently, after the second session, she stopped putting so much pressure on herself to decide between these men; the crying spells stopped.

Another way to help clients understand themselves and their feelings is to point out the *connection between physical symptoms and feelings.* Because we usually can't see what our clients experience, we'll need to ask, "So when you're depressed, what happens to you physically?" or "What kind of sensations do you notice when you have an anxiety attack?" Some clients have difficulty seeing the connection between physical symptoms and emotional reactions. Our pointing out the connections has the potential to help our clients better understand not only what they're feeling but also how to manage.

Darlene, a fifty-eight-year-old secretary who was single and without any living family, didn't see the connection initially between her stomach pains and the conflict in her office. Once she understood that her stomach acted up under stressful conditions, she learned to combat her discomfort with exercise and relaxation techniques. She also discovered that she experienced more relief when she expressed her feelings to me than she did complaining to her doctor.

Unfortunately for many of our clients, getting rid of depression, anxiety, or ambivalence isn't always an immediate option; sometimes the only real option is for a client to learn to tolerate discomfort. In order to help these clients manage painful feelings, we'll want to plan for strategies that allow our clients to function in the midst of turmoil. The rest of this chapter will highlight interviewing techniques that foster this kind of therapeutic work.

Providing Encouragement

When people are depressed, anxious, or caught in the throes of substance abuse (the three most common problems brought to therapy), they're usually skeptical that their situation can improve. We'll want to *make encouraging comments* directly, such as "Yes, I'm optimistic that you can change this," or "Your willingness to consider these issues is a very positive sign," or "I can see this is difficult, but if you can be patient, we'll eventually make progress."

Along this same line, *pointing out progress* is essential. Our clients need to know when we see evidence that they're getting better, managing something difficult, coping more appropriately, or delaying gratification in order to achieve or accomplish goals. The clearer and more specific we can be, the more likely our clients will be able to use that information to cement improvement.

There are others things we can do during an interview that foster the inspiration to continue working toward goals. For instance, *pointing out positive attributes* not only strengthens the attribute but also builds the client's self-confidence and cuts into feelings of low self-esteem brought on by having to seek help. When I ask how clients have reacted to a previous session, I've noticed how frequently they recall my positive comments about their progress, hopeful reminders to focus on themselves, or expressions of confidence in their abilities.

Even *humor* can demonstrate optimism because it lightens intensity and makes clear that even though things are bad, we can still share a funny moment. This is the kind of humor you might use with a friend, to point out faults, struggles, the ridiculousness of too much effort, or the futility of trying to control someone else. It may take the form of *gentle teasing*. For example, Corinna, a thirty-three-year-old secretary with a history of sexual abuse, came to counseling because her husband left her for another woman.

Corinna maintained, "I can't stand it."

I noticed that she did, in fact, stand it. At first, not very well—she spent mornings vomiting and crying from nerves—but she eventually got to work and managed her two children and her job.

Eventually, I could *tease* her when she was presented with new obstacles, by saying, "I suppose you're going to tell me you can't do this either." The teasing conveyed my confidence that not only could she take the loss of her husband but also that she was strong enough to handle both the jest and the new complication.

Over the years, I've noticed a striking reluctance on the part of graduate trainees to offer their observations about progress to their clients. I suspect they're so focused on figuring out what's wrong that they lose sight of what's right. The proverbial pat on the back doesn't occur to them.

Providing Feedback

Our observations aren't worth much unless we can use them to help our clients understand themselves better. We need to give our clients the type of feedback that serves as a catalyst or a jumping-off point for moving therapy along. Feedback may take many forms, such as explaining how things fit together, pointing out contradictions between what the client has said and what you've noticed, or reinforcing what works.

When we work with our clients in session on, for example, breathing from the diaphragm or tightening and relaxing their hands, we can offer advice to help them improve their techniques. Or, when our clients practice saying what they want to say to important people in their lives, we can check on clarity and intentions, and give suggestions that might help make things go better. These opportunities for practice are enhanced when we participate by providing feedback.

The following are some useful guidelines for providing feedback:

- *Be descriptive rather than evaluative.* Describe your observations clearly without sounding judgmental, harsh, or parental. For example, rather than saying, "You must be getting something out of running yourself into the ground," you might say, "I've noticed that you talk about feeling exhausted, but you keep taking on more projects. What do you think?" We want to avoid making our clients defensive.

- *Make it understandable.* Make sure you use language, metaphors, or descriptions that your clients can relate to when you express yourself. Think about how to make what you say useful, practical, and down to earth. Avoid jargon and keep your language age appropriate.

- *Avoid being argumentative.* If you can explain your feedback in terms that relate to what's going on now, during therapy, you reduce the need for argument: "You've just explained that you want your mother to understand how you feel, but from what you've just said, I wouldn't get it. I might understand better if you said something like . . ."

- *Be flexible.* When you discover that a client is irritated by something you've pointed out, investigate by saying, "It seems like you're [whatever you notice]; how does this fit with your perception of things?" It may be necessary to back off, at least for the time being, until the client is more receptive.

- *Focus only on things your client can actually change.* We need to take care to make sure we're addressing behavior, thoughts, and feelings that our clients can actually change. Our clients can't immediately change a personality disorder, but they can make a better choice in a given situation. It is therefore better to say, "I've noticed that you judge yourself pretty harshly after you drink. Have you thought about the consequences of getting drunk tonight?" rather than "You need to stop drinking."

• *Recognize your client's choices.* It's up to our clients to decide what they will use. After all, even we don't swallow other people's feedback "hook, line, and sinker," so we shouldn't expect our clients to, either. We need to respect our clients' responsibility to decide what's useful. Ask if any of what you have said makes sense or is useful: "How are you reacting to what I've said?" or "Does any of this seem useful?" Furthermore, whenever our clients *ask for feedback,* they're apt to be more receptive, so we'll want to take advantage of these times.

Using Silence

One of our most powerful tools is nothing: silence. But we need to give careful consideration to why we are being silent. Most people in American mainstream culture find it awkward to sit in silence for more than a few seconds. When we wait to speak, we'll want to think about what we're doing with eye contact: Are we looking at the client or away? Each conveys a different message.

When we look at the client, we convey that we're waiting; it's her turn to talk. We do this when we want the client to make the next move. We're saying, nonverbally, that we want our client to express something.

When we look away, we leave it open. We're giving time for reflection, some thought. This silence conveys, "We're both thinking about this, and when one of us comes up with something, that person will talk."

When you can't tell what's going on, you can ask for help: "What's going on here?" or "You're not talking. I'm wondering what you're thinking," or "You seem to be waiting for me to say something, and I'm not sure what to say." If it's uncomfortable, you can talk about that as well: "This seems awkward to me. How is it for you?" The point is that silence is part of the interview, and we need to understand what's going on when no one is speaking.

Using Self-Disclosure

Self-disclosure is both verbal and nonverbal and conveys anything from demographic to personal information. It also includes information about our reactions to what's going on in therapy. Research informs us that therapists who self-disclose are preferred to therapists who don't and that clients prefer therapists who provide "reassuring" rather than "challenging" disclosures.[4] In other words, our clients like it better when we disclose positive feelings (for example, "It helps me understand when you express yourself so clearly") rather than negative ("It's really hard on me when you don't talk"). Most important, our disclosures should facilitate our clients' work and not serve as a self-indulgent way to let off steam or deal with our own anxiety.

Our stories take the pressure off the client. When they include information the client needs to incorporate, the stories educate. When they demonstrate that others have overcome similar difficulties, they provide hope. Appropriate statements even have the advantage of communicating more than one message at a time. Here are some guidelines to keep in mind when we're thinking about revealing information about ourselves and our lives:

- *Find the right balance.* Too little disclosure creates distance, but too much can make you seem disturbed or self-absorbed.
- *Don't use too much time.* Make it brief, and return the focus to the client with comments like "How does this fit for you?" or "Is [what I explained] similar to your experience?"
- *Don't ask clients to keep your secrets.* Never ask clients not to reveal something you have disclosed.
- *Notice the effect on the client.* Even though some clients like it when we disclose, we'll want to make sure our disclosures don't have adverse consequences, such as getting our clients to take care of us or our problems. We can check their reaction by asking, "How does what I've said affect you?" or "What's your reaction?"
- *Make sure it's useful for the client.* When we disclose our reactions or other information, the primary purpose should be to help clients further their progress, not provide narcissistic gratification for ourselves.

Providing Explanations and Interpretations

Very often, clients want explanations and interpretations about what's going on. People are most receptive when they initiate inquiries: "Why do I do this?" "How come my life is so hard?" "Why am I always waiting to be loved?" A client's asking for information raises two important considerations. First, we need to determine why this client is raising this question at this time. Second, we need to determine how to handle our client's requests for information.

When clients raise questions that they can actually answer for themselves, it's wise to redirect their questions by pointing out, "That's a great question. What do you think?" On the other hand, sometimes we need to investigate together: "These are my observations, what are yours?" or better yet, "How about telling me what you think, and then I'll share my impressions."

Oftentimes, mental health information is needed to allay fears or to further understanding. When a client asks, "Am I going crazy?" or "Do other people have problems checking their smoke alarm fifty times in a single day? What does this mean?" we'll want to provide explanations that respond to the concern behind the questions and that are honest, accurate, and useful.

So the answer to "Am I going crazy?" might be "No, you're not going crazy, but when you drink heavily you probably can't think very clearly, so it makes you feel crazy." Or, "Most of us feel pretty crazy when we don't get enough sleep, and you've been pushing yourself pretty hard." Or, "Not being able to control your wife's smoking pot seems to really preoccupy your thinking; no wonder you're not attending to details." Or, "Maybe we need to understand your fears better. Can you explain more about what makes you think you're losing control?"

Making Interpretations

We can also use *interpretations,* or explanations, that provide clients with insight into issues and conflicts outside their conscious awareness. This time-honored technique was considered by Freud to be the cornerstone of therapeutic work and involved the therapist explaining to the client the reasons or causes of behavior and feelings. The purpose of an interpretation is to help our clients gain more understanding of the roots of their feelings as well as a greater appreciation for how they've acquired certain patterns of behaving, responding, and interacting with others.

We might use an interpretation to explain our suppositions about how the events from our client's childhood continue to influence her in the present. For instance, "I can understand why it's so hard for you to express your anger at your husband today. It seems to me that your fears about precipitating the same kind of destructive behavior you saw in childhood with your father are still with you today."

We can personalize an interpretation by pointing out how earlier events influence reactions to you and to therapy, such as, "Because of your fears of expressing anger in childhood, you seem to have a hard time trusting me to respond appropriately when you express anger during therapy. What do you think?"

Making an effective interpretation has to do with more than ensuring the accuracy of the content; the challenge lies in the when and how of your delivery. When we give an explanation prematurely, it bounces off, makes the client defensive, or ruptures rapport. If it's given too late, we're inefficient. In other words, timing is crucial.

It's best if we can raise questions and then let our clients make their own interpretations. We can prompt them with lead-ins like these:

Do you see any connections between [your childhood, or previous relationship, or interaction with me] and now?

Do you want to understand [situation, yourself, or feeling] better?

Why do you think you end up in the same emotional place so often?

What do you think led you to feel this way?

How did you learn to respond in this manner?

When we do offer our own interpretations, it is wise to take advantage of "teachable" moments, the times when our clients are most receptive. This usually occurs after you have developed enough rapport to ensure that your client is confident in your judgment as well as secure about your intentions not to cause harm. Interpretations are more likely to be well received when we use jargon-free language that matches the client's understanding of psychological matters.

Most important, whenever we make an interpretation—but especially if we've made a fairly bold statement that seems jarring—

we'll need to understand the effect of our interpretation on the client. It's important to check with the client to see if what we've said makes sense and if the client agrees. We can accomplish this by asking, "How are you reacting to what I said?" or "How does this fit for you?"

Using Metaphors

Some therapists use *metaphors* to make things clearer. By assigning visual images to a particular feeling, we help clients identify and expand their understanding. For example, to explain passivity we might try, "You seem like a cork in the ocean, pushed around by whatever wave comes along," or ". . . a leaf in the wind caught up in currents; one minute you're blown one direction, the next another."

Metaphors are not "one size fits all." They're only effective when they fit the clients' understanding and circumstances. When our clients add their own understanding to the metaphors by supplying new images, we know they can use these images to help them think about their feelings and behavior. When the "fit" is right, the use of shared language and visual imagery between client and therapist adds to rapport and provides tools for mental work.

For example, one metaphor I've found very helpful with people who have troubled backgrounds is to explain that "your feelings from these earlier events are like a lake. When it rains (current trouble), puddles develop. If the puddle is too close to the lake (if your old problems resonate with new dilemmas), the puddles merge with the lake, making it hard to tell the difference between the lake and the puddle. But that's what we need to do during therapy: separate the lake from the puddles. In other words, we need to separate your old feelings from the current ones so that we can keep you from reacting out of the lake when we have only a puddle." One client of mine responded to this metaphor by labeling the feelings that originated during his childhood as "the lake effect." He was able to use this metaphor to designate the feelings from his childhood that he needed to sequester in order to more appropriately manage the events that occurred in the present. In other words, he could respond to his supervisor's criticism with disappointment instead of the rage he felt about his stepfather's abusive criticism.

Challenging Assumptions

One of the most obvious ways we modify our clients' thinking is to *challenge their assumptions*. When our clients draw conclusions that seem unfounded—"I'll never love again," "Nobody likes me"—we can ask them to explain the basis for their assumptions. If necessary, we can challenge erroneous assumptions directly by offering other ideas for clients to consider.

Janine, for example, maintained several erroneous assumptions. First, she assumed she had to choose between the two men in her life. Second, it hadn't occurred to her that she didn't have to remarry if she didn't want to. As we talked, she learned that other people's disapproval did not mean she had to change herself; she realized she'd rather tolerate disapproval for having sex with two different men than alter her behavior. When I pointed out my observations of her thinking, she could more clearly see what she was thinking and then make choices accordingly. She learned that her anxiety derived from her assumption that in order to gain approval she had to behave in a manner she wasn't comfortable with.

In fact, we discovered the reason why she was so much more comfortable after the second session: she had changed some basic thinking. She didn't have to decide between these two men. Furthermore, after another session she was clear that she didn't want to make any changes in the next few years. She gained insight into how she kept herself busy, and therefore anxious, in order to avoid facing what she really wanted. Once she realized that she could accept herself as she was, she found it easier to explain herself to the people she was close to.

Confronting

When our clients have difficulty seeing things that are important for progress, we need to consider using confrontation. It is wise to remember, however, that confrontations are very difficult to choreograph in a manner that demonstrates basic respect for the client's intelligence and autonomy. We'll probably want to avoid lecturing, badgering, and admonishing our clients to understand things that are probably already crystal clear to them. For example, recently I attended a conference on the treatment of substance abuse problems. The presenters were excellent, but their example of how to do a confrontation is, in my opinion, the exact opposite of what's necessary. Their handout reads as follows:

Sample of an Appropriate Confrontation

What you're saying is that you can't find the time to go to a meeting. What I hear is that lots of other things are more important to you than going to a meeting. I see that as denial, meaning some resistance on your part to accepting the fact that you've lost control over alcohol. It seems that way to me because if you really accepted your limitation with alcohol and your need to abstain completely from using it, then hardly anything would be more important than getting into a program that offers you hope. I think you'd find the time to go for treatments, even every day of the week, if you had a potentially terminal illness and if treatment could mean the difference between life and death. That is the way it is with alcoholism. It's an illness; it's chronic and progressive, and it can lead to premature death. How do you feel about that?

Imagine being on the receiving end of this well-intentioned lecture. How would you feel? Would you feel inspired to get started, ready to tackle this problem, or eager to learn new skills? Obviously, the information is correct. Certainly the necessity of getting all this across to an alcoholic makes sense. But what also seems clear is that this is way too much information to convey at one time. It sounds like a sermon. It's not likely to stimulate thinking, provide encouragement, or challenge the client to improve.

Instead, we'll want to use questions or statements in our confrontations that are designed to increase our clients' readiness to work on something or to prompt receptivity to comprehending what we want them to understand. Keep in mind that we can only confront when we've demonstrated enough empathy that our clients know we're trying to understand them, or when we've established enough rapport that clients can trust us to be working in their best interest.

We're not talking about arguing a point or harping on a theme; rather, we want to raise issues in a manner that allows clients to draw their own conclusions. For example, I wanted Mike to consider the effects of his depression on Karen, his girlfriend. So I said, "How is it that you expect Karen to want to be around you when you're always so unhappy and demanding?"

Deflecting his responsibility, he responded, "If she cared, she'd be there."

"What's to care about?" (adding strength to the confrontation).

"I'm nothing; anyway she doesn't."

Ignoring his comment and pointing out his motivation: "It sounds to me like you'd like her to care about you. Have you thought about how you can make that happen?"

Incredulous, he answered, "You mean me, something I could do?"

"Yes, there are probably things you could do that would make it more likely that she would like to spend time with you."

Confrontations start from a position of normality, what should be expected, then ask the client the question, Why don't you see this? When we make a confrontation we need to stay focused on where we're going, because our clients usually do what Mike did; that is, they'll make attempts to change the focus and deflect attention away from their responsibility.

Some clients experience extreme reactions as though they were common and ordinary (such as drinking too much or breaking furniture when angry). This too might call for a confrontation, a question with a message. For example: "I'm wondering why breaking furniture seems normal to you?" or "How is it that you don't consider what this does to your children?" or "How come you have to be perfect?"

For the therapist, the hardest part of a confrontation is keeping frustration in check, especially when the client avoids your "wisdom." It's helpful to remember that you can't force, and that extra effort won't help; in other words, don't get trapped into arguing. Rather, remember that your job is to point out the obvious; what the client takes from the confrontation is a matter of choice. And finally, you don't have to rely on one opportunity. You'll probably get another chance to restate your confrontation if the problem continues.

Giving Advice and Support

One of the more interesting characteristics of our clients is that most of the time they already know what to do even before they come to therapy. And certainly by the time they've gone through an initial session, they've got some understanding of what they'd like to accomplish. Susan, for example, may know that she needs to take better care of herself. (She knows that drinking every night, smoking, and not exercising will eventually create trouble.) Clarissa knows she should end her affair if she wants to improve her marriage. Ellen is clear that she should stop bingeing and vomiting. Tanya assumes she ought to sleep more. (Three hours a night isn't enough rest for her to function without being irritated and fatigued.)

The problem, as Willard Gaylin points out, is that "knowledge does not inform conduct."[5] Therefore we don't want to make the mistake of profoundly pointing out what our clients already know. When we do, our clients are apt to sit in silence but assume "therapy is useless—I know I should . . ." We know we don't want to patronize our clients with parental advice they've already heard six thousand times. On the other hand, Sullivan wisely warns us: "All in all, when you can't reassure a person except by magic the sensible thing is not to try. When you don't know anything in particular to say, don't say it."[6] Our challenge is to find a way to get our clients to do something for themselves without fostering dependency on us.

Support and advice can strengthen rapport and help our clients move forward—as long as we don't overdo it. When we give too much advice or offer up lots of excuses for bad behavior in the name of being supportive, we cheat our clients out of learning how to support themselves. In fact, any time we can get our clients to do something for themselves rather than rely on us, we've taken a step forward.

On the other hand, there are times when information is essential to making progress with problems; sometimes "down home," commonsense advice really helps. "You need to get some sleep!" or "Has it occurred to you that his jealous and possessive behavior isn't going to change?" or "Your drinking is contributing to your depression."

This sort of "everybody knows it" information needs to be tempered: "Since I know you've already thought about this, why doesn't it work?" I've discovered that sometimes what seems obvious, isn't. Frequently, we need to help our clients work out plans.

Assigning Homework

Obviously, therapy time is limited, so we'll want our clients to continue working when they're not with us. Most likely our clients will also want to continue working, thinking, and managing difficult feelings between sessions. Therefore, it's wise to ask clients what they would like to focus on between sessions, what they would like to try out, or how they would like to manage. When they are the ones who decide what's needed, they're likely to be more motivated than if we make the assignments. Our task should be that of fine-tuning their ideas into workable, reasonable, and manageable steps.

On the other hand, sometimes our clients don't know what to do. If what they should work on seems obvious to you, and clients haven't discovered it on their own, you certainly can make suggestions. But you'll really want to think this one through carefully. Beginning therapists often assign homework because it makes them feel useful. Consequently, they select elaborate assignments that sound textbook perfect but that really aren't very practical.

Find out what the client thinks: Does she really believe she'll practice her systematic desensitization hierarchy and deep muscle relaxation, when she scarcely has time to attend to work and family? Does he think he'll record the antecedents of his crying spells, when he's working a construction job all day? Can you really imagine a rebellious teenager committing to giving up pot next week? We need to make sure that the homework or practice the client decides on is "doable." We don't want to set people up to fail.

Closing the Session

We need to find ways to bring closure to what's happened during the hour. First of all, it's a good idea to warn clients that the session time is coming to an end so that they're not caught off guard. Our clients might press for more time, so we'll need to be clear that this is all the time you can give them. You might want to say, "We've only five minutes left, so let me give you some feedback here." That also keeps the therapeutic framework clear. Most of the time, we want to end sessions on time (except in emergencies, which we'll discuss in the next chapter).

It helps to *summarize what's happened during the session.* Summaries help by pointing out how you see what has happened. You might say something like "We haven't made much progress, and in fact, everything still seems pretty confused. But we'll keep working on this." Then talk about rescheduling. More optimistically, you might summarize with "You've covered a lot of important issues, and it sounds like you'd really like to try talking with your daughter about the conflict you're having. Is that how you see what we've done today?"

It's often helpful to say, "We've covered some important issues. Do you have any questions before we stop?" If the answer is yes, answer the question briefly or explain that it will take more time and that you'll attend to that during the next session. If the answer is no, stand up and move toward the door.

So far, we've discussed cases and situations that don't pose much difficulty. And certainly, the more experience we have, the more likely we can handle what comes along. But now we want to turn our attention to those special situations that tax us. No matter how much experience we have doing therapeutic work, each hour provides new opportunities to learn.

Notes

1. Sullivan, H. S. (1954). *The psychiatric interview.* New York: Norton, p. 227.
2. See note 1, p. 34.
3. Garfield, S. L., & Bergin, A. E. (1994). Introduction and historical overview. In A. E. Bergin & S. L. Garfield (Eds.), *Handbook of psychotherapy and behavior change* (4th ed., pp. 3–19). New York: Wiley, p. 8.
4. Hill, C. E., Mahalik, J. R., & Thompson, B. J. (1989). Therapist self disclosure. *Psychotherapy, 26,* 290–295.
5. Heaton, J. A., & Wilson, N. L. (1995). *Tuning in trouble: Talk TV's destructive impact on mental health.* San Francisco: Jossey-Bass, p. 213.
6. See note 1, p. 229.

Chapter Six

Managing Emergencies and Crisis

Most of us have been in an urgent situation that required immediate action but in which we also felt too frightened and confused to know what to do. When our clients contact us in a similar state, they're likely to be feeling completely overwhelmed by their feelings, behavior, and thoughts. Everything they know about solving problems seems inadequate for the circumstances at hand, and they're incapacitated by the fear that whatever they do, the situation will only worsen. In short, they feel pushed to the brink. For example:

Matt came in for an emergency appointment. He sat down sobbing, answered a few questions, then explained that he didn't want to live like this.

Beth told her roommate that she had taken a bottle of Tylenol, after explaining that she wished she was dead. Her roommate called me.

Carol, a forty-one-year-old special education teacher, got sexually involved with one of her fifteen-year-old students on an overnight camping trip. The next day, she told her husband what she had done, then took a loaded gun from the closet and said she was going back to the woods. Because I had seen her husband on another matter several years before, he called me.

Joanne's husband of twenty-six years left her a note saying he wasn't coming home. She sent me an e-mail message describing this and asked, "Do you think I should come in?" She explained that she hadn't eaten for two days, was confused, and hadn't slept.

An officer from university security called me to evaluate Jeffrey, whom they found wandering around the library talking to himself. When I arrived, Jeffrey explained, "I can't go home. They're eating my brains—not with forks but with their radar. They're going to expose me. They think I think about sex too much. I know what I can do to get even, but they won't let me tell you."

Although each case has its own unique circumstances, these situations are alarming for therapists because some action needs to be taken, usually right away, and more than likely, we're the ones called on to make decisions about what to do. In more practical terms, we'll be called on to defuse potentially violent or explosive incidents, provide alternatives to suicidal impulses and intentions, or integrate appropriate strategies for managing tensions. We may also need to assist by calming and soothing victims or reassuring and supporting family members and workers who take care of those involved. (That's a tall order!)

Most experts agree that an immediate intervention which is culturally relevant and socially supportive can facilitate an individual's return to normal functioning.[1] In fact, with our help, a crisis can become an opportunity for our clients to learn skills that foster improved adaptation to other stressful events.[2] However, to turn crisis into opportunity, we'll need to make a number of decisions. First, we'll have to consider whether we'll need outside help. Second, we'll need to decide what our responsibilities are and with whom they lie. Finally, we'll need to use interviewing strategies that promote resolution of the crisis.

Responding to High-Risk Situations

Differentiating between "real" emergencies, in which quick and direct action must be taken, and those crisis situations that allow for time is important. We've already discussed (in Chapter Two) making assessments about the potential for harm by evaluating a client's ideation, intentions, and impulsivity (the three I's). We'll have to take immediate action whenever our assessment leads us to conclude that there is a high risk for

- *Self-inflicted harm.* It's important to consider not only explicit verbal and behavioral threats of suicide but also other types of potentially self-destructive formulations, such as reckless intentions of driving at high speeds while intoxicated, or delusional thinking, such as believing one is able to fly.
- *Harm to others.* This involves threats to others that are coupled with both the motivation to act and the capacity to cause harm.
- *Inability to engage in self-care.* An intervention is required whenever clients are too disabled, drugged, or deranged to manage their affairs, care for their children, or care for such basic needs as food, sleep, and personal hygiene.
- *Trauma.* Certain situations, such as accidents, assaults, or significant losses, call for crisis intervention because intervention lessens the possibility that those affected will develop the symptoms of Post-Traumatic Stress Disorder.[3]
- *Any action that we're legally mandated to report.* In most states, we must inform authorities if we are aware of child abuse or abuse of someone who is disabled or elderly. We are also mandated to warn an intended victim or notify the police. It's important to know your legal obligations because there is considerable variation between states.[4]

Whenever the aforementioned conditions escalate to a point at which there's a possibility of danger to our client, us, or someone else, we'll need to be prepared to act promptly and effectively. And we must do this in a manner that not only promotes our client's welfare but also protects our client's basic rights.[5] Here are some things to keep in mind as you juggle these requirements:

Never put yourself in danger. Most efforts that might be characterized as heroic are not only futile but also dangerous to you and to those who may have to protect you.[6] Instead of waiting for the police, I once made the mistake of trying to stop a man from hitting his girlfriend by stepping between them. I was threatened and almost assaulted before police intervened. My actions made the police work more difficult, to say nothing of the stress I created for myself. So "Rule Number One" is, don't ever use physical means to restrain or overpower someone—get help from law enforcement or medical personnel first.

Get help quickly. If a client is dangerous, it's best to act quickly and not take chances. If someone leaves your office with a loaded gun and is threatening to kill her spouse, you can't sit there paralyzed with fear, hoping she will come to her senses. You'll have to take action (even if you can't find your supervisor). This is not the time to worry about offending, changing the subject, breaking promises, or looking ridiculous. Adversity has taught most experienced therapists that it's usually best to err on the side of caution. When someone's life is in danger, there is no other priority. Even the Red Cross first aid manual advises that the first step in an emergency is to call for assistance; only then do you try to help.

Don't be afraid to admit that you can't handle the situation. Too often beginners think they're expected to manage the unmanageable. More experienced therapists usually know that it's wise to admit that you're in over your head, that you don't know what to do or can't do what's required. For example, when Sophia told me that she had experienced what she thought was a seizure earlier that day, I was concerned. She explained that she was shaking and believed she lost consciousness because she ended up on the floor even though she didn't remember falling. She explained that she had no history of medical, drug, or alcohol problems that might have accounted for what happened. At the time of our session, she appeared fine, but I felt that a medical doctor needed to decide if it was all right for her to continue with her daily routine.

Unmistakably, this wasn't a decision I could make on my own. The fact is, we have an ethical responsibility not to take on tasks that we aren't trained to manage. We may need to seek appropriate consultation, as was the case with Sophia, but often we must call 911 for emergency assistance. (As it turned out, Sophia's neurologist decided her seizure was, in fact, stress induced. But having that diagnosis validated by a physician was essential before I could use psychotherapy to treat this problem.)

Use common sense. Using your best judgment, do what makes the most sense to incur the least amount of harm. Generally, we should resort to the least intrusive intervention that provides protection for those involved in the situation. Here is some commonsense advice for emergencies:

- Maintain the appearance of calm.
- Talk slowly.
- Don't be afraid to tell people what to do, particularly if you seem to be the most rational one on the scene.
- Be firm. Keep what you say simple and clear.
- Ask those people who are too upset or wound up to be of assistance to leave. (Encourage them to go somewhere else to take care of themselves. Advise them on how to best do this.)
- Enlist the help of those who are able to remain calm.
- Don't argue or threaten someone who is violently acting out.
- Keep breathing, and advise others to do the same. Practice deep breathing with those who need it.
- Remind yourself and others that you are doing the best you can with the information you currently have available.
- Stay with those who need assistance until help arrives.

Maintaining Your Professional Role in an Emergency

It's not always easy to be clear about our role in an emergency. Considering that people caught in a crisis are often distraught or in a state of panic, it's not really surprising when they want us to have all the answers, to know exactly what to say, and to be able to take steps to "fix" it. Juggling emotional requests and professional responsibilities in the midst of crisis can make it difficult to draw on our best judgment.

Being Clear About Roles

It can be hard enough to oversee professional roles in an office setting with a single client, but emergencies often involve lots of other people who are also upset. Frequently these people contact you. A medical doctor wants to know what to do with her patient. The police officer wants to know whether to take this person to jail or the psychiatric hospital. If it's a friend or relative of a client, you'll need to be careful about protecting confidentiality. If it's a friend of a friend, it's sometimes hard to know who we're assisting.

Let's be clear. When it comes to professional priorities, the following sequence generally prevails:

1. Take care of basic safety.
2. Protect your client's right to confidentiality as best you can.
3. Provide consultation to others, if it's appropriate.

Each of the situations mentioned in the cases listed at the beginning of the chapter illustrate the importance of determining what our obligations are and with whom they rest. Sometimes the circumstances require us to work with others who are close to the clients. This was certainly the case with Beth and Carol.

Beth (the young woman who ingested Tylenol) had been a client of mine several months before, and she was willing to talk with me on the phone. She explained that she wanted to die but would go to the hospital with her roommate, Cindy. Because Beth's behavior had been unpredictable, Cindy and I decided that it was best to have the emergency squad transport her to the hospital for a medical evaluation. I agreed to meet them at the hospital and stayed on the phone with them until the squad arrived.

Carol's husband had been a client three years ago. (I had seen him for six sessions in a successful treatment of panic disorder associated with his fear of flying in airplanes.) He wanted consultation on what to do with this emergency. The immediate situation was potentially life threatening and required police action to find Carol and remove the gun. My role was to provide consultation for her husband, who had been my client, but I also needed to inform him that I would have to notify Child Protective Services because I had knowledge of Carol's sexual involvement with a minor. He was angry that we couldn't "handle" the situation without creating more scandal. I explained that it was a legal requirement that Child Protective Services be called. (Incidentally, it's also wise to indicate that you believe the laws make sense because they are designed to protect vulnerable people.)

These cases illustrate our need to establish the difference between a consultation and a therapy contract. Carol's case, in particular, also underscores the need to make sure that those involved understand that the protection of confidentiality only extends to our clients and can be broken if there is clear and present danger or if the law requires.[7]

Sometimes, it's our responsibility to provide mental health consultation to the person who is requesting our help, such as the police officer who wanted to know what to do with Jeffrey, or to a potential client, such as Joanne.

Jeffrey needed to be evaluated for the possibility that his bizarre behavior and delusional thinking were precipitated by drug use. He denied taking any drugs when the officer was present in the room. When I asked the officer to stand outside the door and then asked the question again, Jeffrey said, "Maybe I took some Zoloft, or a hit of acid. I'm not sure." When I asked, "How much Zoloft?" he said he didn't know and asked me not to tell the police. I explained to Jeffrey that we would need to figure out how best to take care of him. He insisted everything was fine, even though he was not oriented to place, date, or time. The police officer and I agreed that Jeffrey should be taken to the emergency room at the hospital to run a drug screen. Then I explained to Jeffrey that we were going to take him to the hospital, but I didn't explain any details because he was not rational enough to comprehend what was going on.

I had never met Joanne, nor was I sure why she decided to use e-mail to contact me or what she wanted me to do. So I answered her e-mail with a message expressing my concern for her welfare and informing her of how to contact me or the local mental health clinic for services. I also included the number of the twenty-four-hour hotline in case she needed someone to talk to after hours. She called me for an appointment. She needed care quickly, and I was able to set up her session within twenty-four hours. Had this not been the case I would have needed to refer her to someone who could see her sooner.

Unless you really believe it will make things worse, it's generally advisable to explain what you intend to do so there won't be surprises. If you've called the emergency squad, explain that to your client. In Carol's case, certainly her husband needed to be informed of the actions that had to be taken. Because he was upset about the necessity of informing the authorities, it was very important to take time to communicate both empathy for his position and the rationale for reporting what his wife had done with her student. None of our obligations is more demanding than that of maintaining confidentiality.

Maintaining Confidentiality

When there is pressure from police, friends of victims, family members of psychotics, or others responsible for providing safety and shelter for our clients, it's easy to get confused about what we should tell to whom. Confidentiality is at the core of our profession, and we must be the ones who keep our obligations clear to those involved.

For example, both Beth and Jeffrey, as legal adults, insisted that their parents and family not be called, and I had to respect that right. But after the medical aspects of these emergencies were stabilized, we still needed to plan for what to do next. You can't "warehouse" people in the emergency room of a general hospital, and in both of these cases, these individuals were not stable enough to manage on their own. Beth was still threatening suicide, and Jeffrey needed to be watched until the effects of the drugs he had taken wore off.

Typically, it's not necessary for a therapist to have a release of information when disclosure is necessary to prevent clear and imminent danger to the client or others, or when legal requirements demand that confidential information be revealed.[8] Jeffrey was sent to a temporary facility for crisis management called Respite Care. Because that agency was now responsible for Jeffrey's care, it was possible for me to release necessary information to those involved with his care at this new facility.

However, many emergency situations do not involve an imminent threat or legal obligation. These cases can also be complicated by the involvement of family, friends, doctors, police, and school personnel, who all want information. Most of the time people are understanding and supportive if you take the time to explain that you can't talk about certain aspects of what's happened because of your client's right to confidentiality. The bottom line is that unless you are faced with a life-and-death situation, you can't provide information without getting a release of information.

When you feel it's beneficial for you to talk to a roommate, a family member, or a close friend, explain this to your client and ask permission to supply necessary consultation. For example, I needed a release of information from Beth so that I could talk with Cindy about what was going to happen next. Fortunately, Beth agreed. If the situation requires it and you don't have a release of information form, write one out on a piece of paper: "[Name of client] gives permission to [your name] to talk to [whomever] about [what you want to discuss, such as advice on how to help Beth]." Then ask the client to sign the paper. You can get a proper release form signed later.

If your client won't sign a release of information and you ardently believe that friends and family need help and support to manage their reactions to the crisis, arrange for a colleague to provide the necessary consultations. In this way you protect your relationship to your client while ensuring that others receive the advice and support they need.

Seeking Consultation for Yourself

You can see that crisis situations involve conflicting needs and demands; we'll need to be prepared to juggle these complications. It's usually helpful to get consultation and support from colleagues to ensure that we're not missing the obvious, that important issues are adequately attended to, and that we're using the best available resources. In addition, it is a very good idea to keep a written record of the steps we took to ensure that we were acting in the best interest of all concerned, in the event that any conflict develops.

Although it's wise to seek consultation whenever we're involved in a crisis, not all situations are as volatile as the ones we've been discussing. More often we can try to defuse the crisis by using interviewing skills to reach some manageable resolution.

Interviewing Clients in Crisis

As therapists, we have to be able to think on many different levels simultaneously; in no situation is this need clearer than in a crisis interview. What makes this task so demanding is that these interventions require us to assume certain responsibilities that we usually don't exercise during our regular sessions. First of all, we have to be more directive, because crisis situations often require decisions that clients may not be ready or able to make on their own. Second, we'll need to be aware that our own anxiety can lead us to overlook significant issues as we search for the best course of action. Finally, we must be more vigilant about managing the risk of danger to the client or others.

As if these responsibilities were not enough to worry about, we also have to identify the issues and events that triggered the crisis, defuse associated feelings, and then, most important, help clients develop strategies that will foster resolution and adaptive coping (not to mention somehow managing to stay calm while doing all this). With all this pressure, it's no wonder that crisis work can be challenging and stressful, especially when it's with a client the therapist is seeing for the very first time. What follows is a more detailed description of the skills and responsibilities called for when interviewing someone in crisis.

Focusing the Interview

In crisis, our clients often feel out of control and swept away by a flood of emotion. Clients typically comment that they feel as though they're ranting and raving, or just babbling—on any account, not making sense. For example, in an attempt to describe how desperate he felt, Matt launched into a convoluted explanation of his father's alcoholism and then drifted into an explanation of his son's drug use, his girlfriend Becky's rejection, and his problems at work. And Joanne started off her appointment by describing the entire history of her twenty-year marriage.

In short, these clients didn't bring themselves any closer to labeling what they were feeling, much less figuring out what they needed to do about their situations. Without some active guidance, it's likely that both clients would have continued to use the entire session to express their distress. Not much else would have been accomplished. And more than likely, these clients would have left their appointments just as upset as they were when they arrived.

To assume temporary control of what is discussed, we'll need to be gentle but firm. Our manner and words should convey both why we're providing direction and empathy for how the client is feeling. For example: "I can see that you're distressed and that you have a lot of things on your mind, but I think it would be helpful if during this interview, we try to clarify what we need to do to best take care of you." This kind of statement accomplishes two important objectives. First, it lets your client know in a reassuring way that, from time to time, you may need to interrupt, direct, or offer concrete suggestions. Second, it clarifies that the health and safety of the client and others is the first priority.

For example, Matt couldn't sleep and wasn't eating, and his ruminations about suicide made work and care for his children difficult. I needed to suggest medication and focus his attention on managing his suicidal impulses before we could think about tackling the problems that precipitated this crisis.

Certainly, there will be sessions in which the amount of time you have to work is at a premium. Pointing out time constraints can also be an effective way of focusing your client's attention on what needs to be done. For instance, I might say, "Matt, I understand that you've got a lot on your mind. We only have an hour today, so we need to stay focused on what you're going to do for the next two days. After you get some rest and a little relief, we'll be in a better position to talk about how you can deal with Becky."

When clients drift or bring up other issues, it's essential to remind them of the importance of staying on task. Such shifts should be handled with empathy: "Matt, I can understand why you want to talk about Becky, and it's clear how important she was to you, but now we need to focus on how you're going to manage these suicidal thoughts when your children are with you."

Whenever a therapist is ambivalent about taking control, it increases the likelihood that the crisis will worsen. Most clients detect the therapist's self-doubt and lack of confidence and consequently feel even more anxious. For example, Amy, one of our graduate trainees, saw John on an emergency appointment because he was suffering from panic attacks. Amy needed to provide direction to defuse this emergency but was unsure about how to do this.

After talking for over an hour, John appeared more panicked than ever. Because I was her supervisor, Amy wisely sought me out. Together we finished the interview. I provided the structure by establishing what needed to be discussed, and Amy did a fine job of referring John for medication and teaching him some techniques to manage his panic. Amy was able to see how clear control over the discussion and direct action to manage the symptoms facilitated John's relief.

Making Sense of a Crisis

When clients cry uncontrollably, feel overcome with rage, or are confused by voices, they usually want to know why it is happening. Helping these clients make sense of what they're experiencing is an important step toward regaining a sense of control. Sometimes, the connection between the client's symptoms and the events that precipitated them is pretty obvious. But this isn't always the case. Many clients are not only overwhelmed by what's happened but are also confused by their own responses.

It is also difficult for clients to appreciate that the way they're reacting may be "normal" given the circumstances. When I explained to Joanne that most people would feel pretty overwhelmed if they were trying to manage the stress of losing a twenty-year marriage while juggling the demands of daily responsibilities, she felt relieved. Knowing that her responses were both normal and understandable made her feel more comfortable.

In a similar way, it's often helpful to point out that what a client refers to as an "overreaction" makes sense in light of the client's history. For example, Joanne's reaction to her husband's leaving was magnified because her parents had divorced when she was twelve, and her current circumstances reminded her of how horrible that early experience was for her.

There are many ways of shedding light on the connection between the client's symptoms and the issues and events that precipitated them. Sometimes we can help the client make more sense out of what's happening by asking simple questions. With Matt, the event that really created his intense feelings of being out of control was clarified when I asked, "When did you start feeling so hopeless?" He started to cry and explained, "I don't understand how she could stop loving me. It doesn't make sense. Ever since she told me not to call her, I just feel like I'm losing it." This clarified that the breakup of his relationship with Becky was the primary event that precipitated his crisis.

Identifying the precipitating events or "telling the story" often helps. Joanne, for instance, hadn't told anyone that her husband had left. She was afraid it wasn't right to discuss these matters at work; she anticipated that her family would be judgmental, and she was concerned that her friends would feel burdened. So she kept everything to herself. Once she was able to describe the events that precipitated the breakup of her marriage, she was better able to understand her reactions. As she described her husband's affairs and constant attention to work, and her long-standing feelings of isolation and neglect, she sighed and then concluded, "I've never told anyone how unhappy I was. Maybe it's good that he left." Subsequently, she felt better and more in control of her responses.

Correcting Distorted Thinking

"I won't ever stop crying." "No one will ever love me again." "I can't stand this pain." "I'm worthless, and so is my life." This is just a small sample of the erroneous assumptions Joanne made. During a crisis, our clients often jump to these unsubstantiated conclusions because they're not thinking clearly and they're frightened. "What if" thinking both dominates and torments: what if he leaves; what if she doesn't; what if I die; what if I don't; what if I lose it; what if I never get any sleep. These poorly thought out assumptions are easy enough to understand but still need to be challenged.

It's not that our clients launch into such irrational thinking because they're stupid or don't understand the irrational nature of their thoughts. In fact, their awareness that their thinking isn't rational only creates more frustration because they're unable to use that knowledge to alter their reactions.

Often, our clients tenaciously hold onto this illogical thinking because they lack information. One of the best methods of altering this type of thinking involves presenting straightforward information about the effects of divorce or the loss of a loved one, or about the process of recovering from an assault.

More often, though, we are faced with having to invest time and energy in uncovering the client's fundamentally flawed assumptions about life and "personhood." Albert Ellis offers us a list of such faulty assumptions:[9]

An adult must be loved or approved of by virtually every significant person in his or her community.

One should be thoroughly competent, adequate, and achieving in all possible respects if one is to consider oneself worthwhile.

Human unhappiness is externally caused, and people have little or
   no ability to control their sorrows and disturbances.

One's past history is an all-important determinant of one's present
   behavior, and if something once strongly affected one's life, it
   should indefinitely have a similar effect.

There is invariably a right, precise, and perfect solution to human
   problems, and it is catastrophic if this perfect solution is not
   found.

If something is or may be dangerous or fearsome, one should be
   terribly concerned about it and should keep dwelling on the
   possibility of its occurring.

Certain people are bad, wicked, or villainous, and they should be
   severely blamed and punished for their villainy.

It's awful and catastrophic when things are not the way one would
   very much like them to be.

It's easier to avoid than to face certain life difficulties and self-
   responsibilities.

One should become quite upset over other people's problems and
   disturbances.

Some clients are receptive to hearing that their thinking may
be clouded by the events related to their crisis. When we point this
out, we create an opening for interrupting their reactions.

Matt explained that his life didn't seem worth living without
Becky. He wept, "She seemed so right, and I'm so lonely. I can't
believe she could just stop loving me. No one will ever care
about me like she did. I can't see going on like this. I'm such a
loser."

You can see, of course, the many irrational beliefs embedded
in what he was explaining. But you can also see that he was very
upset and desperate. A hard-line lecture on the nature of his faulty
thinking would surely have been counterproductive. Therefore, I
needed to be attentive to providing empathy and support while I
introduced the idea that his assumptions about himself and his life
were not only adding to his misery but also unwarranted.

"Matt, you seem to feel hopeless about yourself and your situation. From my point of view, it looks like you've lost perspective and
aren't evaluating yourself or your future realistically. Does what I'm

saying make any sense to you?" This opened the door but didn't provide any real relief.

"Of course, I know that, I just can't help thinking I'm better off dead than dealing with this pain."

"Matt, I'd like to help you deal with this pain, because what you're doing isn't working very well."

"I know, and I don't want to hurt my children, but I can't stand this."

"Can you make an agreement that you will not harm yourself while we try to work on this?"

"Yes, I can, even though losing myself hardly matters."

"You've pointed out that it will matter to your children. Now let's try to talk about what you can do to manage. It looks like talking about your thoughts and feelings about Becky only makes you feel more desperate. We can get back to that later on. Now we need to take care of you."

You can see from this brief description of dealing with Matt's crisis that I had to keep redirecting his attention away from his distorted and helpless thinking and onto concrete strategies for coping with his present circumstances.

Disengaging from Intense Emotion

Matt's reaction was typical of clients in crisis: he couldn't disengage from his pain. When clients are caught off guard by intense reactions of grief, guilt, anger, or sadness, it's hard for them to consider anything else. It helps to establish that there are reasons for their feelings as well as variations in the intensity of their reactions.[10] Like waves during a storm, feelings during a crisis come in and then recede, only to be followed by another blast. This perspective can be very difficult to establish during an emotional tidal wave.

The first step in helping a client calm down is to tolerate, if not actually invite, the opposite. More specifically, sometimes catharsis or "venting" provides relief. The easiest method of getting clients to talk about their feelings is to ask about them. And it's often helpful to express a desire to understand: "I really want to understand how this makes you feel. Can you help me out here?"

These questions and our paraphrases of what we're learning let our clients know that we understand how they feel. Our clients are unlikely to trust us to help them manage their feelings unless they know we're comprehending what they're going through. As obvious as this notion is, when we're worried about "fixing" things it can be easy to lose sight of the importance of communicating empathically.

Certainly, the last thing we want to do is provide trite reassurances, such as "That's not so bad," "Others have felt worse," or "You'll get over this soon." Likewise, sound-bite solutions like "Don't worry," "You shouldn't be so angry," or "She wasn't good for you anyway" only reinforce our client's frustration with not being able to comply. In fact, giving this kind of response is usually the worst thing you can do because it demonstrates that you don't understand just how helpless, hopeless, and isolated your client is feeling.

We can also take steps to "inoculate" or protect the client from future panic by pointing out that eventually all this distress will subside but that until things settle down, there will be some difficult times ahead. We can point out the potential for gaining strength by tolerating painful feelings while the client learns from this situation.

On the other hand, when some clients are in crisis, a focus on certain feelings can be counterproductive because the feelings generate destructive coping strategies such as entertaining suicidal impulses, cutting themselves, attacking other people, or abusing substances. Therefore, we'll need to be careful to ensure that talking about painful feelings actually helps. Under these circumstances it may be wiser to provide specific instructions for avoiding feelings that precipitate acting out. Because this strategy might seem unconventional to some clients, it's helpful to point out why you think it's a good idea not to express certain emotions. We'll need to be attentive to our clients' receptivity to this idea before developing strategies to avoid their more destructive reactions.

Let's return to Matt as an example. When he thought about Becky, he got more despondent. But nonetheless he was drawn to obsessive thoughts about his relationship to her. In fact, Matt acknowledged during his first session with me that the more he talked about Becky the worse he felt and the more he annoyed his friends with his incessant descriptions of his pain.

It helped to point out to Matt, "It seems like *you* think that you'll make some headway with this problem by talking about your feelings about Becky. Eventually this might help, but I notice how talking about your relationship doesn't lead you to figure things out. Actually, this kind of talk with your friends seems to be undercutting your confidence, because it leads you to feel suicidal and only makes you feel worse about yourself. Can you see how focusing on these feelings isn't getting you anywhere?"

"Yes, but what can I do to stop it?"

"What have you already tried?"

Surprisingly, Matt was clear about this subject: "At work I stay busy so I keep my mind on what has to get done in a day. I don't feel as bad then, but I'm not sure that will solve this problem."

In an effort to get him to see that he had some control, I suggested, "Can we agree that at this point we're trying to make sure you can function and that this strategy you're using at work seems to get you through the day? Maybe it would be a good idea to try this at other times."

Fortunately, Matt could see the logic in using what was already working for him. The point here is that as therapists we need to notice whether or not talking about what's painful helps our client. If it doesn't help, we need to help clients find alternative strategies for tolerating their most uncomfortable feelings. On the other hand, if talk about feelings provides relief and resolution, it's probably wise to encourage our clients to use this tactic.

Dealing with the Threat of Violence

Some crises are more frightening because there is a serious threat of harm to the client or others. Furthermore, our clients are often aware that we'll take the steps outlined earlier in the chapter. For example, when clients are plagued with thoughts of violence or overcome with a desire to harm themselves, they're also terrified to let us know. They're often fearful that we'll do something like lock them up in a hospital, where they will have even less control. On the other hand, they usually want us to do something to ensure their protection. The key here is to get clients to be forthcoming about how tenuous their self-control may be.

Whenever we're dealing with the potential for destructive acting out, we're obligated to discuss our responsibilities to protect the client and the public from harm. As mentioned earlier, each state has different specifications and requirements, but therapists are usually obligated to make some effort to prevent violence, trauma, and self-inflicted injuries.[11] Consequently, as we explore alternatives with our clients we'll need to integrate our goals of providing adequate protection for the client and the public. Furthermore, we've usually got to document in writing that we've made appropriate suggestions for both protection and needed treatment to ensure that there is a record of our efforts.

Sometimes it helps clients to make a contract not to act on their impulses to harm themselves or others. I try to explain the need for a contract by pointing out that a contract will make it easier and safer for us to work together: "If we can agree that you won't act on the feelings you're talking about, it will leave us freer to talk about what's going on. Would you be able to agree not [to hurt Fred, or to hurt yourself] for [whatever amount of time seems reasonable]?"

However, because making this kind of commitment doesn't guarantee that these feelings won't recur, you will need backup plans for what clients will do if they have trouble keeping to the agreement. For instance, you might make arrangements with the client to call you, report to the emergency room, call a crisis phone service, go to a shelter for domestic violence, or contact some other reliable resource.

In these kinds of situations, you may also want to consult with a colleague or a supervisor about your impressions and intentions. When you're under supervision, you have an obligation to make sure that your supervisor approves of any choices you make regarding clients who could be at risk, dangerous, or suicidal. Even when we're licensed, if we have any doubt about obligations, responsibilities, or agency policies we should ask for advice from colleagues.

In summary, a contract with a client not to hurt himself or someone else should include the following:

- The amount of time agreed to (such as two hours, four days, or six weeks). The point is to agree on an amount of time that allows for some relief but that also seems manageable to the client.
- Backup plans for emergencies.
- A written agreement signed by the client and therapist.
- Careful case notes on what was discussed and agreed to.

- Specifications on consequences. If the client violates the agreement by not attending appointments or by failing to follow other terms, the therapist will call emergency service personnel or others needed to ensure the safety of those involved. (This information may or may not be included in the written document signed by the client, but there should be careful notes on what was discussed regarding these matters.)

When people are unwilling to make commitments not to harm themselves or others, we must take action that will minimize or eliminate risk factors. Sometimes this means hospitalizing the client, which must be done if a client is clearly bent on killing himself. All therapists must be aware of procedures and facilities that are locally available for the management of people in severe distress. And all therapists must be aware of procedures that need to be followed when the client doesn't voluntarily agree with what we believe is best. Anytime we begin at a new facility or take on a new practicum assignment, we have a professional obligation to know about the resources available in the community that we may be required to use during emergencies.

Moving from Analysis to Problem Solving

Begin locating strategies for resolution by making sure there is agreement about the problems you're working on. By summarizing your understanding of the precipitating events and associated feelings, you can make sure that the two of you are "on the same page." In addition, these summary statements pave the way for you to shift the focus of the interview toward problem solving: "We'll need to spend time discussing what we're going to do to help you manage. Are you ready to think about that now?" Or, "I think we understand what started this and how you're feeling [say what that is], but now we need to focus on what you can do when you leave my office. Would that be all right?"

The following sections cover some strategies to keep in mind as we consider creating workable options with our clients in crisis.

Look for Successful Coping

We'll need to know what our clients are already doing that seems useful and adaptive. Listen for signs of self-care, protection, and self-acceptance. Make sure you point out what you notice. In crisis, our clients are often so focused on what's wrong they can't see what they're already doing to cope.

Furthermore, our clients' plans may need to be altered or fine-tuned to be more adaptive. For example, Joanne sat frozen in her chair at night, terrified that something awful would happen. We talked about how she was at least able to survive her fears without doing anything destructive to herself or someone else. In addition, without suggestion from me, Joanne had already tried some deep breathing exercises she learned in her Lamaze class, and in fact these techniques did help her to sleep. After some discussion, she realized she never experienced these fears during the day. We recognized that we could build on these solutions.

As we discussed some of her adaptive daytime strategies, we envisioned that she could interrupt her paralyzing nighttime rituals by playing music and calling her mother. I suggested that she might also take the advice of my friend and colleague, Sheila Williams; that is, she needed to change the channel on her mental radio. In Sheila's words, she needed to dial in another mental station. Rather than focus on her inadequacies, she needed to tune in another station that was more calming, soothing, and confident that eventually this situation would improve.

Many clients have forgotten that they've probably weathered other circumstances in the past that seemed initially daunting. These past experiences are important for us to know about, and our clients need to recall what they did that helped them at those times. So make certain to ask about this.

Encourage Self-Care

Clients in crisis forget to eat and sleep, and seem impervious to the notion that they need to soothe themselves. We can help them plan to take the responsibility for these activities. At times, we may even sound like the proverbial "mom": what did you have for breakfast; when did you go to bed; you don't really think getting drunk helped, do you; you need to eat more; you can't expect yourself to function when you don't take care of yourself.

Instead of just admonishing our clients for not taking care of themselves, we also need to help our clients understand what's getting in the way of adequate self-care. Getting them to be more self-reliant in these ways can require a lot of patience and persistence. For example, Matt assumed that he was "a loser" and therefore deserved the pain he felt. He needed to be reminded that no matter what he had done, he could still accept the responsibility for taking care of himself.

Mobilize Supports

Our clients may be embarrassed or fearful of asking friends and family for help, but most people in traumatic circumstances do better with social supports. We'll need to help our clients consider how best to tap their resources. Sometimes, we'll need to attend to specific details: when do you plan to call your mother; how much time can you spend with Susan; does Alan really help calm you down; it seems like your sister really wants to help you out. (Use your own common sense and best judgment about who helps the client the most, then tell your client.)

Suggest Experimentation

Brainstorm with your client. Think of options that might help and encourage your client to adopt an experimental attitude. If you find something that works, encourage the client to stay with it. After the client builds up a record of success, you can try something more complicated. If one tactic doesn't work, try something else. The point is that we want our clients to be aware that we're not locked into a course of action and that we'll continue to search for alternatives until we find strategies that help. This buys time and creates adaptive options to pick from—the more the better.

Create Concrete Plans

The more distressed the client, the more detailed our plans need to be. Likewise, we need to proceed more slowly by planning for short periods of time. In other words, when our clients are very upset, we may even have to limit ourselves to making plans for two to twenty-four hours and no more.

Here is a checklist of concerns to keep in mind when making concrete, limited plans:

- How to protect themselves from harm
- How to get rest

- When and what to eat
- Who they can be with
- Where they can get emergency assistance at any time, day or night
- How they can manage necessary obligations
- What can be done to create time and places for distress to be expressed—in other words, what kinds of excuses for work or family obligations they can generate to create space to recoup personal resources
- How they relieve their emotional distress
- How to sequence needs and obligations so as to avoid being overwhelmed

We'll need to ask over and over if what we're devising seems actually workable; we want our clients to be able to say, "No, I can't do that," when they are with us. Therefore, you'll need to check in: "It's important that we find something that will work for you, so please, tell me if what we're discussing doesn't work for you."

Express Optimism

By reassuring clients that you've been through this before (other crises with other clients) and that you'll see them through their dilemma, you establish hope that their problems will eventually work out. Avoid guarantees, but express assurance that good self-care will result in a positive outcome.

Arrange for Checkpoints

Generally, people need more frequent monitoring when they're distressed. If you are not the best person to do this monitoring, help your clients identify a reliable alternative, someone who will help them sort out what to do next as well as offer support toward accomplishing objectives. Check-ins with this person can take the form of phone calls, ten-minute appointments, or whatever else allows clients to feel connected to a source that will allow them to manage this crisis. Once a client is stabilized, the length of time between check-ins can be stretched out.

Marie, one of my graduate trainees, missed this point in her work with Stacey, who she saw on an emergency appointment. Stacey was very distraught after having learned that her fiancé had committed suicide. Marie did a nice job of locating the stressful events, defusing Stacey's feelings, and exploring alternatives for managing her grief. But Marie missed the importance of establishing some way to make sure that Stacey was able to maintain the progress they made during their session together. Marie scheduled their follow-up appointment for two weeks after this emergency appointment. During supervision, Marie and I discussed the likelihood that Stacey would again become overwhelmed with grief during this period between appointments. We agreed that more frequent contacts during this period of crisis (usually a span of six to eight weeks) would lessen the possibility of Stacey developing pathological symptoms or further complications. Consequently, Marie called Stacey and asked if she would like to come in the following week. Stacey was relieved and accepted the invitation, and Marie learned an important lesson.

Make Referrals

Certainly we must be attentive to the need for a medical referral. Many medications offer assistance with anxiety, depression, and sleep disturbance. However, it's important first to gauge the client's receptivity to the idea of using medications, because most clients won't comply with options they disagree with. We need to understand their objections. Some clients fear becoming dependent on the medication and often express the fear that they'll have to take it for the rest of their lives. Others are concerned about side effects. Still others balk at taking medication because they see having to take it as a sign of personal weakness. And a few individuals view the suggestion of medication as a trite dismissal of their pain.

Regardless of the reason for a client's resistance, it can be helpful to say something like "It's clear that not sleeping and feeling this anxious are really not helping you manage [whatever the problem is], and we need to help you calm down so that you can think more clearly. What do you think?" (wait for a response). "Would you be willing to consider medication?"

More serious referrals involve placing someone in a hospital, drug detoxification facility, or shelter for protection. In these cases it's essential that we lay the groundwork for the recommendation by focusing on the client's point of view. If we say, "You're a menace, and we need to get you off the street," the consequences are obvious. On the other hand, it's hard to find a way to raise the issue of hospitalization or protection when we're timid about offending the client.

Again, we're on safest ground when we phrase these suggestions and alternatives as having the potential to ameliorate the client's pain and suffering. For example: "You're clear that you can't sleep and think clearly; you've pointed out that you can't stay away from cocaine. It seems like a hospital might provide you the best opportunity to get some rest, figure out what's happening to you, and buy yourself some time without worrying your family and friends. What do you think?" Of course clients may object, in which case we need to keep going back to the clients' goals and pointing out how good self-care is most likely to help them accomplish those goals.

It's imperative that you be decisive and clear about what you're going to do. If you believe that there is still a risk of danger, as we outlined at the beginning of the chapter, you must take action. If you must call the police, tell your client. If you're going to get your supervisor involved, explain what's going on. If your client objects, paraphrase your understanding of his concern so that he remains clear that you're listening, and then explain again what you plan to do. For example: "John, I can see that you think going to the hospital is not what you want to do. I hope you understand that because we can't be clear that you will be safe in any other way, we need to have you evaluated by the staff psychiatrist; therefore we've called the emergency squad. The squad will [do whatever it does], and you can expect [whatever he can expect]; then we'll be able to make sure you get the help you need so that you won't be dangerous to yourself."

Provide Plenty of Opportunity for Questions

Whenever someone is upset, it's likely that concentration is a problem. Our clients in crisis get mixed up, confused, and distracted. Consequently, we need to help them out by providing ample opportunity for them to understand, by asking if they have any questions. Open the door with lead-ins like these:

Let me know if you're confused.

Do you understand?

Does what we're discussing make sense to you?

Do you have any questions about what we're agreeing to?

Can you imagine yourself being able to follow through on these plans?

Do you have any remaining questions? (most important)

Taking Care of Yourself

Following a crisis intervention, it's usually helpful to get some debriefing for yourself. These situations are alarming to therapists for a variety of reasons. First of all, it's almost always upsetting to be faced with powerful and sometimes volatile emotions without the security of knowing what's going to happen. Most of us are affected by profoundly depressed individuals who see no reason to live. Likewise, most of us are made anxious by a glowering client with a history of poor impulse control or a client who is terrified that his "mind isn't working right." Second, what we do is likely to have an impact on our clients or those close to them, and those consequences can be life altering. Finally, there is the awful possibility that the decisions we make could cause us to be sued or harmed in some other way.

A crisis can leave even the most experienced therapist pretty shaken. We need to heed the advice we give to our clients and talk about what's happened to colleagues who will respect confidentiality and be attentive to our needs for support and understanding. This debriefing experience should enable you to talk about how you were affected by working with clients in crisis as well as to discuss any associations these situations have to events in your own life. You'll then have a better idea of what you need to do to take care of yourself while you recover from the stress generated by these circumstances.

Notes

1. Shelby, J. S., & Tredinnick, M. G. (1995). Crisis intervention with survivors of natural disaster: Lessons from Hurricane Andrew. *Journal of Counseling and Development, 73,* 491–497.
2. Slaikeu, K. (1983). *Crisis intervention: A handbook for practice and research.* Needham Heights, MA: Allyn & Bacon, p. 13.
3. See note 1.
4. Baker, D. A., & Fulero, S. (1997). Decision handed down: Ohio

Supreme Court imposes *Tarasoff* duty on outpatient psychotherapists throughout the state. *Ohio Psychologist, 43*(4), 8–10.

5. American Psychiatric Association. (1994). *Diagnostic and statistical manual of mental disorders* (4th ed.). Washington, DC: Author; American Association for Counseling and Development. (1995). *Code of ethics and standards.* Alexandria, VA: Author; American Psychological Association. (1992). *Ethical principles of psychologists and code of conduct.* Washington, DC: Author.

6. Tryon, G. S. (1986). Abuse of therapists by patients: A national survey. *Professional Psychology: Research and Practice, 24,* 142–152.

7. American Association for Counseling and Development. (1995). *Code of ethics and standards of practice.* Alexandria, VA: Author; American Psychological Association. (1992). *Ethical principles of psychologists and code of conduct.* Washington, DC: Author.

8. See note 7.

9. Ellis, A. (1974). *Humanistic psychotherapy.* New York: McGraw-Hill, pp. 152–153.

10. Michenbaum, D. H., & Turk, D. (1976). The cognitive-behavioral management of anxiety, anger, and pain. In P. O. Davidson (Ed.), *The behavioral management of anxiety, depression and pain.* New York: Brunner/Mazel.

11. See note 4.

Chapter Seven

Practical Predicaments and Ethical Dilemmas
What to Do When . . .

Tom calls you at home at 7:30 P.M., again at 10:30 P.M., and then again at 1 A.M.

Anne hasn't paid her bill.

Bi has bought you a gift.

Kevin, whom you've never met, has called to tell you that Mary Ellen, your client, is having an affair with a woman.

Michael, a graduate trainee, has requested an extra supervision session after terminating with his client, Becky. It seems Becky contacted Michael by e-mail to see if they could continue meeting outside the office for "more talks."

Don has finally gotten the courage to tell you that he had a sexual dream about molesting children. Your phone rings; it's your mother, who informs you that they have just taken your father to the hospital with what might be a heart attack.

At first, these situations may seem unrelated, but they share a common denominator for therapists: people and life can complicate therapeutic plans in very unpredictable ways. Imagine how easy therapy would be, if only our clients did nothing more than show up, talk about their problems, reach solutions in sync with session limits, and pay their bills. It would even be better if we didn't make mistakes or have to balance personal obligations. Unfortunately (or, more appropriately, fortunately), neither we nor our clients live in such a convenient vacuum. All too often we're faced with situations like those described at the beginning of this chapter, leaving us wondering about roles, priorities, and ethics.

Although it might be tempting to view these situations as annoyances, sophisticated therapists are able to use these dilemmas as windows of opportunity. If we really understand our clients, we shouldn't be surprised by odd, inappropriate, or unusual requests and demands; rather we'll transform these events into openings for insight, reflection, and progress. As such, these events become grist for the therapeutic mill. First, though, we'll need to develop skill in converting apparent therapeutic mishaps into occasions where our working alliance is promoted and insight into our clients' problems is furthered.

As a graduate student, trainee, or associate you'll need to be mindful of any agency policy regarding the issues we're going to discuss in this chapter. It's important to be clear about expected procedures so that you can adhere to protocol, properly inform your clients, and handle any strain these practices add to a therapeutic relationship. It's also wise to clarify expected procedures during orientation sessions for new assignments.

As we talk about suggestions for managing these practical issues, you'll want to keep in mind that they are indeed just suggestions. The solutions to these troubling circumstances obviously require specific attention to the unique demands of each dilemma. Nevertheless, it's helpful to have some general direction in mind as you consider options. In this chapter we'll propose some ideas for converting these inevitable predicaments into occasions for a step forward.

Phone Calls Between Sessions

There are many ways to contact therapists between appointments: voice mail, pagers, e-mail, cell phones, home phones, fax machines, messages from secretaries. The point here is to be as clear as possible about when it's appropriate to contact us and how to do so, if necessary. Typically, you will cover this information as part of providing general information about therapy before the client gives informed consent for treatment. We'll want to make sure that clients who are suicidal or in some other special life crisis can reach us if that seems appropriate and fits with agency policies. We'll also want those clients to have backup plans for whom they can call if we're unavailable.

When clients begin therapy I often explain something about how they can handle wanting to call me between appointments. It goes something like this: "If you need to call me between appointments, I know you'll be respectful of my time and won't want to inconvenience me. If you call at a bad time, I'll let you know; then I'll tell you when I can call you back. If it's a real emergency, you'll need to make that clear so that we can take care of it."

You'll also need to be clear about billing for time on the phone. If you bill, you need to make that clear at the onset of treatment. Such information is typically on intake forms or is included in other material such as informed consent forms or information about client rights that explains the procedures you'll be following.

Before we go too far, let's talk about how to deal with these between-session phone calls in a therapeutic way:

Susan called in the middle of the night because she said there was a burglar in her backyard.

Tom called me at 7:30 A.M. because he wanted to make sure that he didn't call the woman who had told him three days ago that she didn't want to hear from him.

Emily called me from work because she couldn't get the paper out of the photocopier.

Derek called because he just molested his seven-year-old cousin. He said, "I'm sure he was asleep, but I can't believe I did this again."

The list could go on and on—our challenge is to figure out what to do about the specific issues raised by our clients when they contact us between appointments.

Address the Immediate Situation

When you get a phone call, you'll *really* need to focus on "why now?" Usually people explain, but not always. For the most part we need to take care of the immediate situation, so we need to make sure we understand what that is. We'll need to help our clients focus on their most urgent concerns by raising direct questions: "Susan, what made you decide to call now?"

Regardless of the client's reason for calling, we don't want to get trapped into doing the long-term work of therapy or providing extra sessions over the phone, just because that client feels inclined to continue talking about their problems now that you're on the line. Instead, we need to keep the focus of the phone call on the short-term objectives of managing the current situation, by providing a brief consultation designed to help the client regain enough composure to cope with the immediate occasion independently.

We maintain this focus by being clear about what precipitated the call and by redirecting any discussion of other issues to the therapy hour. For example: "Tom, I know how lonely you feel, and I can appreciate how long these nights must seem. We can talk about that during our next session. For now, we need to decide how you can manage tonight."

If clients drift into discussions that involve longer-term issues, you may need to set boundaries by explaining, "The issues you're raising are important, but we can't really deal with this over the phone, so we'll need to talk about these things during our next appointment. Do you understand why I'm suggesting this?"

Maintaining these therapeutic limits leaves some clients feeling rejected. But we can make an attempt to head off any feelings of rejection by saying something like this: "I can see that my response upsets you [or whatever else you notice]. It may not seem like it now, but therapy works best when we stick to certain guidelines. One of those guidelines is that we've agreed to work on these problems together only during therapy appointments." Or, "I hope you can appreciate that it is important to me to be able to respond to you and your problems effectively; when we're talking on the phone, I can't do that."

Solve the Immediate Problem

Once you've grasped the purpose of the call, it makes sense to paraphrase your understanding of the client's immediate problem(s); then ask whether the client agrees with your summary. For example: "You've called because the paper is stuck in the copy machine. You're crying and telling yourself what a failure you are because you can't decide how to handle this, is that it?" Or, "You think there is someone in the backyard, but you're afraid to call the police. You're worried they'll think you're a crazy old lady, am I getting this right?"

When people are distressed, they often don't think clearly. We can help solve the immediate dilemma by posing questions that direct our clients to think about solutions to their current situation:

What can you imagine yourself doing?
Who can you get to help you?
How can you distract yourself?
What can you do to take care of yourself in the next few hours?

Generally speaking, the more distressed the client is, the more detailed our plans need to be. In other words, if your client is very upset, plan out what she can do to get through the next four hours, two days, or whatever amount of time seems necessary. Again, phone calls are not a suitable context for working on such issues as alcoholism, bulimia, or recovering from a divorce. However, these calls can be a vehicle for you and your client to brainstorm about practical steps to handle the current problem. For instance: "How can you keep yourself from vomiting for the next two hours?" "Who can you get to be with you?" "Can you call someone to fix the photocopier?" By raising questions that allow clients to come up with their own adaptive answers, we bolster their self-confidence and sense of independence.

For example: "I think we've decided that you need to get someone to fix the photocopier, and you think Bill is someone who is not likely to criticize you. Emily, do you feel ready to do that now?" Or, "Derek, we've decided that a variety of things need to happen; let's see if I'm clear about what we've agreed to: we'll need to make sure that your cousin's parents and Child Protective Services are informed about what you've done, and that you both protect yourself and take responsibility for what you've done. So you've agreed to call your probation officer and your attorney tomorrow. You understand that I'll call Child Protective Services. Is that how you see what we've agreed to?"

Before you hang up, ask for questions. Even if it seems redundant, it's wise to summarize the steps you've agreed to one more time. Because our clients are apt to be confused and upset, you'll want to provide extra opportunities for them to voice any disagreement and clarify any remaining ambiguity.

Maintain Confidentiality

It's not surprising that those people concerned about our clients call us with all sorts of information, advice, and warnings. There are any number of reasons why people decide to call us about someone else: they may be worried and want you to do something; they may have information they assume you should know; or they could be manipulative and intrusive, with a self-serving agenda of their own.

Regardless of what prompted the person to call, you need to establish your role, obligations, and boundaries, because most informers aren't going to be thinking about the ethical guidelines for mental health practitioners. Begin by clarifying both the caller's intentions and the ground rules for the conversation.

We first have to be clear about our ethical responsibility not to reveal the identity of our clients. It's helpful to explain, "You may not be aware of the confidentiality guidelines for mental health providers; I'm not allowed to reveal any information about my clients. In fact, I can't even acknowledge that [this person] is my client."

More than likely your client has already told the caller that she is your client. Even so, we're not allowed to confirm this assumption without a signed release from your client. Another issue to clarify is that although we can receive information, we can't reveal anything. So you may want to add, "I'm sure you can appreciate that our clients' right to confidentiality is protected by law. Therefore I can't reveal anything about my clients; but you can tell me anything you think is important."

On most occasions, I also like to make clear that I'll tell my client what was said. "You need to know that most likely I will need to tell [the client] that you have called and what you have said." This alerts the caller to the notion that you're not going to be keeping secrets from your client.

For example, Kevin called to tell me that he was sure his wife, Mary Ellen, was having an affair with a woman. Kevin wanted me to do something about his wife's "infidelity." It seemed to me that I needed to address two things: his worries and my responsibilities.

Because I was already aware that Mary Ellen had informed her husband that she was in treatment with me, I tried to explain: "Kevin, I can see that you're worried. I hope you can appreciate that since she is my client. . . ."

"I can't believe that you wouldn't want to know how dangerous this is. You must know how much she is hurting our family."

"Kevin, I can see that what you're thinking is causing you a great deal of pain. You need to understand that I'm not the person you should be talking to about this. I'm in a bind here. I can't help you, nor can I reveal anything about Mary Ellen. Since this is really hurting you, I wonder if you'd consider getting some help for yourself." He wasn't willing.

"Well, perhaps you might consider raising the possibility of getting someone to help you and Mary Ellen jointly with this issue." That appealed to him.

By redirecting him to appropriate resources, I felt confident that I had maintained confidentiality and also encouraged him to take responsible action for his concerns.

Not all of these calls provide clear-cut solutions. Frequently, I get calls from residence hall supervisors: "Did you know Carolyn has started vomiting again? Her roommates are complaining, and I don't know what to do." Or from parents: "I found a suicide note in Marianne's room. What should I do?" Or from spouses: "Lily seems manic. What do you think?" As already mentioned, it's almost never a good idea to keep secrets from a client with someone else the client knows.

You might want to think about how you would have handled the situations I just outlined. I encouraged Carolyn's supervisor to express her concern to Carolyn and pointed out that she could get some assistance on how best to manage that discussion by speaking with the counselor assigned to provide consultation to her residence hall. Marianne's situation required direct action. Because I needed to assess Marianne (who was not a minor) as well as handle her mother's anxiety, I arranged an emergency appointment and encouraged her mother to accompany her. Similarly, I suggested to Lily's husband that he talk with her about his worries. When Lily came in for her appointment, we discussed her husband's call.

Billing

It's surprising that many people are more uncomfortable discussing financial matters than they are revealing intimate sexual details. Many therapists, too, are reluctant to discuss financial arrangements for fear such matters seem self-serving or disconnected from the client's trouble. Consequently, both therapists and clients are prone to skirting a candid discussion of these matters. But billing, as well as the emotional reactions to such issues, needs to be a "discussable" subject: "I can see that my bringing up billing issues upsets you. Can you help me understand that better?"

Obviously, it's best if you make billing practices clear from the beginning;[1] you should have policies regarding the following issues:[2]

- Missed appointments (In most cases you can't bill insurance companies for missed appointments; most professionals require twenty-four hours' notice, or they bill the client for the time.)
- Telephone calls
- Reports or letters
- Court appearances
- Extended sessions
- How and when you expect to be paid
- When and how you raise fees
- Sliding scales and any extenuating circumstances for lowering fees
- Procedures for dealing with late payment, such as charging interest, or using collection agencies or small claims court

HMOs and Other Insurance Cases

We'll need to make sure that our clients are clear about what they need to do in order to receive the maximum allowable coverage under their current insurance policy. They'll need to be informed about how copayments are handled and what amount they'll be responsible for (the deductible) before insurance payments begin. Most likely your clients will provide you or your agency with insurance forms; these forms will be completed and signed by you (or your supervisor).

Most services require approval from a managed care company. The process of securing approval for services under managed care involves a series of steps that varies from company to company. Most often the client initiates a request for approval of specific services, and then the company contacts us, the providers, for more detailed information on diagnosis, symptoms, and treatment plans. Typically, the managed care company then approves or disapproves a specified number of office visits. As already discussed, you will want to have an open-handed, straightforward conversation with your clients about how billing is handled, and it's always good policy to stipulate your procedures in writing. If your clients are confused about what's covered on their policy, make sure that their questions are answered before they enter into any firm arrangement for treatment with you.

Increasingly, therapists and managed care companies find themselves at odds over the number of sessions allocated. When you believe that the client needs more sessions than are allocated, consider the following questions:

Does the company have an appeal process? Many do. If so, what does it involve?

Does that process involve releasing more information about the client?

Is the client aware of your concerns about his continuing need for treatment?

Does the client want more services?

Are other options available?

Does the client want to appeal?

Who pays for the time spent appealing a ruling on session limits (writing reports and calling "gatekeepers")?

As part of providing informed consent for treatment, it's our obligation to make sure our clients are aware of any information that we release to insurance companies. For example, Arlene, a fifty-six-year-old, divorced food services worker, was allocated three sessions as part of her employee assistance program. She was able to obtain those services simply by requesting them. If she needed more sessions, she would have to apply for them through the managed care company that governed her medical insurance. After only one session, I became aware that Arlene was bulimic, involved in an abusive relationship, and suffering from depression. We used the second session to discuss options and to manage the current crisis with her lover. Given her circumstances and the limitations on her treatment, I also recommended that she consult with her doctor about the possibility of antidepressant medication.

During our last session, Arlene informed me that she had consulted her doctor, who had given her a prescription for antidepressant medication. But Arlene was so preoccupied with the possibility of weight gain that she never filled the prescription. Instead, she consulted another doctor with a questionable reputation for dispensing diet pills. Assuming that she would lose weight, feel less depressed, and be more able to keep her lover from criticizing her weight, Arlene opted to take these pills instead of the medication her doctor had recommended.

I was in a real bind during that final session. To request more sessions from her managed care company, I would have to reveal her diagnosis as well as her noncompliance with both my and her family physician's recommendation for antidepressant medication. Arlene wanted to manage her eating disorder, but she also knew that her employer could learn about her bulimia, and she feared that her job might thus be jeopardized.

I summarized our dilemma. "Arlene, I understand how desperate you feel about your weight. We've both agreed that even though your weight is not harmful to your health, your fears about gaining weight are dangerous for you."

"I know that, but I can't work on this by myself."

"Arlene, you have some choices to make here. In order to ask for more sessions, which we both think you need, we'll need to inform your managed care company of your diagnosis and our treatment plans."

"I can't take that risk. My employer could find out. Would you hire a bulimic to work in your kitchen?"

Arlene's situation is all too common. We are in a position of having to deal with the limits of HMOs, managed care companies, and employee assistance programs. In these situations, we need to be clear about both our options and the needs of our clients. We'll need to discuss those options with our clients in an effort to arrive at the best available strategy for reaching solutions.

Arlene didn't really get the help she needed. She had the recommendations and the prescription for appropriate medication; she learned some ways to cope with her lover's behavior, but then she decided not to follow through. I believed that with more support from me, she would have been able to confront her misguided choices about taking diet pills instead of antidepressant medication. But because of the stipulations of her mental health coverage, she was too afraid of her employer to risk losing her job, so she ended up opting for a plan that left me with my hands tied.

In most cases, however, we're able to work within the constraints of managed care. As discussed earlier, our goals and treatment plans are usually designed to fall within the directives of our clients' coverage. When there is special need, or when the circumstances change to warrant a request for additional coverage, we'll need to work that out with our clients and appeal together to their HMOs.

Fee for Service

Another option is for a client to pay for services, unless doing so violates your agency's contract with the managed care panel. Some clients lack coverage or prefer not to use it because of concerns about confidentiality.

These clients, too, need clear information in writing about what our fees are and how billing is handled. If you're going to make any exceptions (such as providing a sliding scale), make sure they are also clear from the onset. If you're going to make any changes to the policies listed on the intake forms or provided on written consent forms, it's wise to have the client sign a statement that pertains to alternative arrangements. This is particularly important if you are charging for services related to divorce or custody evaluations.

Your clients need to know if their unpaid account will be turned over to a collection agency. Most ethics codes allow us to enlist such services to secure payment of overdue accounts. However, although such services can spare you the aggravation of pursuing people who choose not to pay, you must be sensitive to how such procedures can affect your reputation.

My years of experience on the Peer Review Committee on Ethical Practice for the Ohio Psychological Association made clear to me that confusing billing practices cause therapists all kinds of trouble. Billing problems are not merely frustrating; they can lead to serious ethical complaints.

Therapeutic Issues

Even in a large practice or agency where a central office manages billing, we need to be informed about how billing is handled. Our clients are likely to appreciate opportunities to raise questions about paying for services, so we'll need to be prepared with correct answers. By asking if clients have any questions about billing, insurance, or payment policies, we'll make sure they know that we see billing as a discussable issue.

Aside from the administrative aspects of getting reimbursed, issues related to billing often dovetail with other problems the client is having. In fact, financial dealings often provide a rich arena in which client conflicts are played out. Because paying bills is a part of behaving responsibly, we'll want to make nonpayment a discussable issue by asking, "What's the matter?" Susan, for instance, came to therapy because she shied away from taking charge of her life.

"The central office has informed me that you haven't paid your bill. I'd like to talk about that. Is that all right with you, Susan?"

Sounding surprised, she answered, "Oh, I thought my husband paid that bill; you know he handles these things."

"Susan, paying your bill is part of our arrangement with each other. It's interesting that you see that as your husband's responsibility."

Along these lines, living and practicing in our multicultural society require therapists to be sensitive to various groups' different beliefs and practices regarding money and payment. Mandy, for example, was seeing José in an outpatient clinic. He was new to the United States and didn't understand that barter arrangements for psychotherapy are considered inappropriate. When Mandy said that she could not accept fresh eggs as payment, José was offended. Mandy had to explain carefully to José that she could appreciate his offer and that it was reasonable; she then explained, in language that made sense to him, why mental health practitioners are discouraged from making these kinds of arrangements, covering the problem of dual relationships and the importance of maintaining clarity about roles. Because she was respectful and sensitive to his request and culture, the therapeutic relationship between them was enhanced.

No-Shows

When a client doesn't show up, we have two basic options: contact the client or ignore it. Most often it's wise to assume that, like the 40 percent of clients who come for only one appointment, this client no longer wants your services at this time. On this assumption it makes most sense to ignore the no-show unless the client calls again to reschedule. If that occurs, you may want to raise the issue. "Vanessa, the last time we met, you made an appointment for the next week but didn't come. Can we talk about what made you decide to do that?"

If you have reason to believe your client is a danger to herself or someone else, you may need to call to establish that you have tried to follow through with your initial agreement for therapeutic work. In this case, you'll need to keep in mind that therapy is most often an elective arrangement and that people have the right to determine how best to solve their problems, which may not include you or your services.

Interruptions

Amy, one of our graduate trainees, was talking with her client Suzanne when a policeman knocked on her door. Amy excused herself and went outside to speak with the officer. He explained that Suzanne's boyfriend had just been found dead after having killed himself the night before. (Suzanne's roommate had informed the policeman that Suzanne was in therapy, so he went to Amy's office.) Amy was stunned, but she invited the policeman in; he explained to Suzanne what had happened. Amy was able to help Suzanne understand that the suicide was not her responsibility and was also able to help her plan for how she would like to handle this tragedy.

The more troublesome interruptions are those that have nothing to do with that particular client or his work. And even though we explain to our receptionist that we're not to be interrupted, and we put signs on the door, interruptions still happen. Your daughter comes to the door saying she's locked herself out of her car; your spouse needs to go to the emergency room; your mother calls from Texas; or your secretary has to leave on an emergency of his own and interrupts to let you know he's leaving. Whatever the reason and no matter how understanding your client is, you can be assured that your client, sitting there in your office, feels cheated. It may help somewhat to inform clients that typically you do not respond to outside intrusions unless there's a good reason.

For example, to Don, who was explaining how worried he was about his sexual dream, I explained, "Don, I've just been informed of a family emergency that I will need to attend to. I want you to know that you will not be charged for this session. Please be assured that I want to give you my full attention, so let's schedule again as soon as possible."

Our first obligation has to be to our family, friends, and other clients who may require emergency attention. If we allow ourselves to be neglectful of other personal responsibilities, we'll burn out quickly. Therefore we need the confidence to know that we can address these issues productively with our clients.

When clients react with anger or can't understand our obligations, this could be a sign of more serious personality difficulties. Individuals with a diagnosis of Borderline, Histrionic, or Narcissistic Disorder may display intolerance for frustration as well as impatience with your needs. If appropriate, such as when the timing is right and the situation allows, we might be able to use their reactions to these situations as an example of an overall pattern of behavior. For example: "Tom, I can appreciate that you were angry when my mother called. Your reaction here seems similar to the other episodes we've been talking about; you end up angry when people close to you express their needs. Do you see the connection?"

Managing Boundaries

Movies depict therapists who fall in love with clients; tabloids tell us about therapists who sexually exploit client after client; newspapers report on therapists who are sued after implanting false memories; talk shows parade "Clients in Love with Their Therapists"; and TV sitcoms outline the foibles of therapists befriending clients. Certainly, these public arenas set the stage for confusion over therapeutic boundaries. And then there are our clients, who are so preoccupied with their own problems that more than likely they're not thinking about the conditions necessary for therapy to transpire.

There is so much disagreement among professionals about the nature of appropriate boundaries that our debating how to handle these matters is not surprising. Nonetheless, professionals generally agree that the answers to three primary questions should determine our conduct:[3]

1. Whose needs—the client's or the therapist's—are being met?
2. Will this activity or exchange interfere with therapeutic progress?
3. Does this activity or exchange place the client in jeopardy?

Clearly, engaging in any social, sexual, or financial arrangement with a client put us in the position of being torn by a conflict of interests. This conflict has to do with several important therapeutic variables: the client's dependence on our opinion and approval, our ability to provide straightforward feedback about our client's behavior, and our own needs. For example, as a therapist, could you tell your client, who happens also to be your stockbroker, that you're concerned about her anxiety? How would she evaluate that observation? Did it stem from your worries about the stock market or about her?

Essentially, we'll have to handle these matters openly, frankly, and with sensitivity to our clients' feelings, because serious misunderstandings can occur whenever therapists don't deal with boundary issues appropriately. Furthermore, it's up to us to initiate discussions whenever there is tension about expectations. To avoid these entanglements, let's look at ways we can set limits that help us avoid complicating the therapeutic process.

Social Relationships Outside of Therapy

Although we might enjoy the company of our clients, and our clients may wish to engage us in a friendship, it's wise to remember that our impact as therapists is compromised by dismantling the clear focus present during therapy hours. Unmistakably, the give-and-take style of social conversation calls for mutual self-disclosure and spontaneous reactions, and that style is simply not suitable for therapeutic interaction. During therapy the focus is always on the client, and we must curb our spontaneous responses in order to promote therapeutic goals.

There are, however, many social situations that arise: clients catch you at parties, stop you on the street, see you at synagogue, run into you in the parking lot, and sit next to you at PTA meetings. More than likely, our clients feel embarrassed or want to avoid explaining how they know you. It's almost always wise to let the client initiate any conversation or acknowledgment, but you also must be prepared to follow up during your next session with a discussion of these chance encounters.

It's important to point out that you understand these meetings can be awkward: "I was aware that it seemed hard for you to handle seeing me the other day. There are many ways we can handle this. For example, we can agree to act like we don't know each other. Or we could say hello and leave it at that. It's even OK to talk about trivial issues not related to therapy. What are you most comfortable with?"

It is interesting that most therapists believe it's OK under certain circumstances to accept social invitations. But most agree that it's not wise to go out to eat with clients after appointments or to initiate or accept party invitations.[4] Clearly, we're more likely to be on safe ground if we don't initiate social invitations or if we consult with colleagues when we receive them. Obviously, though, not all situations are the result of invitations. For example, I play in a women's golf league. Two of my clients also participate in this league, so we are assigned to play together on some occasions. (For those of you not familiar with golf, I should point out that golf is a time-consuming activity that can take up to four hours and involves walking and talking.)

I sought consultation with a colleague who was familiar with the nature of small towns and whom I could trust to give me honest feedback on how best to handle this situation. In both cases, we agreed that the first order of business was to be clear about my clients' diagnoses. If these clients had had Axis II problems, which would mean that the potential for confusion and distortion about relationship issues would be high, I would have made other arrangements. (Other therapists might have gone ahead regardless, but I would have been uncomfortable.) My situation involved one client who had seen me intermittently because of depression and another who suffered from panic disorder; both were capable of clear conversations about how to handle the "golf problem."

On separate occasions, I explained to each client, "This situation is awkward for both of us. I think it's important to talk about how we're going to handle this." Both agreed.

I went on to say, "As far as I'm concerned, it's all right if we're paired together, but I think it would make it easier for us both if we agree that while we're playing, our conversation will be limited to golf or other trivial matters. We'll need to be clear that the only time we'll work on your problems is during our therapy time. How do you feel about that?"

One client had played golf with me as part of a university league before she became my client. The other joined the league while in therapy. In both cases, these clients expressed relief that I had initiated the conversation about how to handle this predicament, as they had been unsure about how to bring up their concerns over the issue.

Incidentally, on separate occasions we were part of the same foursome for golf, and I noticed that they seemed quite comfortable. I, on the other hand, was less self-disclosing than usual and in general was less relaxed. The golf seemed more like work than fun. But both clients accomplished their therapeutic goals, and both made clear that the experiences with me outside of therapy made them feel more comfortable and secure.

What's most important to keep in mind is that our clients don't know what to suggest or how to handle complications: this has to be up to us; we have to offer guidelines and then stick to them. In a more complicated situation, Jessie wanted me to go out for coffee.

She explained, "I'm just not comfortable in an office; it seems so formal. I'd feel better if we went out together like friends."

That opened the door for me to provide information about how therapy works best. "Jessie, I can certainly understand why you'd like to be in a setting that is more familiar and comfortable for you. Let me explain why I think this is *not* a good idea. First of all, if we were in an environment with so much distraction, it would be hard for me to concentrate on you and your problems in the way I need to. Second, I think therapy is different than friendship; it's a professional relationship. In addition, therapy ensures that you do not need to reciprocate like friends do. Not having the obligations of friendship is part of what you are paying for, and that professional relationship provides you the protection and safety necessary to discuss your concerns without regard for these matters."

Friendship isn't the same as therapy, and we must be clear about the distinction. It's not that therapy doesn't at times share the same elements as friendship, in that it's characterized by good rapport, respect, and congruence. But therapy also differs from friendship because it is

Unilateral: the focus is on the client's problems and concerns.

Contractual: the framework is spelled out, and expectations, duties, roles, time limits, and obligations are clarified.

Purposeful: as a goal-oriented relationship, it is supposed to help the client.

Along these same lines, Carol, a woman whom I considered a friend, called me for some advice about her daughter. She explained, "I don't know what's appropriate here. Should I make an appointment?" Because our relationship was likely to continue with mutual friends and many other opportunities to do things together, I suggested, "Carol, we're likely to remain friends, so I think it's best if we meet for lunch to talk. We can talk about the situation and then think about whom I might refer you to if that seems like what you need." We had lunch and talked like friends, mutually disclosing our shared concerns about being mothers; because she needed more focus to solve her problems, we agreed on a referral.

Touch

Let's suppose your client asks for a hug, or says she wants to hold your hand, or would prefer if you sit next to him on the couch. The primary question you must answer is, is this action likely to create a risk for sexual intimacies with the patient?[5] And although you may answer with a resounding "Of course not!" that may not be what the client interprets. Because of the potential for misinterpretation, we'll need to make sure that we in no way communicate that we're interested in any physical contact other than that which could only be deemed professional, sincere, and appropriate to the demands of the situation. To be on the safe side, this should never be more than a handshake, an occasional hug, or a pat on the back.

We must always be careful that we use the opportunity therapeutically. For example, when Aaron asked me for a hug after discussing his dissatisfaction with his wife's refusals of intimacy, I was clear that this wouldn't be a good idea. But I also needed to be cautious about not being rejecting, so I tried, "Aaron, I can understand how much you want physical contact, but I hope you can appreciate why I'm not the person you need to get this from." He understood.

In a more blatant attempt at seduction, Paul kept bringing up sexual dreams that he described in too much detail. Then he asked, "Doesn't this ever turn you on?"

I answered, "I'm confused. Why would you want to put your therapy in jeopardy by trying to turn this into a sexual relationship?"

Then he came back with, "Couldn't I hug you? That would be innocent enough."

"Paul, by sexualizing our relationship, even in fantasy, you protect yourself from really working in therapy. You're not working on your problems, so can you help me understand why that is happening now?" In this way, I minimized reacting to the sexual overtures and refocused on the preeminent issue, which was his avoidance of real therapeutic work.

The primary issue in handling these requests is to keep our clients working on their problems. If we allow ourselves to become the object of personal gratification, we shortchange our clients of the opportunity to solve their dilemmas adaptively.

Gifts

Mental health professionals generally agree that it's OK to accept gifts worth less than ten dollars and that it's always unethical to accept gifts worth more than fifty dollars. They're also clear that we shouldn't give our clients gifts.[6] These guidelines provide some guidance but certainly don't cover the variety of situations encountered by therapists. For example, some clients bake us cookies, bring us plants, give us artwork, or make us jewelry. Others offer services, such as financial advice, messages, or gardening. And although it's obviously tempting to accept the reward with a polite thank you, that's not all that needs to be done.

First of all, we'll need to understand the motivation behind these gestures. Sometimes our clients assume we have made some extraordinary gesture that deserves reward, and quite often they are in fact appreciative of our concern. It's easy to be flattered into assuming we deserve what we're given. But we're paid for what we do; if the service is pro bono we shouldn't receive tangible rewards.

When we're flattered, it's easy to lose sight of our client's less obvious motivations as well as the therapeutic leverage these situations provide. Factors other than gratitude may come into play: she feels obligated; he can't pay his bill; it's a cultural expectation; it's an attempt to curry favor; it's a reenactment of some other issue. In fact, there is meaning to be gleaned each time a client wants to give us something. The important issue for us to consider is what this gift means within the context of what's going on in this particular client's therapy.

Carla, for example, even gave my secretary a gift after she scheduled an emergency appointment. Then she gave me an angel Christmas ornament after I withdrew her from school because she was anorexic and incapable of meeting the demands of a rigorous college schedule. (Mind you, these are routine activities that rarely receive a thank you, let alone a gift.) But Carla always had to offer something. And Carla was miserable. She believed she was the only one who *really* cared—but who could compete with her standards? Boyfriends failed her; roommates were insensitive; friends needed her care, and couldn't be counted on to give back. Carla was alone and starving.

The gift giving became a therapeutic opportunity to point out this maladaptive pattern. "Carla, can you help me understand why you feel like you need to give people gifts for doing the jobs they're paid for?"

At first, she was offended; then she replied, "I never feel appreciated. No one knows how much I do."

I didn't quite get the connection, so I asked, "I'm not sure how this fits in with your giving people gifts."

"I want them to feel what I don't—I know what it's like not to feel worthy of anything."

"Carla, can you see that you're not going to fix *your* pain this way?"

"Don't you think I help them?"

"When you gave me the gift for something I do routinely, I was confused. Then I was worried about what these gestures mean. You're so hungry for appreciation."

"But I can't have it; no one gives like I do; no one cares."

"So you protect yourself by starving and giving."

Carla sighed, started to cry and said, "I hate it."

Needless to say, this didn't stop the anorexia but it was a step forward. Carla was able to see that her giving of gifts wasn't really taking care of her distress; in fact, it contributed to keeping her miserable, alone, and self-righteous.

In a somewhat different situation, when Bi brought me a scarf from Beijing, I understood this as a token consistent with her culture. I accepted graciously and told her I appreciated the thoughtful gift. Then I said, "I think the Chinese tradition of giving gifts is a nice way to acknowledge kindness. We don't do that here, not with professionals who are paid for services. What's it like for you to live in both worlds?" Again this provided a unique opportunity to address the awkwardness she felt about walking between two cultures.

When Claire brought me a box of Christmas cookies, I knew this to be one more example of how she tried to ingratiate herself. She was fifty-seven years old, single, with no living family and few friends. In fact, Claire originally came to see me because she was very upset when her gynecologist left town to take another job. I could only guess that Claire had brought her cookies as well. These gestures were kind, but Claire was blind to how her strategies for initiating relationships were ineffective.

Claire's bringing me cookies provided a therapeutic opportunity. Even though the gift posed no ethical constraints for me (and besides I liked the cookies), it was nevertheless an opportunity to point out how Claire set herself up to feel rejected.

"Claire, I appreciate the cookies and the effort that went into making them. But I'm aware of the situation that brought you here in the first place and how attached you became to Dr. Foster. I'm wondering if that is happening here."

"I just thought you might like some cookies."

"Claire, please understand that I can appreciate that maybe there is nothing more to this. But I'd like you to think about what's happening between us and how similar it is to what brought you to therapy."

"You mean because I made her cookies too."

"You were caught off guard by how important she had become to you, and then you were hurt when you realized that she only saw you as one more patient. I think we need to be careful about that happening again."

It's clear how delicate and how important this kind of interpretation was. This "innocent" gesture served as the doorway into a more thorough exploration of how scared she was to initiate friendships with peers. Establishing this therapeutic boundary provided Claire the opportunity to really deal with her problems. Incidentally, I kept the cookies and thanked her. More important, Claire learned how she hid from "real" relationships which led us to an exploration of this problem.

Business Arrangements

Our clients will not understand the potential for trouble inherent in these dual relationships. After all, during a divorce a dentist can consult a friend who is an attorney, a doctor can care for her son's teacher, and an electrician can wire his partner's house. Our ethics codes prohibit confounding relationships, but it's not always easy to spot these situations.

It makes sense to avoid any business or financial dealings with our clients. Therapists who cosign for loans, write letters of recommendation, or in other ways compromise their position risk not only derailing the therapy but also putting themselves in jeopardy if the situation turns sour. In addition, it's unethical for therapists to accept services from clients in lieu of fees.[7]

Living in a small town or a closed community can really complicate these issues. For example, when the woman who for years had cut my hair went through a divorce, she asked me to handle the mediation. Obviously, that wasn't a good idea for several reasons. First of all, I had a well-established relationship with her, which certainly would have left her husband feeling shortchanged. Second, her more casual relationship with me would have made it difficult for me to confront her. Finally, if I disappointed her, as is sometimes the result in mediation when relationships are conflictual, I might have to find another person to cut my hair. It was my responsibility to explain the problem of a "dual relationship," which she accepted graciously.

Therapist Errors

We all make mistakes. Most of us have double-scheduled hours, been late for appointments, said insensitive things, overlooked important points that in retrospect seem essential, or done something that we're sure was likely to be misinterpreted. When we make these kinds of mistakes, we need to figure out how to address them with our clients.

First and foremost, we'll want to make sure that we are looking out for our client's best interests; therefore we need to take responsibility for our error without making the client responsible for making us feel better. Thus it's probably best to say, "I want you to know that I'm aware it was my fault that this appointment was double-scheduled, so you won't be billed for your next hour. Can you tell me how you feel about my having done this?"

We'll also want to give our clients an opportunity to be angry or confused or to have whatever reactions they genuinely have without our getting defensive and overprotective.

Julie placed me on a pedestal in much the same way she had done with her mother. She endowed me with the power to absolve her guilt and reassure her that "all" would be well. My repeated efforts to point out the destructiveness of this childish pattern failed. But when I messed up her bill by not recording a payment she had made and followed that by not immediately depositing several of her checks (which upset her precise banking procedures), Julie was irate. I apologized. But she was really more angry about my being less than deserving of the pedestal than about my errors. My mistakes provided an excellent opportunity to explore the fallacy of magic she expected from me.

Handling Termination

In an ideal therapeutic world, termination is a process rather than an event and is in progress throughout therapy. As mentioned earlier, this is particularly true now that therapy is almost always limited by the constraints of health coverage. Consequently, we need to talk with clients about termination from the beginning and follow through with regular reminders about our time limits. In addition to those outside restrictions, there are four criteria we consider as we assess our client's readiness for termination.[8]

1. The client's initial *problems and symptoms are reduced* or eliminated.
2. The client has enough *insight to understand the problems and patterns* that made therapy necessary in the first place.
3. The client's *coping skills are sufficient* for the client's circumstances.
4. The client has an *increased ability to plan and work productively.*

Whereas some researchers liken the termination process to a death, others more optimistically point out the positive aspects of accomplishing goals and feeling satisfied with therapeutic progress.[9] There are many ways to increase the possibility that termination will run smoothly:

- Discuss termination from the beginning of therapy by discussing session limits and expected outcomes.[10]
- Allow plenty of time for transition, set up appropriate referrals, and discuss any feelings of abandonment whenever there is need for a premature termination. Frequently, therapists are unable to continue therapy, such as when internships or

practicum assignments end or when other events make it necessary to terminate before goals are accomplished.

- Be mindful of a client's wishes to terminate; if you object, there are apt to be serious complications for the therapeutic relationship. Consequently, it's wise to support the client's wishes.

- Space out appointments as clients get closer to achieving their goals. If you provide opportunities for follow-up visits and refinement of what clients have gained, clients are more likely to maintain progress.

- Avoid making the therapeutic relationship central to the client. Whenever necessary, point out that therapy is no substitute for friendship or family.

- Use termination as an opportunity to say good-bye adaptively, which generally includes expressing feelings, reviewing progress, pointing out adaptive coping, and expressing genuine confidence in the client's ability to manage independently.

- Ask the client to employ self-monitoring techniques, such as keeping a journal, attending self-help groups, using para-professional services, or having check-ins with supportive and helpful friends or family members, if any of these techniques seems appropriate to maintaining therapeutic progress.

- Reinforce the concepts that termination is progress and that independence is valuable.

- Make sure that clients who must stop therapy for financial reasons understand where they can receive support services at a reduced fee or no cost. Follow up by obtaining a release of information to plan for transition by sending a written summary of treatment or by having a phone consultation.

- Be clear about your expectations for termination. Whereas some therapists view termination as a hard and fast limit, others prefer to allow clients to return if they need to. Make sure your clients understand your recommendations for how termination should be accomplished.

- Solicit the client's point of view. You want to understand how your clients perceive what you're doing.

Of course, as with all other aspects of therapy, and even with the best of intentions and planning, termination doesn't always proceed as expected. For example, Michael, one of our graduate trainees, ran into a real thicket with Alicia. Michael tried to help Alicia with compulsive hand washing and obsessive worry over germs. After eight sessions (our agency has a thirteen-session limit), Michael was frustrated: Why can't I get anywhere with this client? She comes for appointment after appointment but she never works on her problems. As Michael's supervisor, I tried to explain that maybe she was trying to impress him, but he couldn't imagine that.

With her sessions running out and with little progress being made, we decided that Michael needed to focus on termination. The procedure was textbook perfect. Four sessions before termination, Michael reviewed therapeutic progress; he outlined the sources of support she might tap into following termination; and he processed a stellar final session during which she explained all of her progress as well as areas she needed to continue to work on. Then he said good-bye.

But that wasn't the end of the story; three days after termination Michael got an e-mail from Alicia:

> I was hesitant about writing this, but then I thought . . . you never know. I was concerned about the ethics of writing to you, so I asked my friend, who's a grad student in Hearing and Speech, about the situation. She assured me that there was nothing wrong with talking with someone who was once only in a professional relationship outside of the office, once you are no longer a client. She said that they had just discussed this topic in one of her classes.
>
> Anyway, I guess I am writing to see if we could maybe continue to talk in an informal setting. I think you helped from a professional standpoint, but I also think I just enjoyed talking to you and to hear how you would "interpret"/discuss different topics. It's kind of odd though, since I know very little about you.
>
> Well, I hope to hear from you, and that you don't think I'm "crazy" for writing this: I know for a fact that I'm not.

Michael was worried that somehow, unbeknownst to himself, he had encouraged this reaction. He wasn't attracted to Alicia; in reality Michael found her difficult and boring. As his supervisor, I didn't think he had done anything inappropriate. But he was, in fact, only a few years older than Alicia; he had listened well, and they had developed a good relationship. In retrospect, he pointed out that over the last few sessions Alicia wore more make-up and seemed more "dressed up." It's likely that a more experienced therapist might have guessed that both her resistance to real therapeutic work and her change in attire stemmed from this developing crush. Under those circumstances, her therapist could have addressed her feelings as a reflection of what was missing from her life and focused therapeutic work on creating a better balance.

Regardless of the origins of this situation, we needed to find a way both to terminate this case and to handle the real issue at hand, her request for a post-therapy relationship. Michael and I decided to start by returning the e-mail with a request that she schedule an appointment to discuss her invitation. We decided that during this appointment, Michael would need to address her request and would be wise to reinforce the limits (no outside relationship) while at the same time pointing out that her initiative in seeking a relationship that supported her interests was a good one. We also agreed that he should bring up his concern about how her wish for this "other" relationship might have affected her therapy.

The session went well. Alicia maintained that she had made considerable progress in learning to talk about herself (more than Michael had realized), and she was optimistic about being able to continue that progress on her own. She expressed appreciation for the sensitive way Michael handled her feelings. Because Michael brought up the necessary issues and at the same time reinforced the termination, both Alicia and Michael came away from the experience having learned something about themselves and therapy.

You can easily see from this last example that the problems and predicaments that present themselves in therapy don't appear in neat little boxes. Instead, we're juggling and balancing as we try to do well by our clients. Nevertheless, there are some common overriding principles that should guide any course of action:

- Establish priorities. Certainly our professional ethics codes provide an excellent place to start.
- Be clear with clients about what you can and cannot do.
- Be willing to admit mistakes.

- Provide clients with an opportunity to express their point of view.
- Seek consultation to monitor your own feelings and to increase your awareness of adaptive alternatives.
- Keep a written record of what you did and why you did it, and include information about the consultations you sought.

Notes

1. Orcutt, M. A. (in press). Resolving/avoiding financial ethical issues with patients. *Ohio Psychologist.*

2. Handelsman, M. M., Kemper, M. B., Kesson-Craig, P., McLain, J., & Johnsrud, C. (1986). Use, content, and readability of written consent forms for treatment. *Professional Psychology: Research and Practice, 17,* 514–518.

3. Corey, G., Corey, M. S., & Callanan, P. (1993). *Issues and ethics in the helping professions.* Pacific Grove, CA: Brooks/Cole.

4. Borys, D. S., & Pope, K. S. (1989). Dual relationships between therapist and client: A national study of psychologists, psychiatrists, and social workers. *Professional Psychology: Research and Practice, 20,* 283–293; Pope, K. S., Tabachnick, B., & Keith-Spiegel, P. (1986). Sexual attraction to clients: The human therapist and the (sometimes) inhuman training system. *American Psychologist, 41,* 147–158; Pope, K. S., Tabachnick, B., & Keith-Spiegel, P. (1987). Ethics of practice: The beliefs and behaviors of psychologists as therapists. *American Psychologist, 42,* 993–1006; Pope, K. S., Tabachnick, B., & Keith-Spiegel, P. (1988). Good and poor practice in psychotherapy: National survey of beliefs of psychologists. *Professional Psychology: Research and Practice, 19,* 547–552.

5. Pope, K. S., Sonne, J. L., & Holroyd, J. (1994). Sexual feelings in psychotherapy: Explorations for therapists and therapists-in-training. Washington, DC: American Psychological Association, p. 180.

6. Borys, D. S., & Pope, K. S. (1989). Dual relationships between therapist and client: A national study of psychologists, psychiatrists, and social workers. *Professional Psychology: Research and Practice, 20,* 283–293; Pope, K. S., Tabachnick, B., & Keith-Spiegel, P. (1987). Ethics of practice: The beliefs and behaviors of psychologists as therapists. *American Psychologist, 42,* 993–1006; Pope, K. S., Tabachnick, B., & Keith-Spiegel, P. (1988). Good and poor practice in psychotherapy: National survey of beliefs of psychologists. *Professional Psychology: Research and Practice, 19,* 547–552.

7.   See note 3.
8.   Kleinke, C. L. (1994). *Common principles of psychotherapy.* Pacific Grove, CA: Brooks/Cole, pp. 226–227; Young, M. E. (1992). Counseling methods and techniques: An eclectic approach. Pacific Grove, CA: Brooks/Cole, pp. 306–317.
9.   Kleinke, C. L. (1994). *Common principles of psychotherapy.* Pacific Grove, CA: Brooks/Cole, pp. 230–231.
10.   Kramer, S. A. (1990). *Positive ending in psychotherapy.* San Francisco: Jossey-Bass.

See note 3.

8. Shafir, E. (1993). Choosing versus rejecting: Why some options are both better and worse than others. *Memory & Cognition, 21*, 4, 546–556.

9. Shafir, E., and so forth. . . . (*probable* reproduction/footnote not visible)

Chapter Eight

Using Yourself
A Therapeutic Challenge

> The day Betty entered my office, the instant I saw her steering her ponderous two-hundred-fifty-pound, five-feet-two-inch frame toward my trim, high-tech office chair, I knew that a great trial of countertransference was in store for me.
>
> I have always been repelled by fat women. I find them disgusting: their absurd sidewise waddle, their absence of body contour—breasts, laps, buttocks, shoulder, jawlines, cheekbones, *everything*, everything I like to see in a woman, obscured in an avalanche of flesh. And I hate their clothes—the shapeless, baggy dresses, or worse, the stiff elephantine blue jeans with the barrel thighs. How dare they impose that body on the rest of us.[1]

Irvin Yalom's candid description of his personal reaction to Betty is neither politically correct nor scientific; it seems dangerous if unleashed and counterproductive if bound up. It's hard to imagine how a therapist could transform this reaction in order to create the foundation for a safe, supportive, and thoughtful environment in which Betty would be able to accomplish the work she needed to do. But that's just what Yalom did. (For a full account of how he took responsibility for his issues, see *Love's Executioner.*)

Yalom could work productively with Betty because he was able to acknowledge these honest reactions to himself; he was able to examine the roots of those responses, and he was able to make careful choices about when and how to use those reactions therapeutically. Using our reactions is the skill we want to talk about now.

No matter how hard we try, at any given moment, everything about us—our characteristics, values, experiences, beliefs, and moods—becomes a variable that influences how we respond to our clients. The following are some basic assumptions about this therapeutic fact of life:

- We're going to react emotionally, cognitively, and behaviorally to our clients.
- Our reactions stem from a combination of our own history and our perceptions about the present.
- There is no right way to feel, but the choices we make about the expression of those feelings have inevitable consequences for us and for our clients.
- Greater self-awareness will increase our therapeutic options.
- Because we will change, it is our obligation to pursue self-awareness throughout our career.

Knowing Ourselves

As therapists, our self-knowledge needs to include both an appreciation for our more persistent attributes as well as a continued awareness of how our more transient moods influence what we're doing. The list of what we might want to understand, analyze, and monitor is endless; for our purposes, we'll concentrate on the characteristics that are most essential for understanding our contribution to the dynamics of therapeutic experience.

Who We Are

Even though research suggests that the age, sex, and ethnicity of the therapist are not associated with the overall outcome of psychotherapy, this certainly doesn't mean that these variables were not attended to during the course of the therapy.[2] On the contrary, any experienced therapist knows that nothing could be further from the truth. More specifically, I'm aware that as a Caucasian female therapist my impact on a white male contemporary is going to be different from my effect on a Native American woman twenty years my junior or an African American male twenty-five years my senior. My ability to anticipate how I will affect the client sitting in front of me is essential to being able to build a good therapeutic alliance.

Even my appearance (and my projection about the effect of my appearance) can have an inescapable effect on a client. For example, I'm very conscious of how my young bulimic clients size me up and down. And I react. When I look at myself through the eyes of my bulimic clients, I see (or project that they see) every ounce of cellulite; I'm aware that they don't want my wrinkles; and they certainly wouldn't like my stretch marks. Even though some of these "flaws" are hidden from their view, I feel criticized. As they speak about their "horribly fat thighs," "bulging butts," or "bloated stomachs," I'm appalled; to me they're beautiful, young, and misguided. If that's what they think of themselves, whatever are they thinking of me? And how am I supposed to help when I can't be what they want? (And they, of course, can't be what they want either.) But, as we shall see, my awareness of these reactions helps me help them.

Likewise, when Leanna, an African American woman, came to the counseling center because of a racial incident, I anticipated that my race would be an issue for her. I had to work hard for her to trust me, but I was also aware that trying too hard would be insensitive. So I handled my concern by raising the issue with her: "Leanna, how is it for you to be talking about this incident with a white woman?"

She looked surprised, then said, "Thank you for asking; it's good. When you tell me that this incident was probably racial, it reaffirms and validates me."

"It sounds like you didn't trust your own reactions, Leanna; almost like you felt validated because of what I said. Does that have to do with my being white?"

"You know, the truth is I do look to white people to validate me."

"How can that be good for you?"

"It isn't."

"Isn't it just that position which led you to the anger that precipitated this event?" (She had bitten an airline official who tried to prevent her from boarding an airplane that she had a valid ticket to enter. She was arrested and charged with a felony.)

"Yes, I hate the anger. I wish I didn't feel this rage, but I do."

"I can see why you're so angry. I know those officials would never have tried to keep me off that airplane. It makes sense to me that you'd be so enraged."

That was a very special moment for both of us. We were linked in our abhorrence over the pain this injustice caused her and in the need to harness her rage. As a white woman, I would never have been subjected to the humiliation of her experience. Meanwhile, she no longer felt so guilty because she could appreciate the reasons for her rage. Fortunately, because of her good judgment and with the aid of legal counsel, Leanna was absolved of the charges and able to get on with finishing her master's degree.

What these examples underscore is that we each bring something unique to every encounter with a client. Generally speaking, the more different we are, whether it's because of age, race, culture, gender, sexual orientation, or values, the more likely it is that we'll carry extra "baggage" into the therapeutic relationship. That baggage contains our stereotypes, projections, and assumptions. When we're aware of our "stuff," we can use that awareness to protect our clients from any damage stemming from these suppositions.

Any tendency to avoid owning up to personally held stereotypes and prejudices is exacerbated in a climate that pressures therapists to be "politically correct." When certain views are deemed "inappropriate," it's difficult to actually acknowledge that we may cart around some pretty "incorrect" sentiments: not liking fat people, judging people when they get sick (they deserved it), or being repulsed by disabilities. When these views are unacknowledged, they can't be counteracted; therefore, they're more likely to influence what happens during therapy. Consequently, we'll need extra effort to unearth these less than acceptable views.

There is other, less obvious demographic information about ourselves that can also be useful in helping our clients relate to us. For instance, information about our marital status, our sexual preference, or whether we have children might help clients feel more confident about our ability to understand. A client who feels out of control with her children might feel more confident working with a therapist who's had firsthand experience being a parent. In other words, occasional limited disclosures about who we are can be used to foster connections by establishing a shared background: "I grew up in San Francisco, too"; "I'm also a first-generation American"; "I remember how hard it was to quit smoking."

Where We've Been

All of us can probably cite pivotal events that had a profound effect on us: a child's drug use; a parent's depression; or a personal struggle with addiction, sexual assault, or an eating disorder. Although we typically don't share this information with our clients, these experiences nonetheless make us feel that we've gained a special appreciation or unique understanding. Sometimes this firsthand knowledge or experience provides motivation, because our original suffering gains meaning when it's used to help others. For example, the pain of surviving sexual abuse seems less traumatic when that same experience is used to help others also recover. Over the years, I've noticed that therapists often want to work with clients who've had the same problems they've experienced.

The challenge for us as therapists is to harness what's positive in these intentions. Albert Ellis, for one, is convinced that the personal experiences of therapists can serve their clients' needs constructively. He describes his own ability to help disabled clients avoid whining and self-pity as being rooted in his struggle to overcome the obstacles of his health problems. In his characteristic way, Ellis noted: "One of the saving graces of having a serious disability—if you really accept it, and stop whining about having it, you can turn some of its lemons into quite tasty lemonade."[3]

Personal experiences can provide the basis for compassion and understanding, but those same experiences can leave therapists vulnerable to distortions in perception. For instance, Michelle, a bright, twenty-three-year-old graduate trainee with significant problems with her own self-esteem, seemed drawn to clients with the same problems. In fact, she also picked this topic for her master's thesis.

Although she knew a lot about this topic both personally and professionally, she wasn't aware of how this created significant distortions in her perceptions. Michelle noticed "self-esteem issues" with Angela, who doubted herself and her choices; she saw Fred as suffering from low self-esteem when he had trouble asking women he was attracted to for dates; and she identified Jennifer, whose father was alcoholic and had abandoned her, as also suffering from low self-esteem.

What was puzzling to Michelle was how blind she was to the self-esteem each of her clients possessed. Angela was very bright, and she prided herself on being able to see both sides of an issue. Fred certainly had plenty of self-esteem when he stepped on the stage with a championship debate team. And Jennifer was confident about her choice to avoid further contact with her father. In fact, other issues not related to low self-esteem contributed to these clients' problems. Michelle's distortions illustrate how personal issues can compromise the way a therapist views her clients. In Michelle's case, they prevented her from seeing any of the strengths her clients had and as a consequence affected the way she worked with them.

With the help of both personal therapy and good supervision, Michelle was eventually able to open the door to a more comprehensive understanding of her clients. But first, she had to accept that her own personal history was adversely affecting her work.

In a similar fashion, our personal history can render us vulnerable if our old issues are restimulated because they resonate with similar problems discussed by our clients during therapy sessions. For example, Barbara had an eating disorder in high school, and although she was no longer anorexic, she still suffered from a mental preoccupation with issues related to weight. She understood her problems and was able to keep them in check for herself. However, when she attempted to run a group for college students with eating disorders, she found herself experiencing an urge to weigh less than those in the group. Even though she was able to point out to her group members how their issues with competition and wanting to be the "thinnest" fueled their eating problems, Barbara seemed oblivious to her own participation in this rivalry. When group members began to recognize what Barbara was doing, they grew resentful, and her therapeutic impact was seriously compromised.

Both Michelle's and Barbara's experiences illustrate how important it is to monitor our own motivations closely, especially when the issues we're drawn to in our clients resonate with our own issues. Gloria Steinem explained this dilemma very well. Although not a therapist herself, her views on helping acknowledge a fundamental concept about the motivation to help. She put it this way: "I began to understand with a terrible sureness that we teach what we need to learn and write what we need to know. I felt drawn to the subject of self-esteem not only because other people needed it, but because I did."[4]

Harnessing the positive motivation that stems from our own experience requires that we be sensitive to cues that our personal problems are getting in the way. Here are some signs to watch for:

- Feeling overwhelmed with emotion when the sensitive area is discussed
- Feeling very confused about how to handle your own issues
- Feeling compelled to talk about yourself and your "answers"
- Shifting your energy and focus away from the client and onto your own troubles or history of trouble
- Having colleagues or supervisors express concern about your behavior or perceptions

Our Opinions

Most of us have opinions about life, love, and morality. Likewise, we have opinions about our clients and the things they do: this marriage is doomed; she's gorgeous; he's stupid to have another child; he shouldn't consider converting; she's crazy to give him money; of course she should have an abortion (or no, of course she shouldn't). These opinions and values might prompt reactions from us, such as "I know what you're talking about, I've been there myself," "As you describe your feelings, it sounds like the way I felt when my mother died," or "Of course, no one wants to go out with you, you're too damned negative!" These reactions are the kind of responses we might have when a friend talks about a problem. Why is it, then, that most therapists feel apprehension about such disclosures?

Our misgivings are based on sound reasoning. Therapy has a long tradition of trying to be value free, and from the onset of our professional training we're taught that expressing our own opinions is tantamount to imposing our personal values and opinions on clients. However, it's highly unlikely that we could, or would want to, sterilize every interaction so that not even a trace of what we believe surfaces. Ironically, psychotherapy research informs us that clients are likely to adopt the personal values and opinions of their therapist during the course of successful psychotherapy, anyway.[5]

Aside from this irony, our reluctance to disclose our opinions and values stems in part from an awareness that our clients are, in fact, "not us." Along with this conviction comes the awareness that what makes sense to us won't necessarily make sense to someone else, and what works for us may be a disaster for the next person. Furthermore, we know that one of the main reasons we need to refrain from talking about ourselves is that we want the focus of our sessions to be on our clients and their problems. For these reasons, the self-disclosures we make as therapists are vastly different from those we make with our friends: most of our disclosures in therapy are likely to be premeditated and carry the weight of our professional calculation, whereas with friends our disclosures are usually based on spontaneity and reciprocity. As therapists we'll need to exercise caution, forethought, and strategy.

For example, a very experienced colleague of mine, who is Jewish, saw a Catholic client with a Jewish boyfriend. He found himself concerned when she described her boyfriend's willingness to convert. He was tempted to say to her, "Have you thought about what this will mean to him in the future?" but realized that such a reaction was deeply rooted in his conviction that Judaism is a threatened religion that needs protection. Fortunately, he realized that making such a comment would not have saved his religion from extinction, and it certainly could have made his client feel guilty. Realizing that he was attempting to steer her thinking in a direction that paralleled his own, my colleague not only refrained from expressing this opinion but also reminded himself to attend to her fears about her parents' disapproval.

Our Values

Most of us arrive in graduate school with pretty clear ideas about who we are and how we should behave. That ease and confidence is often shaken once we're confronted with theories and techniques about doing therapy. Because therapy involves using your personality and style of relating to others as a vehicle for helping them change, we have an obligation to integrate professional knowledge and technique with our personality. Recognizing that we need to learn new skills and wanting to please our supervisors, most of us leave behind our old interpersonal skills and attempt to learn new ones. As a consequence, the gulf between professional and personal functioning actually widens over the course of schooling.[6]

During this period of professional development, we're given new ideas and formulas for how to behave with clients. Not only are we likely to feel unnatural as we take on these new skills, somewhat like wearing clothing that doesn't quite fit, but also we're likely to come across to others as phony. I've noticed over the years that beginning therapists are often trying so hard that they don't seem genuine. More specifically, when trying to be "an expert," they fit the stereotypical image of "men in white coats"—that is, too aloof, arrogant, or pompous. Or when trying to seem compassionate, they seem like the shrinks tailor-made for TV: too ingratiating, voyeuristic, and obsequious. The challenge for us is to be open enough to appreciate how our image of what we're supposed to do interferes with our ability to be genuine.

Avoiding this therapeutic quicksand requires us to balance what we've learned with our own common sense. Here are some pretty common therapeutic mistakes related to our assumptions about what therapists "should" do:[7]

• *Pursuing technique for technique's sake.* Much like trying to fit a square peg into a round hole, some methods, techniques, or strategies are ineffective with some people. It's not surprising that after spending hours and hours studying theory and techniques, we want to try out what we've learned. But trying to dazzle our clients (and ourselves and our supervisors) with sophisticated clinical jargon, complex strategies, or elaborate techniques has the potential to compound problems rather than solve them. We need to keep in mind that new methods may need fine-tuning and that old methods may not work with new clients. Rather than forcing an issue, we need to remain flexible. Pushing inappropriately leads our clients to feel insignificant, pressured, or like guinea pigs.

• *Blaming the client.* Once we've learned what's supposed to work, it's easy to assume that our clients are responsible for their own lack of therapeutic progress. Rather than understand how we need to change, we are tempted to blame the client for not getting better quicker. Just as we each have an idealized image of ourselves, we also cart around expectations for our clients. Especially when they don't "measure up," it's easy to feel annoyed and frustrated. In an effort to hide our boredom, annoyance, or frustration, we're likely to come across as cold or disinterested. Our clients usually pick up these feelings as signs of rejection.

• *Attempting to cure the client prematurely.* Most theories and techniques for brief therapy stress action, and rightly so. In addition, the real world of managed care presses us to seek time-focused resolutions. But when we move faster than what our clients are ready for (by offering advice or premature solutions or by pressing for action), our clients can't help but feel misunderstood.

It's interesting that after about ten years of clinical experience, most therapists succeed in integrating what they've learned with who they are. These therapists express comfort with both personal and professional roles.[8] This integration brings advantages. First, when we're more integrated, we're likely to come across to our clients as sincere and genuine because, in fact, we are. Second, this integration also allows us to tap into our basic motivations to help others, to recognize that we gain from the help we provide, not just financially but emotionally and personally as well.

As Irvin Yalom has wisely pointed out, "I have always felt drawn to patients who struggle with the same issues I do."[9] And, "I think I benefited more than they from our work together. . . . For over fifteen years, I have been a healer; therapy has become a core part of my self-image; it provides me meaning, industry, pride, mastery."[10]

Countertransference

The self-awareness we've been discussing in this chapter is not meant to be an end in itself. Actually, it's the prerequisite for understanding countertransference, or the "gut-level" reactions we have to our clients during therapy. Most therapists acknowledge their share of moments when they're confused, uneasy, or puzzled by their reactions to a client: she bores me; his feistiness is really quite charming; his dependency is pathetic; her attempts at flattery leave me feeling manipulated. Most will also admit to times when they feel charmed, enchanted, or taken aback. Whether feeling guilty about liking a client "too much," disclosing too much or not enough, or blurting out some interpretation that seems to come from nowhere—we're aware that something critical is happening.

Attempting to understand this phenomenon has a long history. Freud made it clear that not only do patients react to therapists through a filter of subconscious material stored up from early experiences, fantasies, and projections, but therapists, too, counterreact through the haze of their own subterranean responses. Whether the material is unconscious or subconscious, Freud understood that what isn't remembered still finds expression in the ways we respond to clients.[11] And like the roots of a tree, these reactions remain underground and largely invisible, while at the same time providing the base for all else that appears on the surface.

Regardless of our theoretical orientation, most of us know it is wise to understand that all our reactions—positive or negative, small or intense, fleeting or chronic—contribute to countertransference. Ultimately, we'll use this self-understanding in two ways. First, this information can serve as a personal signal that allows us to protect ourselves from the strain of the intensely personal work of providing therapy. We'll discuss this aspect in more detail later, but first we'll cover the second but crucial purpose of understanding countertransference: using it to further our clients' goals.

Knowing What to Look For

If we're to take responsibility for our contribution to therapeutic dynamics, we need to be conscious of our countertransference reactions while we're actually working with clients. Here are some basic cues to alert us to the possibility that we're responding to more than what our clients are presenting:[12]

- Being overprotective of clients
- Responding in an oversolicitous manner
- Feeling intimidated by clients' anger
- Rejecting clients
- Being angry, irritated, or annoyed
- Seeking constant reinforcement and approval from clients
- Seeing yourself in your clients
- Developing sexual or romantic feelings toward clients

- Giving advice compulsively
- Seeking a social relationship with clients
- Feeling overly invested in your clients' choices

Most experienced therapists will readily acknowledge that it's hard to get through an hour of therapy without experiencing at least several of these reactions. "You're boring me," was how I felt when Gloria, a forty-year-old homemaker who suffered for years from depression, described her suffering. Even though Gloria made good progress with medication and with incorporating some plans to improve her life situation, she still complained excessively about her husband, Frank. I assumed that my boredom and resulting annoyance, my countertransference reactions, stemmed from my awareness that I couldn't do anything about her husband (after all, he wasn't sitting in my office). But more important, after assessing the dynamics of our interaction, I was convinced that she used her complaints about Frank to gain sympathy from me and as excuses to avoid taking responsibility for making her life better.

"Frank never talks to me; he tells me he loves me over and over but then won't listen to me. I can't [whatever it was that session— take care of myself, get a job, have fun, do something interesting] because we always do what Frank wants."

She needed these excuses because it was hard for her to face how fearful she was about charting her own course of action. Gloria grew up in a critical family and wasn't allowed to make choices in her best interest.

In this situation, I could have used an interpretation: "It seems like you've learned to avoid taking responsibility by making excuses and blaming your husband." But because our relationship seemed strong enough, I decided that a more powerful way of communicating this information would be to disclose my reaction and couple that disclosure with an explanation for why I felt it was necessary.

"I've noticed that it's hard for me to pay attention when you're complaining about your husband. I think that's because your complaining leaves us both powerless; neither of us can do anything about these complaints. Personally, I find it frustrating to be talking about Frank when I can't see that this is going to get us anyplace. What do you think?"

At first, Gloria seemed hurt. "I don't have anyone else to talk to about Frank."

I thought to myself, "It's no small wonder—others probably feel like I do." Tempering this reaction somewhat, I said, "Gloria, I wonder if your friends respond with the same feelings of hopelessness when you talk about your husband." That revelation led to further exploration of how she really wanted attention and involvement. Using my experience of her opened the door for Gloria to develop more adaptive strategies with other people.

As therapists, we'll need to know whether or not our responses stem from our interactions with clients, as was the case with Gloria, or from something else. For example, if my boredom with Gloria was a result of my not having enough sleep or of my being preoccupied with some other matter, certainly that would have called for another therapeutic strategy. Our obligation remains to monitor our own reactions continually so that they can be used to further our clients' goals.

Maintaining Sensitivity to Ethnic Differences

Countertransference reactions most definitely include racial issues and tensions. We need to remain aware, sensitive, and respectful to different ethnic groups' finding certain topics more sensitive than others. Caucasians, for instance, might think disclosures about money are too personal, but conversations about sex are OK. African Americans might think it's OK to talk about money but not sex. Asian Americans might see it as a betrayal to discuss family matters, whereas Hispanic clients might assume it's important to share these experiences. Whenever we barge into areas regarded as "private," we run the risk of alienating clients without ever appreciating why.

Whenever there's a difference in ethnicity between client and therapist, it's reasonable to assume that a certain level of suspiciousness will permeate the therapeutic relationship. There is even some research evidence to suggest that when the therapist is Caucasian, African American clients prefer more self-disclosure.[13] My colleague Sheila Williams who has been in practice as a counselor for more than twenty years and who is African American herself, explains these results by saying, "African American clients are going to find personal disclosure by their therapists infinitely more helpful than information about the therapists' training and education. They need to know if they have good reason to trust their counselor, and knowing what this person is like, as a person, gives them a better basis to make assessments about how caring, concerned, and accepting their counselor is likely to be."

Sheila and I work together with our graduate students (together we coordinate our agency's graduate trainee and internship experiences), helping them discuss their countertransference reactions about racial issues. We've often noticed that making racial issues, biases, and prejudices "discussable" during training sessions allows our trainees to feel safer discussing these issues with clients.

Making Decisions About Disclosure

The various examples and situations we've discussed underscore the importance of deciding what to disclose to our clients about our countertransference reactions. In essence, we are the "gatekeeper" for what's revealed and what's withheld. In discussing this role, Hans Strupp and his colleagues advise therapists to use their feelings and reactions toward clients as important information to be shared in appropriate ways at appropriate times.[14] Of course, the obvious questions then become: What's appropriate? What isn't? How do we best communicate this information?

The only hard and fast rule about disclosing countertransference is to make sure that what we reveal and how it is communicated are in the clients' best interest. But that rule can still leave us wondering how best to accomplish this important requirement. The following sections cover some of the issues to consider when making decisions about disclosing countertransference reactions.

Consider Personal Motivation and Expectations

Whenever we want to reveal countertransference reactions, it's wise to review our motivation carefully.

Am I able to articulate how this disclosure will help my client?

Could I justify these reasons to my colleagues and supervisors?

Is the quality of the relationship strong enough to weather this revelation?

Are other feelings motivating this disclosure?

Am I angry at this client (for taking my time, not paying bills, boring me, or showing me how inadequate I am)?

If we can answer these questions satisfactorily, we're more likely to avoid being self-serving. The best criteria for deciding what's better left unsaid is a rather basic one: material that's not beneficial to therapeutic progress shouldn't be expressed.

In essence, it's probably reasonable to assume that most uncensored countertransference reactions are likely to be counterproductive. Many of these reactions are not only irrelevant to what the client is discussing but also negative a good deal of the time. Telling a client, "Being married to you would be a horror-show," "Your voice is grating on my nerves," or "I'm sick of talking about your eating problem" is not likely to be helpful. Likewise, even complimentary countertransference reactions—"She has beautiful eyes," "He's so funny," "Her appreciation of me feels sooo good"—can be counterproductive if revealing this information leaves the client confused or suspicious about our motivation for pointing out such things.

Our clients may or may not share our assumptions about how much disclosure is appropriate for a therapist. One way to find out what a client expects is to ask. "I could tell you about my experience with cancer, if you think that would be useful," or "I could tell you how you affect me when you're angry; would that help?" Along those lines, if we decide to reveal something from our own history, we're probably wise to follow that with "I'm wondering what you think about what I've just told you," or "After telling you about my experience, I'm wondering how you relate that to your experience," or "How does what I've just told you about my reactions to you affect you?"

Consider Timing

Undoubtedly, it's wise to time feedback so that it corresponds with our clients' receptivity. Even though clients ask for feedback, it doesn't necessarily mean they're truly open to hearing what we might have in mind to say. But generally speaking, when clients question themselves, it's a sign that they're ready to hear something new from us. For example, when a client makes such statements as "I don't understand why she responds to me like that," or "I'm wondering why I don't seem to be close to anyone," it probably indicates an opening to make salient remarks.

More than likely, the feedback they're looking for is rooted in our countertransference reactions. Thus, a response to the last remark might be, "I noticed that I have a hard time feeling close to you; I think it's because you don't say much about your feelings. I understand why that's hard for you, given your background. But it would help me feel closer if I understood more about your feelings. What do you think?"

Maintain Focus on the Client

Unfortunately, there are therapists who are only too willing to jump in with descriptions of how they've coped with some problem or obstacle. When a client tells me that a previous, overly disclosing therapist took up half the sessions talking about her own marriage, it's usually to say that it wasn't helpful. Most clients are too intimidated, though, to confront therapists directly about such self-indulgent behavior and consequently either give up on therapy altogether or move on to try someone else. These inevitable situations make clear the necessity of our being on the alert for a discrepancy in expectations about disclosures and for our taking the responsibility to risk discussing that discrepancy directly. When tempted to disclose personal history, anecdotes, or lessons learned, it's best to make sure this information would be useful—so ask your client.

Another reason to be judicious about discussing our own issues is that when clients manage to get us talking about ourselves, it's usually a sign they've succeeded in getting themselves off the hook. Some clients avoid therapeutic work by asking their therapist for personal information or opinions: "Have you ever had an abortion?" "What does your husband get angry about?" "Don't you think I'm fat?" "Don't you think it's wrong to withhold affection?"

Rather than answering these questions, we would do better to discover the client's original motivation. One way to do that is to point out the obvious: "I'm wondering why you want my opinion. Could it be that you don't trust your own judgment about [whatever it is]?" or "Before I tell you about what *I* think, I'd like to know what *you* think [or what *your* experience of this was like]." This strategy allows us to accomplish two things. First, we deal with the discrepancy in expectations about self-disclosure, and second, both client and therapist are redirected to work on the client's problems.

Keep Disclosures Personal Rather Than Historical

People foster intimacy when they react genuinely to what's going on in the "here and now." For a therapist, that means staying involved mentally and emotionally and then responding genuinely from an awareness of that "present" experience of the client. When we're able to respond in this manner, our clients sense our willingness to understand their most intimate issues. In addition, when we reveal how we're reacting to the client, we set both a precedent and a model for our clients to tell us how they're reacting to us.

Studies have shown that clients find self-involving disclosures (personal opinions and reactions to what's going on in therapy) more helpful to them than remote and uninvolved disclosures (demographic or historical information).[15] Thus, when clients seem unaware of their own feelings, we can try self-disclosure as a method to encourage our clients to consider their own reactions. For example: "When you do that, I feel like you're distancing yourself from me." Or, "It makes me angry; how does it affect you?"

It's the rare client who isn't interested in what his therapist is thinking. Clients are especially curious as to what we think about them: Does he think I'm making a mistake to get married? Does she think I'm crazy? Does he like me? Is she fed up with my problems? Whatever the situation may be, our clients see our reactions as helping them better understand themselves. Our reactions provide an important barometer—a reality check for their views and decisions.

We do, however, have an obligation to differentiate our professional opinions from our personal ones. For example, I might assume that women are better off carrying extra weight than developing an eating disorder (my personal opinion), but I don't have any scientific proof. Consequently, if I offer this opinion to a client, I have an obligation to add that this is only my personal opinion or observation—and not the conclusion of the profession. On the other hand, if I offer the opinion that most people who are depressed do better when they take medication and also receive therapy—I'm able to say that this is both my personal and professional opinion.

Be Supportive

Our clients are most likely to respond positively to disclosures that convey support or encouragement: "I feel good about working with someone who's so willing to try." "It's frustrating for me to go over this again, so I can imagine this struggle is really hard on you." "It's easy to listen to you; your attention to detail helps me understand you." In effect, these disclosures provide motivation, especially when we're able to identify client strategies that seem effective. When our reactions are communicated with the message "I'm telling you this because I want to help," our clients are likely to respond in a positive way.

In those instances when it seems wise to disclose something that may not seem supportive, it's critical that we be careful. We need to make clear that any reactions we share stem from our desire to further our client's objectives and are not rooted in our personal moods, desires, or judgment. Consequently, it's often helpful to include our rationale (or motivation) along with the disclosed reaction; for example: "I've noticed that [whatever it is] affects me [describe your reaction], and I'm telling you this because I hope it will help you understand [something]." More specifically, when I wanted to explain to Sean that raising his voice was intimidating, I said, "Sean, I notice that I feel afraid when you raise your voice. You're saying that you don't want women to be scared of you, and I think yelling contributes to the responses in your wife that you're hoping to minimize. What do you think?"

Provide Clients Ample Opportunity to Respond

Giving clients an opportunity to react to what we've said lessens the chances of offending them. Keeping in mind that it's very difficult to get straightforward feedback from our clients, we'll want to make sure we've provided every opportunity for them to respond. It's often helpful to introduce disclosures with such statements as "I want to make sure that I understand your reaction" or "Correct me if I'm off base here." In addition we can follow with "Tell me how you feel about what I've just said." At the same time, we need to attend to other cues that help us gauge a client's reactions, such as her changing the subject, looking away, or tearing up.

Our responsibilities do not end here, however, because our *unexpressed* reactions, too, can influence what happens during therapy. No matter how much conscientious restraint we're able to muster, we still need to monitor whether or not our countertransference reactions leak through in spite of our best intentions.

Managing Destructive Reactions

As we've seen, if we're going to be effective doing therapeutic work, we need to find ways to manage our counterproductive reactions sensitively, intelligently, and skillfully. Longing for appreciation, or feeling angry, lonely, or frustrated may be very human reactions, but they also carry with them the potential for therapeutic trouble. For this reason, careful monitoring and self-knowledge are essential if we're to prevent acting out our countertransference urges.

Who's Crazy Here?

There have been many times when I've wondered, Who's the client here? I'm responding with calm (but I'm anxious); I'm saying something soothing (but thinking, "This time you really screwed this up"); or I'm saddened by what I'm hearing (but hold back tears). Choosing not to disclose certain reactions carries with it an obligation to act in a manner that's *not* consistent with how we're feeling, which can make us feel as though we're working at cross-purposes. We've already discussed the importance of congruency in building rapport, but when our genuine responses are going to be harmful, we have to resist not only saying what we think but also giving off hints.

We must draw back from being totally honest if our acting on these feelings would shift the focus of the client's work, draw attention to ourselves, or in some other way impede therapeutic progress. But this restraint is hard work and very stressful, so we'll need to

• *Take responsibility for our contribution to therapeutic interactions.* The stress of a heavy work schedule, problems in our personal relationships, and even boredom may be at the root of some counter-transference reactions. We have a professional obligation, however, to assess these vulnerabilities and then take responsibility for their contribution to the therapeutic process: we need to own up to mistakes, take time off during periods of crisis, and ensure that we maintain adequate personal support.

• *Maintain clear limits.* The boundaries of therapy function not just to protect clients; they also protect us. If we stick to the rules of practice for our agency and our professional codes of ethics, we're likely to avoid getting entangled in the ambiguities of social relationships: games, intrigue, seduction, passion, acting out, gratifying personal needs, or placating others.

• *Seek opportunities for appropriate expression.* Conversations with trusted colleagues, supervisors, or personal therapists can help us sort through what we're doing and how it contributes to our clients' behavior. Supervisors and educators can surely help by making it safe enough for students to acknowledge such predictable reactions. In addition, sorting through our reactions with a therapist is perhaps the best way we have of "practicing what we preach."

In a sense, it's wise to see these guidelines as a professional obligation for mental health professionals. Dentists, lawyers, and carpenters are also affected by personal turmoil or work-related stress, but we carry an added responsibility to understand and monitor our emotions with exquisite sensitivity.

Where Are We Vulnerable?

The intense and personal nature of our work can reopen old wounds or prevent new ones from healing. Hans Strupp points out that "the patient is driven—again unconsciously—to ferret out and exploit the therapist's own weaknesses."[16] It goes without saying that one of the main reasons to monitor our own reactions is the need to take care of ourselves. More than likely, during gradate school we're concerned about burning out from all the pressure, but we then discover over the course of a long career that changes are really gradual. Most of us can remember some variation on experiences like these:

- Beth was stone-faced when she said, "My clients tell me about taking drugs, and I see my mother shooting up cocaine. I remember trying to protect her from the embarrassment of knowing that I witnessed her doing this. That's how I feel with my clients—whether it fits or not. I want to protect my clients from knowing how awful their behavior really is—just like with my mother. I go home and cry after listening. I can't see how I'm going to manage."
- Eric sounded very analytical explaining, "I remember my father. I loved him, and I wanted him to care enough about me to stay alive, but he didn't or couldn't; he took an overdose when I was nine. He didn't die then. After that suicide attempt, I was always afraid of his depression. I tried to fix it. Then he finally did it: killed himself. Even though I was older, I'm caught between anger and love. Those feelings seem too close when I listen to my depressed clients."
- Anne came to my office after a long day, sat down, and burst into tears. "These clients make me so sad. But I'm so embarrassed. I can't believe I'm actually crying in your office."

Our compassion and need to help can leave us vulnerable to being deeply affected by our clients' pain. Most therapists experience this secondary posttraumatic stress when we work with very upsetting circumstances. Even when our own problems are under control, we can't always take for granted that our clients' issues won't rekindle some of our own struggles.

Beth, Eric, and Anne all were overwhelmed by their own issues. As their supervisor, I thought that they managed very well when they were attending to their clients. But they all wisely assessed their pain as a signal that they needed to take care of their own problems.

Beth decided that therapy with addicts was going to be too upsetting. She switched her emphasis to health psychology, where she could work with prevention programs. This work was less stressful and more rewarding, and she was able to teach others the strategies that had helped her manage her mother's addiction: yoga, exercise, and valuing a healthy lifestyle.

Eric, on the other hand, wanted to continue his work with depressed people. Aware that this issue was very close to home, he used his own personal therapy as the springboard to an appreciation that he would always feel pain related to his father's suicide; he consequently refocused energy on his work and the people he could actually help, his clients.

Sometimes, reactions are a normal response to abnormal situations. When Anne came to my office she looked distraught. Fighting back tears, she said, "I've got to get this under control. I can't stand talking to these sexually abused women hour after hour and then going home and talking to my husband like nothing has happened. I know this shouldn't bother me, but it does." Anne felt upset for her clients and guilty about her reaction. She was fearful about the implications for her professional development.

My initial reaction was, Anne, you're the sane one here. You react to horrible information with horror. I don't feel that anymore. I see these clients clinically: what's going on, how we can fix this, what needs to happen next. I go home, comfortable, without giving this turmoil much afterthought. I wondered about myself.

What's interesting is that we both doubted ourselves. Because of our discussions about these matters, we each learned something important. I reminded myself that it's easy to get removed from my clients' real feelings. Anne realized that it was possible to get some distance by keeping focused on the present and on what she could do to help. She helped herself by staying involved with her husband, and helped her clients by helping them cope with their pain. I continue to struggle with locating a balance between staying involved and protecting myself.

It's a real challenge to remain clear about how we satisfy our own needs for connection, appreciation, and attention in a manner that doesn't adversely affect our clients. It goes without saying that the best antidote for a career as a therapist is an overall lifestyle that provides for affiliation, development, affection, and good health. The better we cope with our own stresses, the more likely it is that we'll be able to meet the therapeutic needs of our clients.

The following are classic early warning signs for impairment:[17]

- Increased tension
- Fatigue even with sufficient sleep
- Irritability
- Depression

- Boredom
- Withdrawal from family and friends
- Loss of interest in pleasurable activities
- Aggression toward clients
- Impulses to act out sexually
- Feelings of failure
- Increased use of substances

The key to acknowledging that we're headed for difficulty rests in recognizing our own particular brand of trouble: yelling at the kids, working too long, shopping till we drop, playing chess all night on the computer, eating too much, running too far. All these problems stem from doing something too much or perhaps from not doing something else enough.

Emotional exhaustion is the most frequent problem reported by mental health professionals.[18] To avoid this professional pitfall, we need to understand what helps us maintain equilibrium—the type of clients we enjoy, the areas we're most interested in, the amount of time we want or need to work, and finding colleagues who can share our experiences. The point here is that we need to know ourselves well enough to choreograph our days in such a way that we accomplish what has to be done. And because our needs change over time, we need to monitor ourselves continually.

Doing therapeutic work becomes more natural as we develop defenses to manage the stress of dealing with painful feelings, distressing behavior, and the strain of emergencies. Nonetheless, most of us continue to struggle with questions like these:

How can I satisfy my own needs for connection, appreciation, and attention in ways that don't adversely affect my clients?

How do I manage when my compassion and desire to make a difference in people's lives leave me vulnerable to my clients' pain?

What do I do when personal issues that I thought were safely at rest are reawakened by clients who are struggling with the same trouble?

How do I manage when my own trouble erupts (as it will over the course of any career) and I can't concentrate?

Sexual Attraction

Of all the countertransference issues we've been discussing, the one that generates the greatest amount of public attention is a therapist's sexual attraction to a client. Unfortunately, in the popular culture such relationships are often portrayed in highly romantic ways, suggesting that such behavior is not only acceptable but even desirable. Take, for example, the movie *Prince of Tides*. Here we find a psychiatrist embarking on a sexual relationship with her client's brother, with whom she is also consulting about *his* personal problems—in her office, later over dinner, and finally in her bedroom. Not only does she overstep boundaries in the sexual domain, she also enters into an additional dual relationship by paying this man to coach her son in football.

Although most of us agree with our ethics codes that any sexual involvement with clients (and former clients and their close relatives) is off-limits, the problem of appropriately managing attraction still remains a critical one for therapists. We're only human. Sooner or later we'll feel attracted to a client.

What's so challenging about this proposition is that we are not only aware of the potential for damage to our clients but also forced to contend with the anxiety such awareness provokes. Close to 90 percent of all therapists admit to occasionally finding themselves sexually attracted to a client—and they're also very uncomfortable with those feelings. Indeed, about two-thirds of those therapists report feeling guilty about their attraction.[19] The shame, discomfort, and awkwardness that surround the acknowledgment of these feelings only compounds the problem. As common as these feelings are and as disruptive as they can be, most graduate programs offer little training in how to handle such situations.[20]

It is precisely because therapists don't have outlets to discuss such matters and because they assume the prohibitions against sexual involvement have inoculated them against acting out feelings of attraction that therapists are so vulnerable. Let's consider what happened with my client, Greg. We might assume that a Ph.D. from a prestigious university, an APA-approved internship, and ten years of clinical practice would certainly provide Greg with all the book knowledge, supervision, and experience necessary for him to manage his feelings of sexual attraction toward Lisa, his client. But they did not.

Greg smiled and spoke softly when he explained, "Lisa wanted me. She said she wanted to touch me, that she needed me. She told me to hold her. The next thing I knew, I was standing there, near my office door, with my pants around my ankles; I don't know how this happened."

From Greg's initial perspective, he was innocent. He saw himself as a victim, seduced by a needy, demanding client. His blindness to his own narcissism (as revealed by Greg's distorting his client's motivation in order to serve his own needs) was overwhelming and very dangerous.

When he was most vulnerable, Greg projected his longing and desire onto Lisa. When she cried, he held her hand. When she said she was lonely, he accepted her phone calls. When she said she needed affection, he held her. He aggravated these problems with inappropriate disclosures of his countertransference reactions: "When you smile at me, it makes me feel good all over," and "When you wear that skirt, it makes me wonder what it would be like to be your lover."

He initially rationalized these disclosures as helping Lisa understand *her* deep-seated longing for him. Disclosing his projections encouraged his client's seductive behavior. Then he turned the tables and reacted with self-righteous indignation when she responded accordingly. This convoluted pathway toward seduction began as a result of his personal vulnerability, his unacknowledged feelings of attraction, and his inappropriate behavior with his client.

Prior to the lawsuit that prompted his therapy, it's hard to imagine what could have been done to open Greg's eyes to the possibility that he was going to harm his clients, himself, and his family. During therapy, Greg was able to acknowledge his loneliness, his isolation, and his attraction to his clients. He gradually learned that his desire to be seen as powerful, sexy, and helpful got the better of him. He learned, the hard way, that unacknowledged feelings can be powerful sources of distortion. Most unfortunately, Lisa was drawn into his pathology and seriously harmed as a consequence.

When therapists are vulnerable because of unresolved problems of their own (which was certainly the case with Greg), these conflicts become entangled with those of their clients. Certainly, using our clients to satisfy our need for intimacy not only distorts our ability to be objective but also shifts the client to a more powerful position. Most therapists believe the balance of power should rest with the therapist. When a client is in a more powerful position due to the therapist's attraction, several outcomes are likely:

- *The therapist minimizes the client's problems.* When a professional is attracted to a client, the desire to see that client as "beautiful" is apt to blind the attracted therapist to the very reasons or problems that brought the client to therapy in the first place. As a consequence, the client is apt to be misunderstood, not taken seriously, or treated as an object.

- *The therapist distorts the client's helplessness.* The stronger the attraction, the more likely it is that the therapist will want to see herself as pivotal in the client's life. Stepping into the role of "protector" or "rescuer" can result in encouraging dependency instead of encouraging the client to function independently. In addition, seeing a client as fragile, wounded, or infantile provides the rationale for inappropriate behavior that further confuses dependency issues for both therapist and client.[21]

- *The therapist distances himself from the client.* One way for a therapist to manage the guilt associated with sexual attraction is to ignore or distance himself from clients who attract him. Because feelings of attraction often produce dissonance, this conflict can cause a therapist to become remote or cold in an effort to mask his attraction. When therapists hide the warmth and caring inherent in attraction, clients are left in a cool environment, feeling pushed away, unimportant, or disregarded. If we respond to our needs for security rather than our client's needs for a therapeutic relationship, we compromise responsible treatment.

- *The therapist inappropriately manages her vulnerability.* The therapist is influenced by the cultural proscriptions associated with gender and attraction to behave inappropriately. Both males and females feel vulnerable when subjected to the power of attraction. When we're attracted to someone, we're likely to behave in ways that increase the likelihood of those feelings being reciprocated. Because there is evidence that perceived dominance makes men appear more attractive, whereas such dominance in females makes them less appealing, it's likely that men and women behave differently when heterosexually attracted.[22]

We might assume that male therapists attracted to female clients are likely to deal with feelings of "powerlessness" brought on by the attraction by attempting to take control over sessions or the client. On the other hand, female therapists may become more deferential or reserved, or less assertive. Ironically, when I've discussed this issue with graduate students, some females acknowledge acting in a dominant manner when attracted, and some males claim to be more passive. But all readily admit that feelings of attraction toward a client influence their concentration and sometimes their behavior.

When a therapist is attracted to someone of the same gender, taboos about homosexuality may make it more difficult for the therapist to acknowledge the vulnerability associated with attraction. In addition, therapists may awaken to denied homosexual feelings when clients struggle with coming out.

• *The therapist projects his feelings.* Whenever we're attracted, it's reasonable to want these feelings reciprocated. If we're also vulnerable and insecure, the original feelings of attraction may remain outside of awareness (buried, denied, repressed) and subsequently end up projected onto the object of attraction. In fact, most therapists who act out sexually tend to have doubts about their sexuality, are often oblivious to the consequences, and rationalize their behavior by blaming the client for behaving in a seductive manner and making "the situation impossible to resist."[23] Certainly, if a client acts in a seductive manner, such behavior doesn't justify responding in kind, even if we're attracted as well. In addition, considering that most attraction doesn't occur in a vacuum, we would be wise to consider our contribution any time a client appears to be attracted to us.

• *The therapist discloses feelings of attraction to the client.* Professionals are wise to avoid disclosing their feelings of attraction to a client, because there is clear evidence that therapy is harmed by such disclosures.[24] However tempting it might be to seek confirmation that sexual feelings are reciprocated, disclosures of this nature usually derail therapeutic progress by shifting the focus of attention to the temptation of real involvement.

Along the same lines, it also makes sense to avoid the "slippery slope" of rationalizing behavior that might seem innocuous: holding hands, hugging, nonsexual touching, lengthening sessions, lingering in the waiting room to chat. It's easy to see how therapists rationalize away warnings with such statements as

Vera needs me; she really has no one she can talk to. She needs extra time to explain her pain, so I'll extend the hour.

Gretchen is so shy, it would probably help to talk outside of my office over lunch.

Peter's so funny, I'd like to continue seeing him after we terminate.

Laura needs to know that men *will* find her sexy.

These clients' therapists were all tempted to stretch the normal limits of therapy and violate established boundaries. But as mentioned earlier, these boundaries protect us and create the conditions necessary for therapeutic work to transpire. When a therapist assumes immunity to such reactions, these feelings often emerge in more subtle forms. Knowing the warning signs and being on the lookout for distortions can go a long way toward protecting ourselves and our clients. Our first obligation is to recognize the warning signs of attraction:[25]

- Wanting increased time with a particular client
- Feeling powerful and attractive when the client is present
- Experiencing increased pleasure with the client
- Enjoying discussions with sexual content
- Persistently daydreaming about the client in erotic ways
- Thinking about the client when sexually involved with someone else
- Feeling sexually aroused when the client is present
- Feeling vulnerable—wanting approval
- Being dissatisfied with others—noticing that the client makes you feel better than other people in your life
- Being unable to deal with dissatisfaction and trouble in personal relationships
- Feeling that "I could really help this client if I was involved with her. I could really appreciate, support, give pleasure to, or guide this woman."
- Feeling as though you are the only one who can really help
- Experiencing anxiety and guilt when thinking about the client

- Denying that harm will result from changing the relationship to a sexual one

The goal here is not to get rid of attraction—that's not necessary or possible. Our challenge with attraction, as with all our other countertransference reactions, is to make these normal, human responses accessible enough to use them to our clients' advantage. In the case of attraction, it's certainly noteworthy that the very qualities that make therapy an intimate and personal relationship are the same qualities that are precursors to sexual attraction: attractiveness, support, humor, understanding, empathy, genuineness, curiosity, liking.[26] Using the energy and enthusiasm that stems from being in the company of someone we're attracted to, while at the same time protecting ourselves and our clients from the variety of untherapeutic behaviors that can result from an attraction, is best handled by consulting with colleagues and trusted supervisors about the details of each unique situation.

We all have the potential to be our own best instructor. If we can learn to read our reactions and understand what those reactions mean, we can follow that awareness with actions that foster our clients' progress and our own professional development. One of our most important resources for making sure we're on the right track is supervision. We move now to an exploration of how to use these relationships to fine-tune the skills we've been discussing.

Notes

1. Yalom, I. D. (1989). *Love's executioner and other tales of psychotherapy.* New York: Basic Books, pp. 87–88.
2. Beutler, L. E., Machado, P. P., & Neufeldt, S. A. (1994). Therapist variables. In A. E. Bergin & S. L. Garfield (Eds.), *Handbook of psychotherapy and behavior change* (4th ed.). New York: Wiley, p. 258.
3. Ellis, A. (1997). Using rational emotive behavior therapy techniques to cope with disability. *Professional Psychology: Research and Practice, 28,* 17–22.
4. Steinem, G. (1992). *Revolution from within: A book of self-esteem.* Boston: Little, Brown, p. 6.
5. See note 2, p. 242.

6. Skovholt, T. M., & Ronnestad, M. H. (1992). Themes in therapist and counselor development. *Journal of Counseling and Development, 70,* 505–515.

7. Kleinke, C. L. (1994). *Common principles of psychotherapy.* Pacific Grove, CA: Brooks/Cole, pp. 75–76.

8. See note 6.

9. See note 1, pp. 196–197.

10. Yalom, I. D. (1974). *Every day gets a little closer.* New York: Basic Books, p. 230.

11. Sifneos, P. (1979). *Short-term dynamic psychotherapy: Evaluation and technique.* New York: Plenum Press.

12. Corey, G., Corey, M. S., & Callanan, P. (1988). *Professional and ethical issues in counseling and psychotherapy* (3rd ed.). Pacific Grove, CA: Brooks/Cole, pp. 50–52.

13. Watkins, C. E. (1990). The effects of counselor self disclosure: A research review. *Counseling Psychologist, 18,* 477–500.

14. Strupp, H. H. (1992). The future of psychodynamic psychotherapy. *Psychotherapy, 29,* 21–27.

15. See note 5, p. 257.

16. Strupp, H. H., & Binder, J. L. (1984). *Psychotherapy in a new key.* New York: Basic Books, p. 150.

17. Coster, J. S., & Schwebel, M. (1997). Well functioning in professional psychologists. *Professional Psychology: Research and Practice, 28,* 5–13.

18. Mahoney, M. J. (1997). Psychotherapists' personal problems and self care patterns. *Professional Psychology: Research and Practice, 28,* pp. 14–16.

19. Pope, K. S. (1990). Therapist-patient sexual involvement: A review of the research. *Clinical Psychology Review, 10,* 477–490.

20. Pope, K. S., Keith-Spiegel, P., & Tabachnick, B. (1986). Sexual attraction to clients. *American Psychologist, 41,* 147–158.

21. Corey, M. S., & Corey, G. (1989). *Becoming a helper.* Pacific Grove, CA: Brooks/Cole.

22. Sandella, E. K. (1987). Dominance of heterosexual attraction. *Journal of Personality and Social Psychology, 52,* 730–738.

23. Schoener, G. R. (1989). Filing complaints against therapists who sexually exploit clients. In G. R. Schoener, J. H. Milgram, J. C. Gonsiorek, E. T. Leupker, & R. M. Conroe (Eds.), *Psychotherapists' sexual involvement with clients: Intervention and prevention* (pp. 313–343). Minneapolis: Walk-In Counseling Center.

24. Edelwich, J., & Brodsky, A. (1991). *Sexual dilemmas for the helping professional* (rev. ed.). New York: Brunner/Mazel; Pope, K. S., Keith-

232   BUILDING BASIC THERAPEUTIC SKILLS

Spiegel, P., & Tabachnick, B. (1986). Sexual attraction to clients. *American Psychologist, 41,* 147–158.
25.   Gill-Wigal, J., & Heaton, J. A. (1996). Managing sexual attraction in the therapeutic relationship. *Directions in Clinical and Counseling Psychology, 6,* 3–14.
26.   See note 25.

Chapter Nine

Making the Most of Supervision
Dual Perspectives

Throughout this book, we've discussed basic therapeutic skills. These skills can't be learned by reading this book alone, nor any other book for that matter, without also having opportunities to practice. And that practice isn't likely to be very helpful unless it's paired with feedback from others who have experience providing therapy. More than likely we'll assume both the role of supervisor and of supervisee throughout our careers. Consequently we need to know how to make the most out of the supervisory process from both angles: providing supervision and receiving it.

There are many models for supervision, each with a slightly different focus. Some models emphasize teaching skills, some rely on transference dynamics, some explore family systems, and still others lay out interventions and outcomes. Methods of accomplishing these tasks also vary. Some supervisors teach, some "therapize," some role-play, others participate and demonstrate, still others observe and explain. Regardless of their theoretical orientation or training in specific supervisory methods, most supervisors are eclectic and use strategies that fit with the demands of their practice and the obligations of their license.[1] Many of us approach supervising as we have parenting: we're apt to repeat what was done to us, drawing on what we liked while trying to avoid what was most offensive.

There's not much information available on models for being a supervisee. As supervisees, we're rarely given a choice in supervisors, let alone methods, so it isn't surprising that early in our careers we give up thinking about how to make this process work for us. Instead, with our fingers crossed we're left trying to decipher what we need to do, hoping that it all works out in the end. Even so, whether we are in the role of supervisee or supervisor, there's a lot we can do to make supervision suit our needs. For most of this chapter we'll focus on how to make supervision a success for each participant, but first I'd like to digress with an example illustrating what to avoid. Either as supervisor or supervisee, we won't want to reenact the situation in which I found myself many years ago.

> When I first saw Linda, it made sense to me why she felt so lonely and isolated. Even though she was thirty-two and held a secure job as a mail clerk, her bouts of depression over the last eight years left her with no motivation to maintain friendships or ability to establish intimacy. She was afraid of what her depression was doing to her. (This took place in the early 1970s; the medications we currently have weren't available then.) I listened, empathized, and turned to my supervisor.
>
> My supervisor pointed out that I was too passive and not confrontive enough and that I should explore my resistance to being more assertive with clients. I felt confused; no one had ever told me I was too passive. Quite the contrary: I usually got feedback that I was too straightforward. But she was probably right, because I certainly felt very passive with *her*. I didn't tell her I thought she was off base. Instead I tried to "be" what she wanted.
>
> Linda cried when I said what my supervisor had suggested: "You're creating your own trouble. I can't help you if you won't do something." It felt wrong to me at the time, but I said it anyway. Linda got more withdrawn, so I confronted her about that too. Finally she stopped coming. I understood. I wouldn't want someone to tell me what I already knew and couldn't do. But I didn't tell my supervisor what I thought; instead I did what I thought she wanted. I'm sure my supervisor grew even more convinced that I needed to learn to be more expressive and confrontive. (She was right, but I needed to confront *her*—not my client.)

This experience was instructive on many accounts. It illustrates that even bad experiences can be useful if we learn from mistakes. Essentially, I learned about the difference between an "internal" supervisor and an "internalized" supervisor.[2] My internal supervisor is my thinking about what's going on; my internalized supervisor is what I think my external supervisor wants. (Sometimes that *is* what the real external supervisor wants, and sometimes it's a distortion.) When the internal and internalized supervisors are in conflict, doing therapy is very confusing.

For example, during my sessions with Linda my internal supervisor argued with my internalized supervisor so that it sounded like this inside my head:

The internalized voice of my supervisor said, "Speak up, tell her to do something, anything; just do it!"

On the other side, my internal supervisor reacted, "No, no, no! Linda's trying. She already knows what to do. She needs encouragement."

Back to the other: "You wimp, no wonder Dr. X thinks you're spineless."

This only made my internal supervisor defensive: "What does Dr. X know? After all, she doesn't listen to Linda. I do. Dr. X is just trying to get me to be like her." This battle went on with variations on the same theme for most of my sessions with Linda.

Meanwhile, I wasn't really listening to Linda. There's no way to listen carefully if you're fighting with yourself at the same time. I respected my supervisor's views, and I certainly wanted to please her. Because I didn't tell her that I was having trouble with her suggestions, our supervision sessions weren't productive. Even worse, because I was too preoccupied to attend to Linda, I wasn't able to describe either what was transpiring during therapy or what was on my mind at that time. In retrospect, it isn't really surprising that my supervisor drew the conclusions she did about my work. Based on our interactions, her assumptions about my lack of assertiveness were well founded. As for me, I knew how off base I felt when I couldn't (or wouldn't) say what was on my mind.

This unfortunate experience underscores how important it is to have clear communication about the supervisory relationship. Fortunately, most of my supervisory experiences are in stark contrast to this early example. When both supervisor and supervisee deal with each other in an empathic, respectful, and congruent way, the supervisory relationship supports the professional development of both people. The point is that both supervisor and supervisee have an important role to play—not only in making therapeutic work productive but also in making supervision successful. Let's look at how to enhance this professional opportunity.

Making the Most of Being Supervised

At the beginning of this book, we talked about the importance of using observational and assessment skills to understand our clients better. As participant-observers in the supervisory process, we'll use these same skills to notice what can be done to make supervision work effectively. Going back to the example discussed here, it is clear to me now that my behavior precipitated my supervisor's reactions. Trying to do what I thought she wanted without ever expressing my opinion put me in the position of attempting to do something that seemed wrong. But I never expressed this conflict to my supervisor. A self-fulfilling prophecy evolved as my supervisor's reactions prompted me to withdraw further, which in turn only reinforced my supervisor's original impressions of me. What fell by the wayside was the opportunity to discuss what was going on.

Many supervisees react as I did with Dr. X and wait for an invitation to say what they think. Very obviously, waiting was a mistake then and, I would wager, is always a mistake. Supervisees need to take an active role in making supervision work to their advantage. Here are some suggestions on how you can do that.

Size Up Your Supervisor

Because the supervisor has the power to set expectations as well as evaluate compliance, the supervisee remains somewhat at the mercy of what the supervisor requires. But before supervision actually begins, supervisees are wise to get a sense of how their supervisor likes to operate as well as some appreciation for their supervisor's flexibility. By finding out what intrigues her, what's likely to bother him, what expectations she might have, you'll be more likely to figure out the most effective way to work with that person. Therefore, it's a good idea to consider asking your supervisor some questions, such as the following:

How do you like to do supervision?

Can you tell me what you liked about the students you've most enjoyed working with?

Can you give me some examples of situations or students that bothered you?

How can I best prepare for supervision with you?

What kinds of information would you like me to describe?

Do you want audiotapes, videotapes, or written transcripts?

Do you want to review my case notes?

How can I reach you in an emergency? In a "semi" emergency?

How would you like me to handle things when I disagree with you?

This sort of initial conversation can best be handled by listening to the answers carefully rather than by stating what you'd like. Even if the supervisor asks, it's better to think about this carefully before moving in with suggestions. You'll profit more if you can integrate what you're looking for with how your particular supervisor likes to work.

Know How You'll Be Evaluated

It's important to know how you'll be evaluated. Some supervisors take on the responsibility of being very clear about this process, whereas others say little. Again, this is not something to leave to happenstance. It's always better to know what's expected before the real work begins, but it's surprising how rarely supervisees question how they'll be evaluated. There are several things you can do so that you'll be clear about how you will be evaluated:

- Ask to see all evaluation forms. Sometimes there are more than one, with one going to the license board and another to the academic department. Find out what is actually on these forms so that you'll know what criteria will be used to evaluate your work.
- Find out who will receive these evaluations (the license board, the internship supervisor, or the academic clinical director). It's helpful to know how evaluations will be used. For example, will they be part of a grade for a course, information to be included in letters of recommendation, or part of a personnel file?
- Find out who your supervisor reports to and what kinds of information about you are transmitted. (This is particularly

important when supervisors are also in training and so are supervised by another supervisor—a common practice in the beginning phases of training.)

- Find out what kind of records of your sessions your supervisor keeps.
- Find out if you'll have access to those records or reports about your work.
- Discover what information is confidential and what isn't—about you, your clients, and your work.

Again, it is unwise to argue about these matters. Rather, it's best to listen carefully so that you'll be in the best position to decide how you'd like to handle supervision.

Meet Basic Requirements

The basic requirements for certification, licensure, or internship almost always include a specific number of client contact hours and of direct supervision hours. Supervisees are wise to make sure that their current placements and practicum experiences will satisfy the requirements for whatever degree, license, certification, or prerequisites are necessary to get where they want to go. Many practicum placements as well as internship sites offer supervised experience in accordance with agency needs to provide services, which may or may not coincide with those of the supervisee. It is therefore better to remain on the safe side by checking and rechecking requirements and specifications with the accrediting group, academic administrator, or licensing board. This check should include the following:

- The number of hours necessary
- The types of experiences that qualify
- The necessary credentials of the supervisor
- The prerequisites for the supervisee
- The title you can use when you're working ("Psychology Assistant," "Counseling Intern," and so on)
- The paperwork that you and your supervisor must file in order for you to receive credit

Test the Water

As is the case with most relationships, you'll need time to evaluate what's safe and what isn't. Although it's often useful to talk to other people who've been supervised by the same person, it's also wise to assume that each relationship is unique and should be approached without being encumbered by too many preset assumptions.

It might help to try out what you'd like to do with your supervisor using an issue or circumstance that isn't too threatening, before you jump into something that might leave you feeling too exposed. For example, when Sally wanted to discuss how her reaction to her father's alcoholism influenced her work with alcoholic clients, she started off on safer ground. "I notice that I'm anxious talking to clients with drinking problems. Can you help me understand what to do during sessions when that happens?" By keeping the focus on the present therapeutic dilemma rather than more personal data, you might not feel as vulnerable.

Certainly, this is an individual matter. What's ideal for one supervisee may be terrible for the next. And fortunately most of us will have plenty of opportunity to work with a variety of supervisors. When you are beginning with a new supervisor, there are some signs you can look for that might indicate the supervisor's receptivity, sensitivity, and therefore safety:

- Is willing to admit personal dilemmas and mistakes
- Seems clear about not turning supervision into therapy
- Seems interested in your reactions
- Asks questions about your feelings
- Seems nonjudgmental
- Provides useful feedback
- Seems willing to listen
- Is responsive to your concerns

Without some assurance that you're on safe ground with a supervisor, it's probably best to seek additional support from peer supervision or additional consultation, just as long as you don't make the mistake of not informing your supervisor about things he needs to know. This extra support from colleagues can help you sort through how best to approach a supervisor you're worried about.

Be Prepared

Think about each session with a supervisor before you arrive at the door. Make sure you're prepared to do what your supervisor wants. If you're not prepared, don't make excuses; offer an apology instead.

But also think about what would be most helpful to you. Consider making a list of the items you'd like to cover. The clearer you are, the more likely you'll be able to assert those needs appropriately. The following sections cover some possible subjects.

Planning Treatment

Certainly, in the beginning most therapists aren't sure which options, of the very many that are available, are likely to prove most fruitful. Organizing options, deciding where to focus attention, determining whether or not to refer—all can be best determined when supervisors add their observations and recommendations. Many treatment situations leave you feeling stuck. When progress seems stalled, alternative suggestions can jump-start your thinking. Because you as the supervisee-therapist are in the best position to know what has happened during therapy with your clients, it's a good idea to raise issues of concern directly. Clear, straightforward questions help supervisors focus their attention on trouble. For example: How can I bring up termination? Should I bring up her son's alcoholism? Do you think I should try relaxation techniques?

Clarifying Understanding

One of the primary reasons that clinicians need to study psychological theory is because that study helps us provide explanations for the thoughts, feelings, and behavior of our clients. Most definitely, some treatment approaches are better implemented once cases are conceptualized from a particular perspective. Whether it be from an object-related, solution-focused, or other point of view, most techniques work better when we're clear about the theoretical basis for that strategy.

We know that our clients are more apt to make progress when they can make sense out of their feelings. After years of study most of us know something about the theoretical underpinnings of our work. We may, however, still feel quite confused by what we're seeing in our therapy sessions. Certainly, therapy is more productive whenever we're able to translate theory into behavioral terms—supervision is the ideal opportunity to figure out how to put theoretical ideas into action.

Receiving Support

Therapeutic work is often lonely and frustrating. Certainly, in the beginning it can produce a lot of insecurity and self-doubt. It's easy for supervisors to lose sight of how hard it is for supervisees to listen to a long list of their mistakes. Yes, you can remind yourself that remaining open to criticism is the best way to improve, but at times it can be very hard not to get defensive, withdrawn, or argumentative. It might help to alert your supervisor to what's happening with you. Without going overboard with a supervisor ("I'm scared; I'm a lousy therapist"), it might help to reveal your concerns: "I'm worried about how this last session went. As you listen can you point out anything you notice that seemed OK?" Or, "I'm pretty discouraged about what's going on. Can you help me understand this better?" Or, "I wonder if I'm the only one who ever felt so [whatever it is]. Did this ever happen to you?"

Managing Countertransference

Supervision is perhaps the very best place to deal with countertransference issues. But you're not going to be very comfortable with this opportunity if the situation doesn't feel safe. If the conversations about expectations and evaluation procedures haven't already clarified whether or not your supervisor can be trusted with personal reactions, it's wise to find out whatever else you need to know to ensure your protection. It might help to ask, "I'd like to talk about how I felt during my session with X. I'd appreciate hearing your reactions. Would that be all right?"

We may want to discuss intense countertransference reactions to our clients, but if our supervisor is only concerned with behavioral objectives, it's probably not wise to pursue that course of action. Likewise, a supervisor may appear to encourage revelations of personal reactions, only to use those observations as evidence for a negative evaluation. It makes sense to avoid revealing anything that leaves you feeling too vulnerable.

Supervision can be used to help you identify how your personal reactions to your clients and their situations affect what transpires during therapy. It's wise to think through what you want to discuss before a supervisory session so that you avoid stumbling into unnecessary personal revelations. In other words, you don't want to turn supervision into an opportunity for you to solve your personal problems. Rather, the focus during supervision needs to be on how to use yourself and your responses to further your clients' progress.

Because our countertransference reactions are personal ("I feel inadequate with Susan, manipulated by Jason, enchanted by Kyla"), we need to acknowledge that we may not be in the best position to evaluate objectively how to manage these feelings with our clients. Certainly, our supervisors are in a better position to assist us in the often arduous task of knowing what to say and do with our clients. Begin by offering your opinions and observations as well as your suggestions about what to do. ("Because I feel so sad, yet also angry, I wonder if Jason tells me these heartbreaking tales to solicit my concern; I think it would be wise for me to stop the small talk with Kyla.") At the same time, you'll want to remain open to alternative ways of interpreting what's going on. With the questions we raise ("Why does my mind wander when I listen to Susan?") and the comments we make to our supervisors, we set the stage so that our supervisors can give us pragmatic feedback.

Handling Ethical Dilemmas

Most often ethical dilemmas are best discussed with our supervisors. Because supervisors bear the professional burden of making sure that therapy is effective, supervisees have an obligation to keep them informed of any ethical issues precipitated during their work with clients. For example, supervisees should inform their supervisor of any situation that involves a duty to warn ("My client wants to shoot his wife—he has a gun"), conflict of interest ("My client Susan wants to sign up for the yoga class I teach on Thursdays"), inappropriate behavior ("John wants me to hug him at the end of the session. I've done that a few times; now I think it's inappropriate. What should I do?"), or confusion about roles ("My client doesn't know I'm being supervised; I thought the intake counselor already explained that. Now what?").

Ask for Demonstrations, Examples, or Opportunities to Participate

Most people like not only to talk about their own experiences but also to show others how to do what they do well. Unquestionably, examples, demonstrations, and opportunities to participate help clarify exactly what a supervisor is trying to convey. In essence, supervision is an opportunity to apprentice ourselves before we're fully licensed to practice independently. It only makes sense to watch others do what we're trying to learn.

Ask if you can go on an emergency appointment with your supervisor. Ask to watch her do an intake session, a full assessment, a couples intervention, an interview at the jail—whatever she does that you'd like to learn. Seeking involvement demonstrates initiative and is an excellent way to get firsthand experience.

Raise Questions

If what your supervisor is saying doesn't make sense to you, ask him to clarify: "I'm sorry, I just don't seem to understand. Can we run through that again?" If the supervisor is impatient, "I can appreciate how frustrating it is to go over this again, but I just don't seem to be getting this." Or, "I know we're short on time. Can we arrange another meeting?" Remember that no question is too insignificant. In fact, it's usually the little things that create the greatest confusion. Sometimes being confused paves the way to asking your supervisor to help you sort out the confusion: "Something is bothering me here. Can you help me figure out [whatever it is you need]."

Express Your Opinions

Even in the beginning, it's wise to avoid being a passive recipient of your supervisor's methods and techniques. Certainly, you're reluctant to make mistakes, so you hesitate. But this cheats you of the opportunity to develop your own internal supervisor. Whenever you're brave enough to try out observations, insights, and inclinations, you foster the development of your own style. When

you can articulate the reason you did this rather than that, if you
can clarify ambiguities about the way cases are conceptualized and
can think though alternatives carefully, you not only further your
professional understanding but also are less likely to make the mistake of incorporating, hook, line, and sinker, everything your
supervisor says. When you're able to state what makes sense to you
together with a request for feedback, it cues your supervisor to help
you fine-tune what you already have in mind.

Disagree Respectfully

When you disagree with your supervisor you'll have to recognize
that she has the final say. But that doesn't mean you give up all
resistance. In fact, it's wise to voice your concerns. You might consider saying something like "I understand that you think [summa-
rize the supervisor's views], but I see it [this way]. I'm concerned
about how to best manage this so I don't get confused." Or, "I'm
concerned. I can't quite see myself saying that in that way." When
you know something that the supervisor doesn't, you might try saying, "I've learned [whatever]. How does that fit with your views?"

Review What Happened

After supervision, consider what you didn't say:

Are you learning what you need to learn?
What would you have said, if only . . . ?
Were there things you felt reluctant to discuss?
Do you know why you felt reluctant?

It is important to remember that we're under supervision
because we have things to learn. Realizing that our mistakes are
really opportunities for professional growth makes it easier to tolerate criticism and alternative suggestions. Allowing ourselves that
room to learn stems from accepting that doing therapeutic work
defies perfection. There is no one way to do therapy, but there are
alternative and often more effective strategies. If we have trust in
our desire to learn more, to use ourselves productively, and to help
our clients improve, receiving criticism is a small price to pay. Leav-

ing ourselves open to that feedback without being defensive is the very best way to develop more skill.

Providing Supervision

Many mental health professionals will at one time or another be responsible for others with fewer credentials or less experience.[3] Understanding the requirements and responsibilities of providing supervision helps increase our sensitivity to the role of providing assistance to our colleagues. Even though these relationships can be frustrating, exasperating, and confusing, more often than not they are also intellectually exciting, sometimes amusing, and almost always rewarding. Therefore it makes sense to appreciate what's involved in making the most of being a supervisor.

As already mentioned, the purpose of supervision is to apprentice our supervisees. One hurdle to overcome is intrinsic to the need for supervision: in essence, whether they want to be or not, the inexperienced are assigned the task of listening to the more experienced. "There are few old people who have not wished to tie a young person down, hand and foot, and tell her or him the truth about life. Unfortunately, the young person will not listen, and the old person will inevitably come across as, at best, a tedious bore."[4] Even though Carolyn Heilbrun was talking about an attitude with which teachers can easily identify, this classic dilemma is also one for supervisors to take to heart: How do we find ways to make our ideas receivable?

Make Supervision Safe

It's important to remember that those in training are usually anxious, apprehensive about their skills, and fearful of our evaluations. And the less experienced they are, the more likely it is that they'll do all kinds of things that demonstrate their naïveté and lack of skill. That's only to be expected. The supervisor's challenge is to provide feedback that ensures clients are being served responsibly while at the same time creating an atmosphere that is safe enough for our supervisees to be open to feedback. Let's consider how we can do this within the context of the supervisory relationship.

Human nature being what it is, our students' reluctance to tell us when they're struggling is probably the major obstacle we face. After all, it's the rare student who hasn't at one time or another been scared to reveal these kinds of thoughts:

I don't think I can do therapy.

I'm baffled by eating disorders.

If I'm confused about my own sexuality, what can I say to my client?

I've never talked to an African American about anything important.

I don't get it.

I can't imagine myself saying what you just said.

It's one thing to acknowledge these kinds of reactions privately; it's quite another to feel safe enough to risk conveying that information to another person—especially when that other person has the responsibility to make sure that therapy is effective and also possesses the power to evaluate one's performance as well as affect one's job prospects. Nevertheless, the supervisory relationship can flourish only if the risks for open expression of doubts, mistakes, and insecurities are minimized.

To create an environment that's conducive to learning new skills, we'll want to make several points clear:

We all make mistakes. (I've made more than you can imagine!)

Nobody's perfect. (I'm not, and I don't expect you to be.)

It's better to reveal inadequacy than to try to hide it.

It's normal to have intense reactions.

I'm interested in what you think.

I don't have all the "right" answers, just more experience.

It's all right to disagree with me. But because I have to take final responsibility for what happens, eventually we'll need to work out something we can both agree to.

Keep Track of Requirements

Each state and each mental health license has rules and regulations about how much and what kind of supervision is necessary.

In addition, there are many treatment modalities that require specialized supervision, including marriage and family therapy, mediation, and chemical dependency. Along these lines, there are specifications for the types of experiences that will satisfy requirements for that license or certification. And there are the mandates of specific agencies, graduate programs, and internships.

Both supervisor and supervisee have an obligation to make sure they are fulfilling their professional requirements. Ironically, each person's requirements do not always parallel the other's. Nonetheless, supervisors have an obligation to follow the dictates of both their agency and license. For example, a supervising psychologist in Ohio is not supposed to take on more than four supervisees and is expected to provide face-to-face individual supervision for no less than 5 percent of the client contact time.[5]

Not all agencies have the same policies governing supervision. One agency may require three hours of individual supervision for twenty hours of client contact, whereas another may require only one. Some family counseling centers require that supervisors watch each session from behind a one-way mirror. Our responsibility as supervisors is to ensure that both ample time and appropriate methods are used to teach the skills we're hoping to develop.

Assume Responsibility

A primary characteristic of supervision is that supervisors bear the full responsibility for what transpires under their supervision. Consequently, we have an obligation to answer these three questions:

1. Is the training case-appropriate?
2. Does the supervisee have adequate preparation?
3. Can the supervisee and supervisor work together adequately?

As it's our obligation to know whether our supervisees can handle the cases available, we'll need some direct knowledge about the client other than what the supervisee tells us. Most state licensing boards stipulate that the supervisor either meet the client directly, review preliminary assessment data, or review tape-recorded interviews so that the supervisor has firsthand knowledge of what the client needs and whether the supervisee can handle what's necessary. Because it's our responsibility to make sure that those in training succeed with their clients, we need to assess trainees' readiness by finding out whether they

Have already had relevant experiences

Know what to do (book knowledge and clear understanding of the tasks necessary)

Would prefer that the supervisor be there in the room to monitor what's going on

Still prefer to watch the supervisor demonstrate what's to be learned

Know how to handle situations when they feel, "I'm in over my head. Now what?"

In most instances, it makes sense to assume that the less experience the person in training has, the more direct supervision that person will require. As a consequence, our decisions about how much supervision is needed also involve some consideration about how much time we have available and how that time can best be used.

The supervisee is also expected to take direction. Certainly, we operate in good faith with the assumption that supervisees are aware that our license and reputation are on the line, not to mention our professional liability insurance. Because as supervisors we are obligated to be "watchdogs," we must be reasonably confident that we can work collaboratively with those we're supervising.

I remember one instance that was particularly upsetting to Joyce, one of my colleagues. She had a supervisee, Elissa, who became sexually involved with a client. The client sued Elissa, Joyce, and the agency where she was employed. Even though Joyce was eventually absolved of this charge, it was not without a lengthy trial that established that Elissa had deliberately withheld pivotal information about what transpired during therapy with her client. Fortunately, Joyce kept supervision notes that included a summary of her sessions with Elissa. Consequently, she was able to document that she had asked about issues of attraction and that Elissa had denied not only the feelings but also any inappropriate behavior. Eventually, the jury absolved Joyce of any culpability, but this case was a painful reminder that most lawsuits go after everyone: the agency, the board of directors, the therapist, and the supervisor.

It's hard to know what Joyce could have done to protect herself from Elissa's deceit. But if we're not confident that we can trust a supervisee to act appropriately, we have an obligation not to take that student on. Often supervisors in training are simply assigned supervisees without their having any choice; certainly, this is also true for many agencies and training sites. Even so, we shouldn't assume that this means we have to supervise someone we're not confident we can work with well.

Keep Records

Joyce's case also illustrates the need to keep good records of what transpires during supervision. It was very fortunate for Joyce that she had kept detailed accounts of her sessions with Elissa. Without this documentation, this would have been a case of one person's word against another's. Perhaps it's also a reminder that students would be wise to keep their own notes and records about what transpires during supervision.

However, most licensing laws make clear that the primary responsibility for record-keeping rests with the supervisor. And although there is some variation by state and type of license, these records are generally supposed to include the following:

- The supervisory agreement (a contract about what's expected in terms of client contact hours, obligations, commitments for supervisory time, and any other stipulations, such as a waiver of confidentiality)
- The dates of supervision
- Notes regarding supervision
- Notes on specific clients and cases discussed

These records generally must be maintained for five years and be open to inspection by the state board.

Notify Clients

The supervisor has the primary obligation to make sure clients know that their therapist is being supervised. In most states, this information must be written and should include the following:

- A brief description of services
- The name of the supervisor
- A schedule of charges and an indication that charges will be billed under the supervisor's name
- The names and professional addresses of both supervisor and supervisee
- Statements about the parameters of the professional relationship and the availability of the supervisor to meet with the client if requested to do so
- The signatures of supervisor, supervisee, and client

Handle Confidentiality

Inherent in all supervisory relationships is the conflict between the necessity for complete openness from the supervisee and the obligation of the supervisor to evaluate what the supervisee says and does. In essence, the supervisee could disclose material that leads to a poor evaluation. In order to document the evaluation, the supervisor may have to reveal personal information about that supervisee. This dilemma makes clear the limited confidentiality afforded those in training. Some information may be kept confidential, but it may not be clear to either the supervisor or the supervisee what's protected and what isn't when it comes to revealing information to license boards, internship supervisors, or other educational administrators.[6]

Pretending this dilemma doesn't exist is the surest way to create misunderstanding. It's far better to confront the matter head on. As the supervisor, you need to be clear about what kinds of disclosures are required, desirable, or unnecessary for the work at hand. For example, emergencies involving the client, ethical dilemmas about the therapy, or a supervisee's feelings of being unable to manage all necessitate disclosure.

Regardless of clearly stated expectations, it's been my experience that more often than not most supervisees stumble into personal revelations during supervisory sessions without understanding that the protection of clients' confidentiality does not include the therapist-supervisee. If the supervisee's information cannot be kept confidential or must be included as part of an evaluation, it's a courtesy to warn the supervisee.

For example, when Analee told me during supervision that she was struggling with depression that medication hadn't helped and that she was going to begin therapy, I was concerned about her and her clients. She wanted to complete her training assignment, but because she was having trouble concentrating and found her clients' problems too stressful, I had to inform her that she was not in a position emotionally to complete her training assignment. After some discussion, we decided that Analee would be the first one to inform her academic department. Most supervisees appreciate it when we involve them in choices about their training and work. Nonetheless, supervisors must maintain the responsibility to act decisively if the supervisee can't manage therapeutic work.

Build Competence

Certainly the primary task we take on as a supervisor is to enhance the therapeutic skills of those under our supervision. The following are some suggestions on how to help our supervisees:

• *Build on existing skills.* Adding skills is more productive than harping on mistakes. We need to help our students understand what they're already doing that's working. Whenever we notice our supervisees demonstrating skill, making insightful observations, building good rapport, interviewing effectively, and managing complex situations, we need to point out our observations and describe in detail what evidence we're using to draw our conclusions. In addition to building supervisees' confidence, these observations and comments inform supervisees of the criteria we use to make positive assessments of their work.

• *Maintain clarity about what the supervisee needs to learn.* An important aspect of supervision is the ability to assess our supervisees' skill level. This assessment includes not only what the supervisee already knows about providing therapy but also which skills should be added next. For example, in the beginning, students often need to concentrate on effective listening; next they may profit from a focus on case management; and then they may benefit from fine-tuning interviewing skills. Being clear about the specific skills we're trying to teach helps supervisees know where to focus their attention.

When supervisor and supervisee agree on what needs to be learned and how to best acquire these new skills, our supervisees are more likely to be actively engaged in taking on new challenges. Many if not most supervisees are already aware of their shortcomings. Consequently, it's easy for them to be overwhelmed with all they have to learn. When we can help them focus their attention on certain aspects of the therapeutic process, we lessen their discomfort and thereby increase their sense of accomplishment.

• *Be straightforward.* We must assume that our supervisees have blind spots. It helps to offer suggestions with clear descriptions of what they could do differently. After all, it can't help but be frustrating for a supervisee to hear something like "Oh, that was awful!" or "I would have said . . ." We need to help our supervisees by providing clear-cut ideas with the understanding that they will need to develop those ideas in their own style. For example, we might try something like "It seems like we agree that you'll need to find a way to point out that her drinking is creating problems in her marriage. How might you do that?" After the supervisee offers her ideas, we fine-tune with suggestions for improvement: "OK, that's a good start. How about also expressing some optimism that she already has skills that will help her?"

• *Develop multicultural competence.* Our culture is growing more and more diverse; 25 percent of Americans define themselves as an ethnic minority. "By the year 2056 the average United States resident will trace his or her descent to Africa, Asia, Hispanic [American], the Pacific Islands, Arabia, almost anywhere but White Europe."[7] It's essential that our supervisees develop skills in providing services to diverse groups, but this won't happen unless supervisors are prepared themselves. Maintaining cultural sensitivity is an ongoing process that deserves special attention as part of the supervisory process. Certainly, having opportunities to work with supervisors from diverse backgrounds is essential. If you're working in a place that lacks diversity in staffing, you'll need to provide supervisees additional opportunities to interact with members of minority communities so that the skills they develop reflect appreciation for other cultures.

• *Encourage independent thinking.* There is no doubt that advice on how to manage helps supervisees learn, but eventually we want our supervisees to learn to give themselves feedback. Telling them what we would have done or said may dazzle them with our skill but probably won't do much to help them learn to do it themselves. We'll want to help our supervisees decide what they could do or say that would have been better. One way to do this is to review tapes or transcripts with stops for "Can you imagine how your client felt when you said this?" or "Can you think of another way to approach this?" or "I might have tried X. What do you think would be your way of doing something similar?"

Manage Disagreements

Disagreements in supervision are as inevitable as the power structure intrinsic to this relationship. However, because the purpose of supervision is not to make our supervisees into clones of ourselves, we'll want to use these episodes constructively. Although we have the final responsibility for what our supervisees do with their clients, we want to avoid coming across as though we have all the answers and as though a supervisee's ideas aren't worth much. To do otherwise increases the likelihood of our supervisee's internal supervisor being at odds with us. The reality is that there may be times when your supervisee has a better sense of the client than you do.

So we'll want to make every effort to work collaboratively by exchanging proposals and counterproposals until we develop a strategy that the supervisee can put into action. This means, of course, that no one gets her way absolutely and no one loses. Instead we'll search for alternatives that seem workable and include the best of the available options.

Avoid Exploitation

The ethics code for professional counselors stipulates that supervisors have a responsibility to be clear about the power differential between supervisor and supervisee and to discuss the potential for exploitation with their supervisees.[8] One point that must be made clear is the supervisor's obligation not to enter into sexual relationships with supervisees. At one time this was a serious problem in graduate training programs for mental health professionals; in one study conducted in 1979, one out of four female graduate students reported that she had engaged in a sexual relationship with a supervisor or educator.[9] The "exploitation rule" may also reflect that there have been problems with educators and supervisors taking advantage of their students by having them work for low wages in exchange for supervision or having them do research without giving adequate credit.

Personal involvements that end up sour are particularly painful. Ultimately, the supervisor is in a position to exploit the supervisee's admiration and desire for more contact. Some graduate students feel seduced when supervisors offer extra time, listening, soothing, and sometimes physical intimacies. When these students want more than the supervisor can deliver (declarations of love, even more time, special favors, good evaluations, or ongoing relationships), the exploiting supervisor often sets limits and backs off.

Typically this rejection is very difficult for students, most of whom are vulnerable women, to manage. When I've seen clients in this predicament, they express confusion about their attraction; they feel guilty about being disloyal but ultimately grief stricken over the loss of what they'd hoped for, then angry about feeling seduced, and later betrayed when the supervisor imposed limits. In short, these supervisees are devastated.

Rarely will the supervisor even be reprimanded, because most students are too afraid of repercussions if they report problems. More often than not, the supervisor never knows that the supervisee was upset. Nevertheless, the supervisor is ultimately responsible for avoiding not only sexual harassment (unsolicited overtures) but also *solicited* overtures during the period of time that supervision takes place.

Avoid Conflicting Roles

When a supervisee needs counseling or therapy in order to understand countertransference better, to manage impairment, to develop more appropriate styles of interaction, or to deal with personal problems, someone other than the supervisor must provide that service. To be in both roles constitutes a conflict of interest. This rule makes clear that a therapist cannot be in a position of evaluating or having authority over their client's professional work. Most training sites won't even allow trainees to be supervised by their former therapist.

A more difficult challenge is to find supervision for impaired professionals.[10] In Chapter Eight I discussed Greg, who became sexually involved with a client. He underwent a thorough assessment by a psychologist in Minneapolis who had years of experience dealing with sexual exploitation. This psychologist recommended that Greg continue therapy and participate in a period of supervision. (This was in the early 1980s; it should be noted that now many professionals believe that once a mental health professional has violated this prohibition his license should be permanently removed.[11]) As you recall, I provided Greg's therapy, which was protected under the guidelines of confidentiality.

But finding supervision was another matter. No psychologist was willing to take the risk of being identified as his supervisor. The liability was too great, and the few psychologists who volunteered were discouraged by their insurance providers from assuming this risk. In addition, his clients would have to be notified that he was working under supervision.

These complications have led some to suggest that licensed mental health professionals who are impaired and who need supervision should receive the same service but that the supervisor should be called a monitor rather than a supervisor.[12] Others see this as a semantic skirting of the issue. Regardless, these issues present a clear challenge for the mental health professionals who need added supervision following accreditation. State professional organizations have begun to take on the difficulties of providing supervision for mental health professionals impaired by problems with alcoholism, severe stress, or other factors causing mismanagement.

Aside from these dilemmas, providing supervision is an excellent opportunity to enhance professional learning. We all profit from exchanging ideas with those who have different levels of training and experience. As we will discuss now, the suggestions for enhancing the supervisory relationship are also appropriate for our professional contacts with our colleagues.

Peer Supervision

The need for continued feedback, consultation, and the opportunity to learn from different perspectives is always present. Whether we are still in graduate school, in private practice, or part of an agency (when we're no longer under anyone's direct supervision and even when we are)—our peers are a great resource for both professional development and personal consolation. Whether conducted with a group of therapists or on an individual basis, consultations with fellow professionals tend to be collegial and therefore uncontaminated by the pressures of evaluations.

Even though these arrangements can't serve as substitutes for the traditional supervision necessary for documented competency or professional requirements, our peers provide the opportunity for exploring our deeper fears, embarrassing slip-ups, or profound countertransference reactions. For example:

Alan took his client's file out of the office by mistake and now can't find it. He's afraid to tell his supervisor and even more afraid someone else will find it. He worried, "What if I'm thrown out of the graduate program? I can't believe I did this. What do you think I should do?"

When Sue listened to her client explain how scared she was that her husband would leave her, Sue kept thinking about her own marriage and how much trouble she was having. She wondered, "I'm not sure what I should do. Maybe I need therapy, maybe this trouble will get better. I wish I didn't think about my own marriage so much. Do you think I should see a therapist?"

When the lights went out during her session, all Jennifer could think about was, "Now what? I'm so attracted to this client. I know it's off-limits, but it was all so weird. I did fine. We laughed about the lights, and they came back on after about ten minutes, but I couldn't believe I acted so calm when my heart was racing. Do you think she was aware? I hope not."

Max's client, who is eighteen years old, told Max that he became sexually involved with one of his friends, who's only fourteen. Max wondered, "Do I need to report this?"

These dilemmas cry out for an opportunity for therapists to find a sounding board that will give them the safety to figure out what to do next. Although it's important that we select someone with whom we feel comfortable, it's also important that it's someone who is not afraid to challenge our thinking. In other words, we need to strike a balance between the need for emotional support and the need for honest feedback. If we pick someone who's afraid to risk criticizing us, we won't learn anything; on the other hand, if we pick someone who makes us defensive, we're apt to be less than totally candid. After weighing the available options, we'll want to ask someone (or ones) we can trust to help us gain awareness of our cognitive, emotional, or ethical blind spots—someone who knows us well enough to know where we're vulnerable, to know what assets we can muster when the chips are down, and who can be there in odd hours to provide emotional support when we most need it.

Many therapists find supervision groups helpful. There are several models for setting up these leaderless programs.[13] The first step is to pick members. You increase your chances of success if

All participants are willing to agree on the basic responsibilities of being a member.

The group is small enough to allow for participation (four to six people).

Members agree on who will be included.

Members agree on confidentiality guidelines ahead of time.

Everyone has approximately the same level of experience and shares similar interests.

Members decide on the method of making decisions (consensus or voting).

Members establish time limits.

Members agree to topics and the discussion format ahead of time.

Members outline, discuss, and agree to guidelines for constructive feedback.

One common format for this type of group is for members to take responsibility for hosting a session by picking a topic, sharing a case, or presenting an ethical dilemma or countertransference issue (or some combination). It's sometimes easier if the host initiates the structure for her topic by assigning readings, identifying questions, or focusing the discussion. These kinds of situations are perhaps not as intimate as one-on-one consultations, but they have the added benefit of learning about a variety of opinions and reactions.

Most of these groups go well, with members building trust over time. Because these groups tend to be informal and members already know each other, participants don't often talk about how they'd like the discussions to go. Consequently, the ground rules get lost in the ongoing momentum of what's most pressing at the time. Avoiding this pitfall is easier if members agree to some general guidelines before launching into topics. Some basic guidelines might include avoiding the following:

- Complaining about agency policies and practices
- Engaging in one-upsmanship "You should have done it this way!"
- Focusing on the past, on what could have been done; rather, it's better to focus on the future: What will I do now?
- Not creating enough safety for members to provide straightforward feedback
- Changing the topic or shifting the focus

We have a great deal we can teach each other whenever we're willing to listen and to risk saying what we think and expressing how we feel. Providing therapy can be lonely and isolating because of the demands of confidentiality and the responsibility of working toward specific therapeutic goals. Nonetheless, these tasks are enriched when they're shared. Our early experiences with supervision set the stage for the collegial relationships we'll want to develop with our peers.

Notes
1. Watkins, E. C. (1995). Psychotherapy supervision in the 1990s: Some observations and reflections. *American Journal of Psychotherapy, 49,* 568–581.
2. Casement, M. A. (1997). Towards autonomy: Some thoughts on psychoanalytic supervision. In M. H. Rock (Ed.), *Psychodynamic supervision.* Northvale, NJ: Aronson, p. 266.
3. Norcross, J. C., Prochaska, J. O., & Farber, J. A. (1993). Psychologists conducting psychotherapy: New findings and historical comparisons on the psychotherapy division membership. *Psychotherapy, 30,* 692–697.

MAKING THE MOST OF SUPERVISION: DUAL PERSPECTIVES   259

4. Heilbrun, C. G. (1997). The last gift of time: Life beyond sixty. New York: Dial, p. 158.

5. State Board of Psychology. (1996). Ohio psychology law. Columbus, OH: Author, p. 29.

6. Kottler, J. A., & Hazler, R. J. (1997). What you never learned in graduate school. New York: Norton, p. 209.

7. Atkinson, D. R., & Thompson, C. E. (1992). Racial, ethnic, and cultural variables in counseling. In S. D. Brown & R. W. Lent (Eds.), Handbook of counseling psychology (2nd ed., pp. 349–382). New York: Wiley.

8. American Counseling Association. (April, 1995). Code of ethics and standards of practice, F.1.

9. Pope, K. S., Levenson, H., & Schover, L. (1979). Sexual intimacy in psychology training: Results and implications of a national survey. American Psychologist, 34, 682–689.

10. Rodger, D. (1994, May-June). Warning alert concerning supervision of licensed colleagues. Ohio Psychologist, 40, 608.

11. Pope, K. S., Sonne, J. L., & Holroyd, J. (1993). Sexual feelings in psychotherapy. Washington, DC: American Psychological Association.

12. See note 10.

13. Borders, D. (1991). A systematic approach to peer group supervision. Journal of Counseling and Development, 69, 248–252; Marks, J. L., & Hixon, D. F. (1986, September). Training agency staff through peer group supervision. Social Casework, pp. 418–423; Greenberg, S. L., Lewis, G. J., & Johnson, M. (1985). Peer consultation groups for private practitioners. Professional Psychology: Research and Practice, 16, 437–447; Wendorf, D. J., Wendorf, R. J., & Bond, D. (1985). Growth behind the mirror: The family therapy consortium's group process. Journal of Marital and Family Therapy, 11, 245–255.

Afterword

Providing mental health services is a challenging career that changes constantly. The demands of current clinical practice are very different now than they were twenty years ago. Everything from the theories that guide practice to the financing has changed. And no doubt will change again. Nonetheless, certain fundamentals remain:

- We must be attentive to building workable therapeutic relationships with our clients.
- We must be responsive to funding sources.
- We need to maintain sensitivity to diverse groups and cultures.
- We must take care of ourselves in order to maintain the intense concentration that providing therapy requires.
- We have an obligation to protect our clients from our inadequacies.
- We should build strong collegial relationships to ensure opportunities for both professional growth and personal support.

This book was designed to offer some fundamental suggestions for implementing these basic therapeutic skills. It's my hope that each reader can add to these skills by using what is basically helpful, compassionate, and thoughtful from his or her own unique style and personality. Learning to be therapeutic entails a lifelong commitment to continued professional development. Surely our professional organizations as well as the demands of continuing education offer ample opportunity for continued expansion of the basic skills we've been discussing, and there's no doubt that careful adherence to professional ethics also makes providing therapy safer for everyone.

The rewards, too, shall always remain, regardless of changes in clinical practice. Providing therapy helps our clients, but it also helps us. We learn. We have a front-row seat for life. We have the privilege of learning firsthand about the most intimate aspects of other people's lives. We are personally gratified when our clients improve and suffer less pain. And we get paid. Enjoy and prosper.

The Author

Jeanne Albronda Heaton, Ph.D., has had twenty-five years of experience as a psychologist at Ohio University's Counseling and Psychological Services. Beginning with her master's thesis, *Training Paraprofessionals for a Crisis Phone Service,* Heaton has maintained an abiding commitment to the development and education of mental health workers. She teaches part-time in the psychology department and has a private practice in Athens, Ohio. She also co-coordinates the internship and traineeship opportunities for graduate students from both counseling and psychology in her agency.

In addition to her university responsibilities, Heaton is a mediator for the domestic court in Athens County, as well as program coordinator for the board of Milestones, a therapeutic foster care network. She has served on the Ohio Psychological Association's Committee for Colleague Assistance and is currently a member of the Peer Review Committee on Ethical Practices.

Index

Index

and, 208–209; therapist personal filters and, 26–28, 206–208; therapist personal problems and, 105–106, 206–208, 221–224; unexpressed, 220; vulnerability to, 221–224. *See also* Therapists

Crisis management, 147–171; backup plans for, 164, 175; circumstances of, 147–148; collegial consultation for, 155; commonsense advice for, 150–151; concrete plans for, 167–168; confidentiality issues of, 152, 153, 154–155; consultations to nonclients in, 152–153; in dangerous situations, 163–165; decisions of, 148; emotional disengagement versus exploration in, 161–163; experimental attitude in, 167; focus on problem in, 156–157; getting help for, 150; in high-risk situations, 148–151; identifying precipitating events in, 158–159; irrational beliefs and, 159–161; meaning-making in, 158–159; monitoring in, 168–169; objectives of, 155–156; opportunity for questions in, 170–171; phone calls for, 174–175; priorities in, 151–152; problem-solving strategies for, 165–171; referrals in, 169–170; self-care in, 149, 166–167; social supports and, 167; therapeutic interview for, 155–171; therapist control in, 156–157; therapist role in, 151–155; therapist self-care in, 171; written records of, 155. *See also* Danger to others; Danger to self; Violence

Crying. *See* Tears

Cultural differences: and assessment, 64; in barter acceptability, 184–185; and countertransference, 214–215; empathic understanding and, 100–101; in expressiveness, 11; in eye contact, 13; in gift giving/acceptance, 193; in manner of speech, 18; in physical space, 16; respect for, 98; supervision and training in, 252; and therapist self-disclosure, 214–215

D

Danger to others: assessment of, 58–61; confidentiality and, 154–155; contract against, 164–165; crisis intervention and, 148–151, 163–165; lethality determination for, 60–61; risk factors for,

58–59; variables assessed for, 59–60. *See also* Crisis management

Danger to self: assessment of, 52–57, 61–62; being at risk for violence and, 56–57; confidentiality and, 154–155; contract against, 164–165; crisis intervention and, 148–151, 163–165; determining lethality of, 55–56; and pacing of therapy 124–126; risk factors for, 53–54, 56–57; variables assessed for, 54–55. *See also* Crisis management; Violence

Danger to therapist, avoidance of, 149

Debriefing, therapist, 171

Deductibles, 180

Defensive functioning scale, 84

Defensiveness, 112; and diversion, 126–127

Delusions, assessment for, 42–43

Demographic identity, therapist, 203–205

Depersonalization: assessment for, 46; and substance abuse, 49

Depression: melatonin and, 50; speech and, 18

Derealization, 46

Di Clemente, C., 35–37

Diagnosis: classification systems for, 77–79; clinically significant symptoms for, 80–83; consequences of, to client, 84–86; *DSM-IV* multiaxial system for, 79–85; differential, 83; discussion of, with client, 81–82, 85–86; history of, 77–79; information sharing about, 85; making a, 77–86; provisional, 84; rationale for making, 78–79; specifiers for, 83; steps for making, 83–86; symptom assessment and, 33; third-party payer requirements for, 34, 78–79, 84, 85; uncertainty in, 84

Diagnostic and Statistical Manual of Mental Disorders (DSM-I), 77

Diagnostic and Statistical Manual of Mental Disorders (DSM-III), 77

Diagnostic and Statistical Manual of Mental Disorders (DSM-III-R), 77

Diagnostic and Statistical Manual of Mental Disorders (DSM-IV), diagnosis based on, 34; history and background of, 77–79; making a diagnosis with, 79–85; *Quick Reference* version of, 80; "Use of the Manual" section of, 80

Power, balance of, 227–228

Practice settings: diagnosis requirements of, 34; information requirements of, 62; policies of, regarding dilemmas, 174; supervision requirements of, 246–247

Precontemplation stage of change, 36

Predicaments. *See* Dilemmas and predicaments

Premature solutions, 211

Preoccupation, therapist, 105

Preparation stage of change, 36–37

Prescription drugs, 50

Presentation, general, assessment of, 39–41

Presenting problems: assessment and clarification of, 32–38; focus on, in first session, 73–74; summarizing, 75–76. *See also* Assessment

Prince of Tides, 225

Prochaska, J., 35–37

Professional boundaries. *See* Boundaries

Professional filters, therapist, 28. *See also* Technique; Theoretical orientation

Professional identity, therapist, 2, 209–211

Progress, communication of, 111–112, 133

Proxemics, 16

Psilocybin use, signs of, 49

Psychobabble, 20

Psychological symptoms. *See* Symptoms

Psychotherapy: basic skills of, 3–4, 261; effectiveness of, 1–3, 95–96; explaining, to clients, 72–73; in first session, 68–92; fundamentals of, 261–262; harm done by, 3; motivation for, 32–38; objectives of, 128–129; outcomes of, predictors of, 2–3, 38, 96; termination of, 196–199; therapeutic interview of, 120–146; third-party payer demands and, 3–4; work of, 128–146. *See also* First session; Skills, psychotherapy; Therapeutic interview

Q

Questions: to clarify client's feelings, 131, 161–162; to clarify observations, 34–35, 43–44; encouraging client's, in crisis situations, 170–171, 177–178; about interpretations, 137–138; open-ended, 131, 123; specific, 131; to stimulate exploration, 130–131

R

Race: observation of client's, 9; therapist's, 203–205. *See also* Cultural differences

Rapport, 94–117; alliance and, 110–112; assessment of, 112–113, 116; congruence and, 96, 101–104; empathic understanding and, 96, 99–101, 108–110, 113; establishing, 104–114; facilitative conditions for, 95–104; listening and, 105–108; maintaining, 104–114; nature of, 94–95; repairing ruptures in, 113–114; research about, 115–116; rigid techniques and, 115–116; therapeutic respect and, 97–99, 108–110; therapist attributes for, 96; "throw-in" variables of, 116–117; training for, 114–117. *See also* Empathy; Therapeutic relationship

Readiness for change: assessment of, 35–38; of substance abusers, 52

Readiness for termination, assessment of, 196

Record-keeping: for supervision, 249; for therapy, 155, 200

Referrals, in crisis situations, 169–170

Release of information, 154–155

Respect, therapeutic, 96, 97–99; and confrontation, 141–142; demonstrating, 108–110

Responsibility: for countertransference, 220–221; respect for clients', 98; for topic selection, 121

Restimulation, of therapist's issues, 207

Rogers, C., 95–96, 97, 99–100, 101, 116

Roles: in emergency situations, 151–155; in supervisory relationship, 233–258; in therapeutic relationship, 122

Room, position in, 16

S

Secrecy: and phone calls about clients, 178–179; about potential for harm, 163–164; and therapist self-disclosure, 137; of victims of violence, 57

Self-care: in crisis situations, 149, 166–167; mental status assessment and, 39, 46; observation of, 10–11

Self-disclosure, therapist, 136–137; client focus and, 217–218; client response to, 219–220; countertransference and,

214–220; ethnic differences in, 214–215; making decisions about, 215–220; of opinions and values, 208–209; personal versus historical, 218–219; of personal demographic information, 205; of sexual attraction to client, 228; timing of, 216–217
Self-knowledge, therapist, 203–211. *See also* Countertransference; Therapists
Self-perception, assessment of, 46–47
Self-respect, 98–99
Self-talk, observation of, 20
Sensorium, assessment of, 41
Sessions: interruptions of, 185–186; missed, 185. *See also* First session; Therapeutic interview
Sessions, conduct of. *See* First session; Therapeutic interview
Sexual attraction, therapist's, 225–230; acting out of, 225–228; balance of power and, 227–228; of female versus male therapists, 228; homosexual, 228; outcomes of, 227–228; prevalence of, 225; warning signs of, 229–230
Sexual orientation, therapist, 205
Sexual relationships: supervisor-supervisee, 253–254; therapist-client, 191, 225–228
Shaking, interpretation of, 25
Shyness: nonverbal cues of, 13; speech cues of, 17
Silence, client: observation of, 21–23; possible causes of, 22
Silence, therapist, 136
Single sessions, 68–69. *See also* First session
Skills, psychotherapy: of assessment, 31–65; of crisis management, 147–171; for dilemmas and predicaments, 173–200; in first session, 68–92; fundamental, 4, 261; integration of, with outside demands, 3–4; necessity of, 3; of observation, 7–29; of rapport, 94–117; of supervision, 233–258; supervision for developing, 251–253; of therapeutic interviewing, 120–146; of therapist use of self, 202–230; training for, 114–117. *See also* Assessment; Countertransference; Crisis management; Diagnosis; Dilemmas and predicaments; First session; Observation; Rapport; Supervision; Therapeutic interviewing; Treatment plans

Sleep problems, and substance abuse, 49
Sliding scale, 183
Small towns, boundaries in, 195
Social and occupational functioning assessment scale (SOFAS), 84
Social relationships: post-termination, 198–199; supervisor-supervisee, 253–254; therapist-client, 188–190
Social skills training, therapist, 114–115
Social supports, 167
Sociolinguistics, 17. *See also* Verbal expression
Speech: fluency of, 18–19, 109; observing client's manner of, 17–18. *See also* Verbal expression
Spontaneity, client, 112
Steinem, G., 207–208
Stereotypes: about drug users, 51; and listening, 105; and therapist identity, 205
Stress, signs of therapist, 223–224
Structured clinical interviews, 79
Strupp, H., 115–116, 215, 221
Subculture affiliations, nonverbal cues of, 10–11
Substance abuse and addiction: assessment of, 48–52; assessment instruments for, 51–52; and assessment of level of consciousness, 40; and "flight of ideas," 43; over-the-counter remedies and, 50; prescription drugs and, 50; psychological symptoms of, 49–50; signs of, 40, 43, 48–49; stereotypes about, 51
Suicide potential: assessment of, 54–55, 61–62; lethality determination and, 55–56; risk factors for, 53–54, 56; variables assessed for, 54–55. *See also* Danger to self
Sullivan, H. S., 120, 126–127, 144
Summary statement, 130; at session closure, 146
Supervisees, 233–234; assessing readiness of, 247–248; assessing skill needs of, 251–252; competence building for, 251–253; disagreement of, 244, 253; evaluation of, clarification about, 237–238; exploitation of, 253–254; preparation of, for sessions, 240–242; strategies and roles of, for effective supervision, 236–244; therapy and therapists for, 254–255

of, and impact on therapy, 208–209; personal emergencies and responsibilities of, 186; personal filters of, 26–28, 203–211; personal problems of, and impact on therapy, 105–106, 206–208, 221–224; physical appearance of, 204; professional filters of, 28; professional identity of, 2, 209–211; self-care of, in crisis situations, 171; self-disclosure of, 136–137, 205, 214–220; self-knowledge of, 203–211; self-observation of, 26–29, 102; self-respect of, 98–99; stress signs of, 223–224; use of self of, 202–230; values of, 205, 209–211; vulnerability of, 221–224. *See also* Countertransference

Third-party payers: client billing and, 180–183; diagnostic requirements of, 34, 78–79, 84, 85; impact of, on clinical practice, 3–4; information release to, 181–183; and professional filters, 28; and time-limited therapy, 196. *See also* Managed care

Thought/thinking: assessment of, 42–44; clarifying questions about, 43–44; content of, 42; delusions of control of, 42–43; irrational, 159–161; organization of, 43

"Throw-ins," 116–117

Time constraints, 123, 157, 211

Time-limited dynamic psychotherapy (TLDP), 115–116

Timing: of interpretations, 139; of therapist self-disclosure, 216–217. *See also* Pacing

Tissue box, 13

Tone, establishing the, 69–70

Tone of voice, client's, 17–18

Topic selection, responsibility for, 121

Topic shifting, 18–19

Touching: observation of, 16; and sexual attraction, 228–229; therapist-client, 16, 191, 228–229

Training, for rapport, 114–117

Trauma, crisis intervention for, 149. *See also* Crisis management

Treatment plans: development of, 86–92; elements of, 89–90; goal setting for, 86–88; for managed care, 91–92; supervision of, 240

Tremors, interpretation of, 25

Tune-up sessions, 37

Turn signals, 24

U

Unconditional positive regard, 96, 97–99

Unpaid accounts, 183–184

V

Values, therapist, 205, 209–211

Verbal expression, client: elements of, 17; fluency of, 18–19; interaction of, with nonverbal behavior, 23–26; interpretation of, 25–26; laughter in, 21; manner of speech in, 17–18; meaning and choice of words in, 19–21; movement harmonics and, 24–25; observation of, 17–23; pauses in, 21–23; silence and, 21–23; turn signals in, 24. *See also* Assessment; Mental status assessment; Observation

Verbal expression, therapist, 109, 135

Vineland Adaptive Behavior Scales, 46

Violence, 58–61; assessment of, 59–60; clients at risk for, 56–57; dealing with threat of, 163–165; determining lethality of, 60–61; risk factors for, 58–59; secrecy of victims of, 57; therapeutic model for, 61; variables assessed for, 59–60. *See also* Danger to others; Danger to self

W

"Why now?" question, 32–33, 175–176

Williams, S., 166, 214–215

Words: observing client's choice of, 19–21; personal meanings of, 19–20; therapist's choice of, 109, 135

World Health Organization, 77

World Health Organization (AUDIT) structured interview, 52

Wrapping up, in first session, 90–91

Y

Yalom, I., 102–104, 202, 211